Operational Risk
Management

Founded in 1807, John Wiley & Sons is the oldest independent publishing company in the United States. With offices in North America, Europe, Australia, and Asia, Wiley is globally committed to developing and marketing print and electronic products and services for our customers' professional and personal knowledge and understanding.

The Wiley Finance series contains books written specifically for finance and investment professionals as well as sophisticated individual investors and their financial advisors. Book topics range from portfolio management to e-commerce, risk management, financial engineering, valuation and financial instrument analysis, as well as much more.

For a list of available titles, visit our Web site at www.WileyFinance.com.

Operational Risk Management

A Complete Guide for Banking and Fintech

Second Edition

PHILIPPA GIRLING

WILEY

Published by John Wiley & Sons, Inc., Hoboken, New Jersey.
Published simultaneously in Canada.

For general information on our other products and services or for technical support, please contact our Customer Care Department within the United States at (800) 762-2974, outside the United States at (317) 572-3993 or fax (317) 572-4002.

Wiley also publishes its books in a variety of electronic formats. Some content that appears in print may not be available in electronic formats. For more information about Wiley products, visit our web site at www.wiley.com.

Library of Congress Cataloging-in-Publication Data:

Names: Girling, Philippa, author.
Title: Operational risk management : a complete guide for banking and
    fintech / Philippa Girling.
Description: Second edition. | Hoboken, New Jersey : Wiley, [2022] |
    Series: Wiley finance | Includes index.
Identifiers: LCCN 2021052103 (print) | LCCN 2021052104 (ebook) | ISBN
    9781119836049 (cloth) | ISBN 9781119836063 (adobe pdf) | ISBN
    9781119836056 (epub)
Subjects: LCSH: Risk management.
Classification: LCC HD61 .G537 2022 (print) | LCC HD61 (ebook) | DDC
    658.15/5—dc23/eng/20211112
LC record available at https://lccn.loc.gov/2021052103
LC ebook record available at https://lccn.loc.gov/2021052104

Cover Image: © Tuomas A. Lehtinen/Getty Images
Cover design: Wiley

SKY10032314_011022

For my husband, Joe;
my children, Leah, Holly, and Tegwen;
and my stepchildren, Hayley and Allison.

Thank you all for helping me to balance risk
and reward every day.

Contents

Preface

The evolution of operational risk over the past 20 years has given rise to a new profession: the operational risk manager. This book equips the student or practitioner of operational risk with all of the framework elements that are needed in order to establish a successful operational risk framework.

Banks have been working with formalized operational risk frameworks for many years now, but the rise of the digital banking paradigm has brought new entrants into the financial services space who need to manage their risks effectively.

Financial technology companies (fintechs) face the same operational risks as banks, and they are finding that the operational risk practices that banks have adopted are also key to their own survival. Operational risk events and reputational impacts require effective management in both fintechs and in banks, and the approaches outlined in this book provide practical methods that can be applied across the whole of the financial services industry and beyond into other industries.

In the past year, several fintechs have experienced intense regulatory scrutiny and some negative reputational impact, often stemming from operational and compliance weaknesses or failures. An effective operational risk framework can help protect these emerging "banking" companies from future reputational damage and fines.

The speed of digital innovation requires banks and fintechs to look for ways to keep their risk frameworks in touch with the changes that are occurring rapidly in their processes and products, and the operational risk framework needs to adopt a growth mindset to match. Methods of adapting traditional risk management methods to agile cultures are explored in this book.

While best practices and regulatory guidelines are readily available for both the qualitative and the quantitative elements of operational risk, many firms continue to struggle with the practical implementation of operational risk frameworks. This book provides real-life examples of successful methods and tools while facing head-on the cultural challenges that are prevalent in this field.

Today, chief risk officers are finding themselves facing the daunting task of providing assurances to senior management and board members that operational risks are being effectively managed and mitigated. Traditional market and credit risk approaches offer only partial effectiveness in the operational risk field, and this book explores the unique qualitative aspects of operational risk management.

This book also provides insight into some of the (often notorious) operational risk events that have occurred in the past 10 years, with analysis of the JPMorgan Whale event, the Archegos Credit Suisse event, the UBS and Société Générale unauthorized trading scandals, the reputational risk events related to LIBOR and the recent Australian Banking scandals, the Knight Capital technology misstep, and the management of operational risk at the Olympics.

The COVID-19 pandemic's impact on operational risk losses is also explored, along with the effectiveness of preparations for that event.

The author explores how the regulatory framework has evolved over the past few years in response to these events and in response to the recent economic crises and proposes effective approaches to meet both global regulatory expectations and the industry's risk management goals. The regulatory changes that have been implemented or proposed since the first edition of this book are incorporated throughout the framework to provide the latest guidance and practical steps that can be taken to meet those rising expectations.

The proposed framework provides practical steps to ensure effective identification, assessment, monitoring, and mitigation of operational risks. In starker terms, how can you find it, size it, watch it, and kill it (or choose to accept it)?

Operational risk is an elusive risk category, but it can be managed using best practices that have grown up in the industry over the past few years. This book provides both the new and the experienced operational risk professional with tools and best practices to implement a successful operational risk framework and to embed operational risk management more deeply in their firms.

Acknowledgments

Thank you to my agent, John Wright, for his engagement, support, and encouragement, and to Bill Falloon at John Wiley & Sons for taking me on as a new author over 10 years ago and for welcoming me into the Wiley community. Thank you to the whole Wiley team, especially my editors, Purvi Patel and Manikandan Kuppan, for their careful and diligent shepherding of the manuscript and Samantha Enders for her book design.

Thank you to Cathy Hampson, Jon Holland, Nicole Hubert, Lorinda Opsahl-Ong, Ilya Rozenfeld, David Silverman, Mark Taylor, Jedediah Turner, and Jan Voigts—my friends, colleagues, and peers who generously agreed to review portions of the first edition of this book, and to Nancy Foster, Kevin Oden, and Spyro Karetsos for taking on the second edition and for all of their thoughts and suggestions. This is a much stronger work as a result of your excellent insight and in-depth knowledge of the field of operational risk. I am grateful to you all for taking time to review and improve the manuscript when you are very busy managing operational risk on a daily basis. Any remaining weaknesses and errors in the book are entirely my own doing.

Thank you to all of the risk teams that I have worked in over the past 15 years; I have learned so much from all of you.

Thank you to both ORX and IBM FIRST for providing external loss data for analysis with a generous spirit and remarkable efficiency.

Thank you to Penelope Vance for coaching me through the entire process for the first edition, for asking all the right questions at the right time, and for continuing to be a voice of reason at all times.

Thank you to GARP for generously allowing the reuse of content that I wrote for one of their course textbooks.

Finally, a special thank you to my children, Leah, Holly, Tegwen, Hayley, and Allison, for their patience with me as I wrote, and to my husband, Joe, for his constant encouragement that I could, and should, write and rewrite this book.

CHAPTER 1

Definition and Drivers of Operational Risk

This chapter examines the definition of operational risk and its role in the management of risks in the financial services sector, including fintechs and digital and traditional banks. It outlines the formal adoption of operational risk management for regulated banks under the Basel II framework. The requirements to identify, assess, control, and mitigate operational risk are introduced, along with the four causes of operational risk—people, process, systems, and external events—and the seven risk types. The definition is tested against the 2012 London Olympics. The different roles of operational risk management and measurement are introduced, as well as the role of operational risk in an enterprise risk management framework.

THE DEFINITION OF OPERATIONAL RISK

What do we mean by operational risk?

Operational risk management had been defined in the past as all risk that is not captured in market and credit risk management programs. Early operational risk programs, therefore, took the view that if it was not market risk, and it was not credit risk, then it must be operational risk. However, today a more concrete definition has been established, and the most commonly used of the definitions can be found in the Basel II regulations. The Basel II definition of operational risk is:

> . . . *the risk of loss resulting from inadequate or failed processes, people and systems or from external events.*
>
> *This definition includes legal risk, but excludes strategic and reputational risk.*[1]

Let us break this definition down into its components. First, there must be a risk of loss. So for an operational risk to exist there must be an associated loss anticipated. The definition of "loss" will be considered more fully when we look at internal loss data in Chapter 7, but for now we will simply assume that this means a financial loss.

Next, let us look at the defined causes of this loss. The preceding definition provides four causes that might give rise to operational risk losses. These four causes are (1) inadequate or failed processes, (2) inadequate or failed people (the regulators do not get top marks for their grammar, but we know what they are getting at), (3) inadequate or failed systems, or (4) external events.

While the language is a little awkward (what exactly are "failed people"?, for example), the meaning is clear. There are four main causes of operational risk events: the person doing the activity makes an error, the process that supports the activity is flawed, the system that facilitated the activity is broken, or an external event occurs that disrupts the activity.

With this definition in our hands, we can simply look at today's newspaper or at the latest online headlines to find a good sample of operational risk events. Failed processes, inadequate people, broken systems, and violent external events are the mainstays of the news. Operational risk surrounds us in our day-to-day lives.

Examples of operational risk in the headlines in the past few years include egregious fraud (Madoff, Stanford), breathtaking unauthorized trading (Société Générale and UBS), shameless insider trading (Raj Rajaratnam, Nomura, SAC Capital), stunning technological failings (Knight Capital, the Nasdaq Facebook IPO, anonymous cyber-attacks), and heartbreaking external events (hurricanes, tsunamis, earthquakes, terrorist attacks, and a global pandemic). We will take a deeper look at several of these cases throughout the book.

All of these events cost firms hundreds of millions, and often billions, of dollars. In addition to these headline-grabbing large operational risk events, firms constantly bleed money due to frequent and less severe events. Broken processes and poorly trained staff can result in many small errors that add up to serious downward pressure on the profits of a firm.

The importance of managing these types of risks, both for the robustness of a firm and for the systemic soundness of the industry, has led regulators to push for strong operational risk frameworks and has driven executive managers to fund and support such frameworks.

Basel II is the common name used to refer to the "International Convergence of Capital Measurement and Capital Standards: A Revised

Framework," which was published by the Bank for International Settlements (BIS) in Europe in 2004.

The Basel II framework set out new risk rules for internationally active financial institutions that wished to continue to do business in Europe. These rules related to the management and capital measurement of market and credit risk introduced a new capital requirement for operational risk. In addition to the capital requirement for operational risk, Basel II laid out qualitative requirements for operational risk management, and so a new era of operational risk management development was born.

The Basel II definition of operational risk has been adopted or adapted by many financial regulators and firms and is now generally accepted as the standard. It has been incorporated into national regulations across the globe with only minor adaptations and is consistently referred to by regulators and operational risk managers. Many regulators have simply adopted the Basel definition into their national regulatory frameworks as is, but it is interesting to note that the Office of the Comptroller of the Currency (OCC) has adopted a definition that underscores the impact of operational risk on a bank's resiliency as well as on its financial condition:

> *Operational risk is the risk to current or projected financial condition and* **resilience** *arising from inadequate or failed internal processes or systems, human errors or misconduct, or adverse external events.*[2] *[emphasis added]*

JPMorgan Chase has adapted the definition as follows:

> *Operational risk is the risk associated with an adverse outcome resulting from inadequate or failed internal processes or systems; human factors; or external events impacting the Firm's processes or systems. It includes compliance, conduct, legal, and estimations and model risk.*[3]

Deutsche Bank applies the European Banking Authority's *Single Rulebook* definition, which closely matches the original Basel II definition:

> *Operational risk means the risk of losses stemming from inadequate or failed internal processes, people and systems or from external events. Operational risk includes legal risks, but excludes business and reputational risk and is embedded in all banking products and activities.*[4]

Under the Basel II definition, legal events are specifically included in the definition of operational risk, and a footnote is added to further clarify this:

Legal risk includes, but is not limited to, exposure to fines, penalties, or punitive damages resulting from supervisory actions, as well as private settlements.[5]

This is a helpful clarification, as there is often some tension with the legal department when the operational risk function first requests information on legally related events. This is something that will be considered in more detail later in the section on loss data collection.

The Basel II definition also specifically *excludes* several items from operational risk:

This definition includes legal risk, but excludes strategic and reputational risk.[6]

These nuances in the Basel II definition are often reflected in the definition adopted by a firm, whether or not they are governed by that regulation. However, these exclusions are not always applied in operational risk frameworks.

For example, some banks have adopted definitions of operational risk that include reputational risk. For example, Citi's definition includes reputational risk:

Operational risk is the risk of loss resulting from inadequate or failed internal processes, people or systems, or from external events. It includes the reputation and franchise risk associated with business practices or market conduct that the Company undertakes.[7]

Operational risk has some similarities to market and credit risk. Most importantly, it should be actively managed, because failure to do so can result in a misstatement of an institution's risk profile and expose it to significant losses.

However, operational risk also has some fundamental differences from market and credit risk. Operational risk, unlike market and credit risk, is typically not directly taken in return for an expected reward. Market risk arises when a firm decides to take on certain products or activities. Credit risk arises when a firm decides to do business with a particular counterparty. In contrast, operational risk exists in the natural course of corporate activity. As soon as a firm has a single employee, a single computer system, a single office, or a single process, operational risk arises.

While operational risk is not taken on voluntarily, the level of that risk can certainly be impacted by business decisions. Operational risk is inherent in any enterprise, but strong operational risk management and measurement allow for that risk to be understood and either mitigated or accepted.

We will be looking at ways that operational risk management and measurement can meet the underlying need to accomplish five tasks:

1. **Identifying** operational risks.
2. **Assessing** the size of operational risks.
3. **Monitoring and controlling** operational risks.
4. **Mitigating** operational risks.
5. **Calculating capital** to protect you from operational risk losses.

These five requirements occur again and again in global and national regulations and are the bedrock of successful operational risk management.

In addition to putting these tools in place, a robust operational risk framework must look at all *types* of operational risk. Seven main categories of operational risk are defined by Basel II, and we will explore them in the next section.

Before we dive into how operational risk impacts the financial services industry, let's take a step back and see how other businesses have been addressing operational risk.

At the time of this writing, the Tokyo Summer Olympics (delayed from 2020 to 2021) were still in some doubt, with controversy raging as to whether attendees should be allowed in the stands. The Tokyo Olympics Committee were struggling to manage the games under the pressure of the biggest operational risk event in recent history, the COVID-19 pandemic. Taking a look back at a prior Olympics might give us some insight into how the current Olympics management team is managing its complex operational risk profile today.

The 2012 Summer Olympics and Paralympics in London, England, provide an interesting case study in how operational risk is managed in such a scenario and a practical view into how the basic elements of operational risk management have been applied outside of the financial services sector.

2012 LONDON OLYMPICS: A CASE STUDY[8]

At the end of the summer of 2012, the Paralympic flame was extinguished in London, bringing the Summer Olympics and Paralympics to a triumphant close. By all accounts both Games were a resounding success, and there was much proud puffing of British chests and declaring of "Happy and Glorious!"

Before the opening ceremony, then–London mayor Boris Johnson had admitted that there would be "imperfections and things going wrong" as the capital coped with the Olympics.[9]

However, at the opening ceremony, London 2012 Olympic Chairman Lord Sebastian Coe confidently declared: "One day we will tell our children and our grandchildren that when our time came we did it right."[10]

It is unlikely that Lord Coe and his team turned to banking regulations to assist them in this task, but the Games do offer us an interesting opportunity to assess whether the Basel II operational risk requirements stand up to a "real-world" test. Was Lord Coe an excellent operational risk manager? Will we ever see him as a headline speaker at a future risk conference? (Spoiler alert: He has my vote.)

The Basel requirements are designed to ensure that there is an adequate framework in place to manage any risks resulting from failed or inadequate processes, people, and systems or from external events. These were exactly the risks that faced the London 2012 team as they prepared to unleash a global event on the crowded city of London. The four main causes of operational risk were there in abundance:

People: Nervous athletes, opinionated officials, aggressive press, terrorists, disgruntled Londoners, (missing) security guards, confused volunteers, crazed fans, lost children, heads of state, visiting dignitaries, and the list goes on.

Processes and systems: Stadium building and preparation, ticket sales, transportation, opening ceremonies, closing ceremonies, managing the Olympic Village, cleaning, feeding, running races, organizing matches, safety checks of the parallel bars, awarding medals, playing anthems, global broadcasting, keeping that darned flame alight, and the list goes on.

External events: Two words—London weather.

In the most recent BIS Sound Practices document, the rules require risk management activities that identify and assess, monitor and report, and control and mitigate operational risks. Was this how Lord Coe pulled it off? Did he ensure that the London 2012 team excelled in all of those practices?

The Basel rules also provide seven categories of risk for us to fit any operational risk events into.[11] The risk categories certainly seem comprehensive to those of us in the banking industry, but do they truly capture all operational risks? The categories we are given to work with are:

- **Internal Fraud:** Losses due to acts of a type intended to defraud, misappropriate property, or circumvent regulations, the law, or company policy, excluding diversity/discrimination events, which involves at least one internal party.

- **External Fraud:** Losses due to acts of a type intended to defraud, misappropriate property, or circumvent the law, by a third party.
- **Employment Practices and Workplace Safety:** Losses arising from acts inconsistent with employment, health, or safety laws or agreements; from payment of personal injury claims; or from diversity/discrimination events.
- **Clients, Products, and Business Practices:** Losses arising from an unintentional or negligent failure to meet a professional obligation to specific clients (including fiduciary and suitability requirements), or from the nature or design of a product.
- **Damage to Physical Assets:** Losses arising from loss or damage to physical assets from natural disasters or other events.
- **Business Disruption and System Failures:** Losses arising from disruption of business or system failures.
- **Execution, Delivery, and Process Management:** Losses from failed transaction processing or process management, from relations with trade counterparties and vendors.

We will learn more about these categories later, but first we will test them out in the real world.

Test One: Do the Seven Basel Operational Risk Categories Work in the Real World?

Let's take a look at the categories and see if they match up with those salacious Olympics headlines that popped up over the summer:

- **Internal Fraud:** "Olympic Badminton Players Disqualified for Trying to Lose"[12]
- **External Fraud:** "London Olympics Fake Tickets Create 'Honeypot' for Criminals"[13]
- **Clients, Products, and Business Practices:** "Empty Seats at Olympic Venues Prompt Investigation"[14]
- **Employment Practice and Workplace Safety:** "Dispute Between London Olympics and Musicians Union Heats Up"[15]
- **Execution, Delivery, and Process Management:** "NATB Calls London Olympics Ticket Distribution a Failure"[16]
- **Damage to Physical Assets:** "Olympic Security Shortfall Called 'Absolute Chaos'"[17]
- **Business Disruption and System Failure:** "London 2012: Traffic Jams and Impact of Games Lanes"[18]

Certainly, the Olympics raised risks in each of the categories. Indeed, over 17 years of working in operational risk with clients ranging from banks to commodities shipping firms and from law firms to tourism and hospitality conglomerates, I have found that the Basel seven categories have proven remarkably resilient and comprehensive.

Test Two: The Risk Management Tools

Managing the Olympic Games and Paralympic Games was without doubt an enormous challenge in operational risk management. So the next test, and surely the more important one, is whether the Sound Practices requirements cover the bases. (*Note*: We will not be discussing why baseball is not an Olympic sport as it did manage to make an appearance at the Tokyo Games in 2021.)

Risks did materialize, and the headlines were at times brutal, but the final wrap-up headlines were consistently positive. Did the London 2012 team avert disaster by applying the tenets of good operational risk management? Did they identify and assess, monitor and report, and control and mitigate the risks?

Yes, they did. In the Annual Report of the London Organising Committee of the Olympic Games and Paralympic Games Ltd. (LOCOG),[19] the team outline the "principal risks and uncertainties" that they face and describe their methodology for managing these risks as follows:

> *Management use a common model to **identify** and **assess** the impact of risks to their business. For each risk, the likelihood and consequence are identified, management **controls** and the frequency of **monitoring** are confirmed and results reported. [emphasis added, p. 33]*

To be a stickler for accuracy, I will concede that the word *mitigation* is referenced only for budget risks and security risks, but it is clear in the report that mitigation of the risks identified was the key purpose of the risk management activities. In addition, according to their own website,[20] the London Prepares series, the official London 2012 sports testing program, helped to test vital areas of operations ahead of the London 2012 Games.

The Basel rules were first published in 2004, and the main tenets of operational risk management have not changed fundamentally since that time. It is interesting, and somewhat comforting, to see that the language of operational risk management has become remarkably consistent—the same risk categories and the same tenets of best practices apply whether you are a bank or an Olympic Games.

Then–London mayor Boris Johnson admitted that there would be "imperfections and things going wrong"[21] as the capital coped with the Olympics. For the record, I like this as a new definition for operational risk. Operational risk management does not ensure that nothing will go wrong, but instead focuses on identifying and assessing what can go wrong, on monitoring and reporting changes in risk, and mitigating and controlling the impact of any events that are threatening to occur or that have occurred and need speedy and effective cleanup.

It's real-world risk management, and that is why operational risk managers get so passionate about their discipline. Operational risk exists in every industry and in every endeavor. It exists in massive global multimedia extravaganzas and in small local events. It does appear that the Basel operational risk management rules are applicable across the board. Job well done, Bank for International Settlements.

Now whether we need to have all of these rules and also hold bucket loads of capital in case something happens anyway—well, that's a different discussion for a different chapter (Chapter 12, "Capital Modeling").

For now, we can agree that an excellent motto for an operational risk department would be Lord Coe's confident declaration that "one day we will tell our children and our grandchildren that when our time came we did it right."[22]

The London Olympics nearly 10 years ago gave us a valuable insight into how practical the financial services operational risk frameworks are. However, these frameworks have been stretched to their limits by the recent and ongoing devastating operational risk world event—the global COVID-19 pandemic. This event has impacted financial services, and banks have used their operational risk frameworks to manage their response, and nonbanks have turned to the same practical tools to manage the risk and mitigation of the global pandemic. We will explore this further in Chapter 17.

OPERATIONAL RISK MANAGEMENT AND OPERATIONAL RISK MEASUREMENT

There are two sides to operational risk: operational risk management and operational risk measurement. There is often tension, as well as overlap, between these two activities. Basel II requires capital to be held for operational risk and offers several possible calculation methods for that capital, which are discussed later in Chapter 12. This capital requirement is the heart of the operational risk *measurement* activities and requires *quantitative* approaches. As a result of the global economic crisis in 2008, Basel III was established and provides new guidance on operational risk capital that simplifies the capital approach. At the time of this writing, the new approach was scheduled to come into effect in January 2023, having been delayed from its original due date of January 2022 as a result of the COVID-19 pandemic.

In addition, firms must also demonstrate effective *management* of their operational risk, and this requires *qualitative* approaches. A successful operational risk program combines qualitative and quantitative approaches to ensure that operational risk is both appropriately measured and effectively managed.

Even if a financial services firm is not under a regulatory requirement to measure and manage its operational risk, doing so is a critical element of an effective risk management framework to ensure the fintech or bank's successful execution of its business plan. The Basel framework provides an excellent structure under which these risks can be effectively managed and measured and so in this book we look to that guidance to assist in constructing an effective operational risk program that is appropriate for the firm.

Operational Risk Management

Helpful guidelines for appropriate operational risk management activities in a firm can be found in Pillar 2 of Basel II:

> 736. **Operational risk:** *The Committee believes that similar rigour should be applied to the management of operational risk, as is done for the management of other significant banking risks. . . .*
> 737. *A bank should develop a framework for managing operational risk and evaluate the adequacy of capital given this framework. The framework should cover the bank's appetite and tolerance for operational risk, as specified through the policies for managing this risk, including the extent and manner in which operational risk is transferred outside the bank. It should also include policies outlining the bank's approach to identifying, assessing, monitoring and controlling/mitigating the risk.*[23]

There are several important things to note in these sections. First, operational risk should be managed with the same rigor as market and credit risk. This is an important concept that has many implications when considering how to embed an operational risk management culture in a firm, as will be explored later in Chapter 5.

Second, policies regarding risk appetite are required. This is no easy task, as articulating a risk appetite for operational risk can be very challenging. Most firms would prefer to have no operational risk, and yet these risks are inherent in their day-to-day activities and cannot be completely avoided. Recently, regulators have been very interested in how firms are responding to this challenge, and there is much debate about how to express operational risk appetite or tolerance and how to manage against it. This will be explored further in each of the framework sections in upcoming chapters.

Finally, policies must be written that outline the bank's approach to "identifying, assessing, monitoring, and controlling/mitigating" operational risk. This is the heart of the definition of operational risk management, and the elements of an operational risk framework need to address these challenges. Does each element contribute to the identification of operational risks, the assessment of those risks, the monitoring of those risks, and the control or mitigation of those risks? To be successful, an operational risk framework must be designed to meet these four criteria for all operational risk exposures, and it takes a toolbox of activities to achieve this.

In the operational risk management toolbox are operational risk event data collection programs, risk and control self-assessments, scenario analysis activities, key risk indicators, and powerful reporting. (See www.wiley. com/go/girling2E for access to sample toolbox templates.) Each of these elements will be considered in turn in this book.

Operational Risk Measurement

Operational risk measurement focuses on the calculation of capital for operational risk, and Basel II provides for three possible methods for calculating operational risk capital. Basel III simplifies the methods down to one. These methods are discussed in Chapter 12. Some firms choose to calculate operational risk capital, even if they are not subject to a regulatory requirement, as they wish to include the operational risk capital in their strategic planning and capital allocation for strategic and business reasons.

The Relationship between Operational Risk Management and Other Risk Types

Operational risk often arises in the presence of other risk types, and the size of an operational risk event may be dramatically impacted by market or credit risk forces.

EXAMPLE

One of Gamma Bank's business lines offers retail customers the ability to trade bonds. One of the customers calls the broker at Gamma Bank and instructs the broker to buy Andromeda Corporation bonds for the customer's account. The trade is executed, but it is mistakenly booked as a sell instead of a buy; this will result in a significantly larger loss if the market moves up.

The cost of making the customer whole will now be much higher than if the market had remained stable. In fact, there could be a gain if the market drops. It is clear, then, that market risk can magnify operational risk.

There are also events that include both credit and operational risk elements. If a counterparty fails and there was an operational error in securing adequate collateral, then the credit risk event is magnified by operational risk.

While market risk, credit risk, and operational risk functions are usually run separately, there are benefits in integrating these functions where possible. The overall risk profile of a firm depends not on the individual market, credit, and operational risks, but also on elusive strategic and reputational risks (or impacts) and the relationships among all of these risk categories.

Additional risk categories also exist—for example, geopolitical risk and liquidity risk. For these reasons, some firms adopt an enterprise risk management (ERM) view of their risk exposure. It is important to consider the role of operational risk management as an element in ERM and to appreciate its relationship with all other risk types. The relationships among risks are illustrated in Figure 1.1.

This ERM wheel illustrates that all risk types are interrelated and that central risk types can have an impact on risk types on the outer spokes of the wheel. For example, a geopolitical risk event might result in risks arising in market risk, credit risk, strategic risk, liquidity risk, and operational risk.

Similarly, reputational risk, or reputational impact, can occur as a result of any risk event and so is at the center of the ERM wheel. This is just one possible model for the relationship between risk types and simply illustrates the complexity of effective ERM. Operational risk sits on the ERM wheel and is best managed and measured with that in mind.

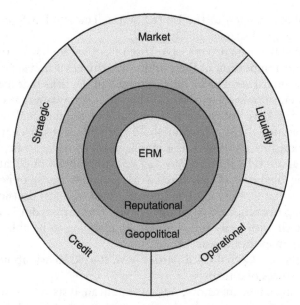

FIGURE 1.1   Enterprise Risk Management Wheel

EXAMPLE

A country's government banned trades in a particular type of derivative. This ban could result in market risk (the value of the derivatives plummets), credit risk (counterparties who are concentrated in this product might fail), strategic risk (the business model might rely on growth in that product), and operational risk (certain activities might now be illegal).

DRIVERS OF OPERATIONAL RISK MANAGEMENT

Operational risk management has arisen as a discipline as a result of drivers from three main sources: regulators, senior management, and third parties.

In addition to Basel II and III, there are other regulatory drivers for operational risk management, including Solvency II, which imposes Basel-like requirements on insurance firms, and a host of local regulations such as the Markets in Financial Instruments Directive (MiFID) legislation in Europe and the Sarbanes-Oxley Act (which includes risk and control requirements for financial statements) in the United States. The regulatory evolution of operational risk is discussed in Chapter 2.

Additional business drivers have arisen from within banks and fintechs. One of the most important of these additional drivers is that senior management and the board want to be fully informed of the risks that face the firm, including operational risk exposures. They are fully aware that operational risk events can have catastrophic financial and reputational impacts. An effective operational risk program should provide transparency of operational risk exposure to allow senior management to make strategic business decisions that are fully informed by any operational risk implications.

A strong operational risk framework provides transparency into the risks in the firm, therefore allowing for informed business decision making. With a strong operational risk framework, a firm can avoid bad surprises and equip itself with tools and contingency planning to be able to respond swiftly when an event does occur.

Furthermore, external third parties have started to ask about the operational robustness of a firm.

Ratings agencies, investors, and research analysts are now aware of the importance of operational risk management and often ask for evidence that an effective operational risk framework is in place and whether sufficient capital is being held to protect a firm from a catastrophic operational risk event.

KEY POINTS

- Operational risk is defined in Basel II as the risk of loss resulting from inadequate or failed processes, people, and systems or from external events. This definition includes legal risk but excludes strategic and reputational risk.
- Firms adapt the Basel II definition to their own needs.
- Both qualitative and quantitative approaches are needed to effectively manage and measure operational risk.
- Operational risk is a key element in an ERM approach.

REVIEW QUESTIONS

1. Which of the following best meets the Basel II definition of operational risk?
   a. A basket of options expires with a value of zero.
   b. A client refuses to pay his invoice.

    c. A wire transfer is sent to the wrong account.

    d. A government expropriates all foreign-owned assets.

2. The main causes of operational risk are generally accepted to be

    a. People, processes, systems, external events.

    b. People, processes, systems, internal events.

    c. Processes, systems, events.

    d. People, events.

NOTES

1. S644, "International Convergence of Capital Measurement and Capital Standards: A Revised Framework," Bank for International Settlements, 2004.

2. *Comptrollers Handbook: Corporate and Risk Governance*, Version 2.0, July 2019, Office of the Comptroller of the Currency, 5.

3. JPMorgan Chase & Co. Annual Report, 2020, 85.

4. Deutsche Bank Financial Report, 2020, 99.

5. See note 1, footnote 90.

6. See note 1.

7. Citi Annual Report, 2020, 64.

8. As featured in issue 9 of *Risk Universe* and reproduced with their permission.

9. www.independent.co.uk/news/uk/home-news/things-will-go-wrong-as-london-holds-olympics-says-boris-johnson-7952706.html.

10. www.bbc.co.uk/sport/0/olympics/18906710#TWEET179228 (no longer available).

11. Annex 9, "International Convergence of Capital Measurement and Capital Standards: A Revised Framework," Bank for International Settlements, 2004.

12. http://edition.cnn.com/2012/08/01/sport/olympics-badminton-scandal/index.html.

13. www.bloomberg.com/news/2012-07-26/london-olympics-fake-tickets-create-honeypot-for-criminals.html.

14. http://sports.yahoo.com/blogs/olympics-fourth-place-medal/empty-seats-olympic-venues-prompt-investigation-224320331–oly.html (no longer available).

15. www.billboard.biz/bbbiz/industry/legal-and-management/dispute-between-london-olympics-and-musicians-1007687952.story#I1ptQC1VdfjCF9xS.99.

16. www.ticketnews.com/news/natb-calls-london-olympics-ticket-distribution-a-failure081213258.

17. www.cbsnews.com/8301-33747_162-57473130/olympic-security-shortfall-called-absolute-chaos/ (no longer available).

18. www.bbc.co.uk/news/uk-england-london-18962856.

19. www.london2012.com/mm/Document/Publications/Annualreports/01/24/09/33/locog-annual-report-2010-11.pdf.

20. www.london2012.com/about-us/london-prepares-series/ (no longer available).

21. See note 9.

22. www.bbc.co.uk/sport/0/olympics/19023771.

23. See note 1.

CHAPTER 2

The Regulatory Push

The regulation of operational risk was globally founded on Basel II and later refined in Basel III. This chapter discusses the regulatory response to the Basel Capital Accords (commonly known as Basel I, Basel II, and Basel III) that were presented by the Basel Banking Committee of the Bank of International Settlements in 1988, 2004, and 2010 and that were intended to provide a robust capital framework and risk management approach for internationally active banks.

The focus of this chapter is on (1) the history of the Basel Accords; (2) the rules of the Basel Accords; (3) the adoption of Basel II in Europe and (4) in the United States; (5) the impact of the financial crisis and resulting European and U.S. regulatory changes, including the Dodd-Frank regulation in the United States; and, finally, (6) the introduction of Basel III and its impact on operational risk management.

HISTORY OF THE BASEL ACCORDS

The Basel Accords were developed by the Bank of International Settlements (BIS), which is headquartered in Basel, Switzerland. The BIS describes its mission and activities as follows:

> *Our mission is to support central banks' pursuit of monetary and financial stability through international cooperation, and to act as a bank for central banks. To pursue our mission we provide central banks with:*
>
> ■ *a forum for dialogue and broad international cooperation*
> ■ *a platform for responsible innovation and knowledge-sharing*

- *in-depth analysis and insights on core policy issues*
- *sound and competitive financial services*[1]

The BIS was originally established in 1930 to assist with the management of reparation loans post World War I, but it soon transitioned into a body that addressed monetary and financial stability through statistical analysis, economic research, and regular meetings between central bank governors and other global financial experts. The BIS has successfully expanded its global reach in recent decades and between 1995 and 2020 grew its membership from 33 member central banks or monetary authorities to 63.

At the time of this writing, the global representation at the BIS accounts for about 95 percent of world GDP and includes the following members:

Bank of Algeria
Central Bank of Argentina
Reserve Bank of Australia
Central Bank of the Republic of Austria
National Bank of Belgium
Central Bank of Bosnia and Herzegovina
Central Bank of Brazil
Bulgarian National Bank
Bank of Canada
Central Bank of Chile
People's Bank of China
Central Bank of Colombia
Croatian National Bank
Czech National Bank
Danmarks Nationalbank (Denmark)
Bank of Estonia
European Central Bank
Bank of Finland
Bank of France
Deutsche Bundesbank (Germany)
Bank of Greece
Hong Kong Monetary Authority
Magyar Nemzeti Bank (Hungary)

Central Bank of Iceland
Reserve Bank of India
Bank Indonesia
Central Bank of Ireland
Bank of Israel
Bank of Italy
Bank of Japan
Bank of Korea
Central Bank of Kuwait
Bank of Latvia
Bank of Lithuania
Central Bank of Luxembourg
Central Bank of Malaysia
Bank of Mexico
Bank Al-Maghrib (Central Bank of Morocco)
Netherlands Bank
Reserve Bank of New Zealand
Central Bank of Norway
National Bank of the Republic of North Macedonia
Central Reserve Bank of Peru
Bangko Sentral ng Pilipinas (Philippines)
Narodowy Bank Polski (Poland)
Banco de Portugal
National Bank of Romania
Central Bank of the Russian Federation
Saudi Central Bank
National Bank of Serbia
Monetary Authority of Singapore
National Bank of Slovakia
Bank of Slovenia
South African Reserve Bank
Bank of Spain
Sveriges Riksbank (Sweden)

Swiss National Bank

Bank of Thailand

Central Bank of the Republic of Turkey

Central Bank of the United Arab Emirates

Bank of England (United Kingdom)

Board of Governors of the Federal Reserve System (United States)

State Bank of Vietnam[2]

Over the years, the BIS has established several standing committees to take on the important financial topics of the day. It was heavily involved in supporting the Bretton Woods System in the early 1970s, and tackled the challenges of cross-border capital flows and the importance of financial regulation in the late 1970s and 1980s. In 1974, the G10 nations[3] formed the BIS Basel Committee on Banking Supervision (BCBS) to address shortcomings in the regulation of internationally active banks:

> *The Basel Committee comprises 45 members from 28 jurisdictions, consisting of central banks and authorities with formal responsibility for the supervision of banking business. Additionally, the Committee has nine observers including central banks, supervisory groups, international organisations and other bodies. The Committee expanded its membership in 2009 and again in 2014.[4]*
>
> *Institutions represented on the Basel Committee on Banking Supervision*

Country/jurisdiction	Institutional representative
Argentina	Central Bank of Argentina
Australia	Reserve Bank of Australia
	Australian Prudential Regulation Authority
Belgium	National Bank of Belgium
Brazil	Central Bank of Brazil
Canada	Bank of Canada
	Office of the Superintendent of Financial Institutions
China	People's Bank of China
	China Banking Regulatory Commission
European Union	European Central Bank
	European Central Bank Single Supervisory Mechanism
France	Bank of France
	Prudential Supervision and Resolution Authority

Germany	Deutsche Bundesbank
	Federal Financial Supervisory Authority (BaFin)
Hong Kong SAR	Hong Kong Monetary Authority
India	Reserve Bank of India
Indonesia	Bank Indonesia
	Indonesia Financial Services Authority
Italy	Bank of Italy
Japan	Bank of Japan
	Financial Services Agency
Korea	Bank of Korea
	Financial Supervisory Service
Luxembourg	Surveillance Commission for the Financial Sector
Mexico	Bank of Mexico
	Comisión Nacional Bancaria y de Valores
Netherlands	Netherlands Bank
Russia	Central Bank of the Russian Federation
Saudi Arabia	Saudi Central Bank
Singapore	Monetary Authority of Singapore
South Africa	South African Reserve Bank
Spain	Bank of Spain
Sweden	Sveriges Riksbank
	Finansinspektionen
Switzerland	Swiss National Bank
	Swiss Financial Market Supervisory Authority (FINMA)
Turkey	Central Bank of the Republic of Turkey
	Banking Regulation and Supervision Agency
United Kingdom	Bank of England
	Prudential Regulation Authority
United States	Board of Governors of the Federal Reserve System
	Federal Reserve Bank of New York
	Office of the Comptroller of the Currency
	Federal Deposit Insurance Corporation

In 1988, the BCBS published the Basel Capital Accord[5] (commonly known today as Basel I) to provide a framework for the consistent and appropriate regulation of capital adequacy and risk management in internationally active banks. In 2004, the Basel Committee published a revised framework, which came to be known as Basel II.[6] Today, the Basel Committee is made up of five groups: the Policy Development Group, the Supervision and Implementation Group, the Macroprudential Supervision Group, the Accounting Experts Group, and the Basel Consultative Group; each of these groups has task forces and working groups that are formed as needed.

By its own admission, the Basel Committee has no legal authority over member central banks, but it relies on them to commit voluntarily to the standards that it sets:

The BCBS does not possess any formal supranational author-ity. Its decisions do not have legal force. Rather, the BCBS relies on its members' commitments, as described in Section 5, to achieve its mandate.

Section 5. BCBS members' responsibilities

BCBS members are committed to:

a. *work together to achieve the mandate of the BCBS;*
b. *promote financial stability;*
c. *continuously enhance their quality of banking regulation and supervision;*
d. *actively contribute to the development of BCBS standards, guide-lines and sound practices;*
e. *implement and apply BCBS standards in their domestic juris-dictions within the pre-defined timeframe established by the Committee;*
f. *undergo and participate in BCBS reviews to assess the consist-ency and effectiveness of domestic rules and supervisory practices in relation to BCBS standards; and*
g. *promote the interests of global financial stability and not solely national interests, while participating in BCBS work and decision-making.*[7]

However, the U.S. Federal Reserve, along with the majority of member central banks, moved forward with national regulatory implementation of most of the Basel Committee recommendations such that they became man-datory for the banks in their jurisdictions.

As a result of the global economic crisis of 2008, the BCBS implemented further standards focusing on credit and liquidity risk management and further bolstering the capital requirements of global financial institutions. These additional standards are known as Basel III.

RULES OF THE ACCORDS

The Basel Accords outline rules for financial institutions and for the national regulators who supervise those institutions.

Basel I

In 1988, the BIS Basel Committee on Banking Supervision published the "International Convergence of Capital Measurement and Capital Standards" (commonly known then as the Basel Capital Accord and today as Basel I). The report aimed to "secure international convergence of supervisory regulations governing the capital adequacy of international banks" (1988, p. 1). Balin outlined the four "pillars" of Basel I as the Constituents of Capital, the Risk Weights, a Target Standard Ratio, and Transitional and Implementing Agreements.[8]

Basel I focused on credit risk and assigned different weightings (0 percent, 10 percent, 20 percent, 50 percent, and 100 percent) for capital requirements, depending on the level of credit risk associated with the asset. Later amendments to Basel I added further weightings to accommodate more sophisticated instruments. The Target Standard Ratio set a minimum standard whereby 8 percent of a bank's risk-weighted assets had to be covered by Tier 1 and Tier 2 capital reserves.

There were no requirements to either manage or measure operational risk under the Basel Accord.

The Basel Accord was adopted with relative ease by the G10 nations that were members of the Basel Banking Committee at that time, including the United States. In the United States, the Basel recommendations were codified in Title 12 of the United States Code and Title 12 of the Code of Federal Regulations.

The Basel Accord (Basel I) was seen as a safety and soundness standard that would protect banks from insolvency, and the minimum capital requirements provided a standard below which regulators would not permit a bank to continue to conduct business. However, regulators soon began to question whether Basel I adequately captured the risks of the increasingly complex and changing financial markets. In addition, banks were able to "game" the system by moving assets off balance sheet and by manipulating their portfolios to minimize their required capital while not necessarily minimizing their actual risk exposure.

Basel II

As pressure mounted for a revised approach, the Basel Committee responded by proposing a revised Capital Adequacy Framework in June 1999. They described the new proposed capital framework as consisting of three pillars: "minimum capital requirements; . . . supervisory review of an institution's internal assessment process and capital adequacy; and effective use of disclosure to strengthen market discipline as a complement to supervisory efforts."[9]

Comments and discussions were held over the next few years, with the newly broadened membership of the Committee providing a global perspective on the proposed changes. The "International Convergence of Capital Measurement and Capital Standards: A Revised Framework" was issued on June 26, 2004, and served as a basis for national rule-making to reflect the Basel II approaches. The Basel Committee outlined the goal of the revised framework as follows:

> *The Basel II Framework describes a more comprehensive measure and minimum standard for capital adequacy that national supervisory authorities are now working to implement through domestic rule-making and adoption procedures. It seeks to improve on the existing rules by aligning regulatory capital requirements more closely to the underlying risks that banks face. In addition, the Basel II Framework is intended to promote a more forward-looking approach to capital supervision, one that encourages banks to identify the risks they may face, today and in the future, and to develop or improve their ability to manage those risks. As a result, it is intended to be more flexible and better able to evolve with advances in markets and risk management practices.*[10]

On July 4, 2006, the Committee issued an updated version of the revised framework incorporating additional guidance and including those sections of Basel I that had not been revised. The revised framework is almost 10 times the length of Basel I, running to more than 300 pages. For the first time, operational risk management and measurement were required.

Basel II consists of three pillars: Pillar 1—Minimum Capital Requirements, Pillar 2—Supervisory Review Process, and Pillar 3—Market Discipline.

Pillar 1

The major changes to the capital adequacy rules were outlined in detail in Pillar 1. Basel II required banks to hold capital for assets in the holding company, so as to prevent banks from avoiding capital by moving assets around within its corporate structure.

Credit Risk   Pillar 1 offered three possible approaches to calculating credit risk: the standardized approach, the foundation internal ratings based (F-IRB) approach, and, finally, the advanced IRB approach.

Under the standardized approach a bank could use "authorized" rating institution ratings in order to assign risk weightings and to calculate capital.

Under the IRB approaches, the banks were able to take advantage of capital improvements on the standardized approach by applying their own internal credit rating models. Under F-IRB, a bank could develop its own model to estimate the probability of default (PD) for individual clients or groups of clients, subject to approval from their local regulators. F-IRB banks were required to use their regulator's prescribed loss given default (LGD) and to calculate the risk-weighted asset (RWA) and the final required capital.

Under advanced IRB (A-IRB), banks could use their own estimates for PD, LGD, and exposure at default (EAD) to calculate RWA and the final required capital.

Market Risk   Pillar 1 also provided market risk capital requirements, based mainly on a value at risk (VaR) approach.

Operational Risk   Finally, Pillar 1 introduced a new risk category: operational risk. As discussed in Chapter 1, operational risk is defined in Basel II as the "risk of loss resulting from inadequate or failed internal processes, people and systems or from external events. This definition includes legal risk, but excludes strategic and reputational risk."[11]

Pillar 1 offered three possible methods to calculate capital for operational risk: the basic indicator approach (BIA), the standardized approach (TSA), or the advanced measurement approach (AMA).[12]

Under BIA, capital was simply calculated from a percentage (set at 15 percent) of the average of the previous three years' revenue. TSA offered different percentage weightings depending on the business line—ranging from 12 percent for retail banking to 18 percent for sales and trading. AMA offered banks the opportunity to develop their own risk-based model for calculating operational risk capital. AMA required that the model include four elements: internal loss data, external loss data, scenario analysis, and business environment and internal control factors. These three methods are summarized in Figure 2.1.

While Pillar 1 offered three possible methods to calculate operational risk capital, most large banks found that their local regulator required them to pursue an AMA approach. In addition, even where a bank was not required to take an AMA approach to calculating capital, their regulator often advised them that they should adopt best practices and that best practices require them to ensure they have fully developed all four elements of AMA.

Therefore, the standard for a strong operational risk framework is based on the effective development of internal and external loss data systems, appropriate use of scenario analysis, and effective development of business environment and internal control factors.

BASIC INDICATOR APPROACH	THE STANDARDIZED APPROACH	ADVANCED MEASUREMENT APPROACH
$\sum avg\ 3yr\ gross\ revenue \times \alpha$ α is 15%	$\sum avg\ 3yr\ gross\ revenue \times \beta$ β for each business line is: Corporate Finance Trading and Sales — 18% Payment and Settlement Commercial Banking — 15% Agency Services Retail Banking Retail Brokerage — 12% Asset Management	Regulator approved, internal risk model, which includes the following inputs: Internal Loss Data External Loss Data Scenario Analysis Business Environment Internal Control Factors

FIGURE 2.1   Three Capital Calculation Approaches for the Treatment of Operational Risk under Pillar 1 of Basel II

Recent Basel guidance requires banks to adopt a more simplified standardized approach to capital calculation that is driven only by the business activities of the bank and the internal loss history of the bank. However, whether or not the AMA elements are still used as direct inputs into a capital model, they are still considered vital elements of a sound operational risk management framework.

Capital Reserves   Finally, under Pillar 1, a bank had to hold capital reserves of at least 8 percent of their total credit, market, and operational risk-weighted assets:

$$\frac{capital}{market\ risk + credit\ risk + operational\ risk} \geq 8\%$$

Pillar 2
Basel II introduced Pillar 2 requirements as follows:

This section discusses the key principles of supervisory review, risk management guidance and supervisory transparency and accountability produced by the Committee with respect to banking risks, including guidance relating to, among other things, the treatment of interest rate risk in the banking book, credit risk (stress testing, definition of default, residual risk, and credit concentration risk), operational risk, enhanced cross-border communication and cooperation, and securitization.[13]

Pillar 2 outlined how the regulators were expected to enforce soundness standards and provided a mechanism for additional capital requirements to cover any material risks that had not been effectively captured in Pillar 1.

Pillar 3

Pillar 3 provided methods for disclosure of risk management practices and capital calculation methods to the public. The purpose of Pillar 3 was to increase transparency and to allow investors and shareholders a view into the inner risk practices of the bank.

ADOPTION OF BASEL II IN EUROPE

In the European Union, Basel II was codified through the European Parliament through the Capital Requirements Directive,[14] which required member states to enact appropriate local regulations by January 1, 2007, with advanced approaches available by January 1, 2008.

ADOPTION OF BASEL II IN THE UNITED STATES

In the United States, the plethora of regulators added to the complexities of implementation.

Securities and Exchange Commission Amendments to the Net Capital Rule

U.S. investment banks needed to select a global Basel II regulator, and the Securities and Exchange Commission (SEC) looked for ways for them to be able to select the SEC as that regulator. To support this, the SEC adopted rules that allowed for consolidated supervised entities (CSEs) to apply to the SEC for regulatory supervision for Basel II. The five large U.S. investment banks took this opportunity: Goldman Sachs, Morgan Stanley, Bear Stearns, Merrill Lynch, and Lehman Brothers successfully applied for CSE status.

The SEC moved swiftly to make changes to its net capital rules to reflect Basel II standards,[15] and the five investment banks were quickly approved for Basel II supervision by the SEC.

U.S. Regulators' Adoption of New Regulations to Apply Basel II

Meanwhile, the remaining U.S. banks were waiting to see whether U.S. banking regulations would be amended to apply the Basel II rules to them.

Questions were raised on the appropriateness of the rules, and the audacity of the European Union in driving these global standards was hotly debated in Congress. Pressure was mounting from the regulators and the banks, and international political tensions were increasing as banks waited for the United States to move forward with Basel II rules.

On September 25, 2006, the Federal Banking agencies (the Office of the Comptroller of the Currency [OCC], the Board of Governors of the Federal Reserve System, the Federal Deposit Insurance Corporation [FDIC], and the Office of Thrift Supervision [OTS]) came together to collect comments on the adoption of Basel II rules in the United States through two Notices of Proposed Rulemaking relating to capital requirements: New Risk-Based Capital Rules for Large or Internationally Active U.S. Banks in accordance with Basel II, and Market Risk Rule.

On November 2, 2007, the Federal Reserve Board approved final rules to implement new risk-based capital requirements in the United States for large, internationally active banking organizations, stating:

> *The new advanced capital adequacy framework, known as Basel II, more closely aligns regulatory capital requirements with actual risks and should further strengthen banking organizations' risk-management practices.*
>
> *'Basel II is a modern, risk-sensitive capital standard that will protect the safety and soundness of our large, complex, internationally active banking organizations. The new framework is designed to evolve over time and adapt to innovations in banking and financial markets, a significant improvement from the current system,' said Federal Reserve Board Chairman Ben S. Bernanke.*[16]

On July 20, 2008, the Federal Reserve, OCC, OTS, and FDIC reached agreement regarding implementation of Basel II in the United States. There would be mandatory Basel II rules for large banks, and opt-in provisions for noncore banks, as had been proposed in the Notices of Proposed Rulemaking (NPRs).

The new standards were to be transitioned into over a parallel run period, with Basel I–based capital floors being set for the first three years.

Pillar 2 guidance was provided later, resulting in supervisory guidance being published on December 7, 2007.[17] The Pillar 2 guidance provided for an Internal Capital Adequacy Assessment Process (ICAAP) for the implementation of Pillar 2 standards in a bank. The final rules were published in the Federal Register, mostly through amendments to Title 12.

IMPACT OF THE FINANCIAL CRISIS

The global economic crisis that began in 2007 led to much soul-searching by governments, regulators, and the BIS as they sought to understand how the Basel frameworks had failed to protect the global economy.

The Limitations of Basel II

Global political pressure resulted in the BIS Basel Committee on Banking Supervision revisiting Basel II to consider what further regulatory and capital enhancements were needed in order to ensure global financial stability. Former – SEC Chairman Christopher Cox himself was vocal about the need for regulatory reform, stating that "in March 2008, I formally requested that the Basel Committee address the inadequacy of the Basel capital and liquidity standards."[18]

The Group of Twenty (G20) met regularly to address concerns regarding global regulatory requirements and capital adequacy. They established a Financial Stability Board (FSB) to address these concerns and to make recommendations for change, and the BIS worked closely with the FSB and the International Monetary Fund (IMF) to develop new recommendations to enhance the Basel framework. In April 2010, the G20 met to review a report prepared by IMF and FSB and "the main message coming through this document from central banks and regulators is that priority number one is Basel III," two sources involved in the G20 process said.[19]

Indeed, the G20 agreed to introduce Basel III by the end of 2012. Proposals for an updating of Basel II were put forward by the Basel Committee on Banking Supervision in December 2009 in two documents: "Strengthening the Resilience of the Banking Sector"[20] and "International Framework for Liquidity Risk Measurement, Standards and Monitoring."[21] The Committee gathered comments and feedback, and the main recommendations were:

- An increase in Tier 1 capital.
- Additional capital for derivatives, securities financing, and repo markets.
- Tighter leverage ratios.
- Setting aside revenue during upturns to protect against cyclicality of markets.
- Minimum 30-day liquidity standards.
- Enhanced corporate governance, risk management, compensation practices, disclosure, and board supervision practices.

European Response to the Crisis

The Committee of European Banking Supervisors (CEBS) produced the "Guidelines on the Management of Operational Risk in Market Related Activities"[22] in October 2010. They placed a heavy emphasis on the importance of strong corporate governance, an area that many saw as one of the key causes of the financial crisis. This document supplemented the earlier "Guidelines on the Scope of Operational Risk and Operational Risk Loss"[23] and rounded out the European detailed guidance on the implementation of a robust operational risk framework under Basel II.

This guidance was used by European regulators as a measure against which to assess the operational risk frameworks of European banks.

U.S. Response to the Crisis

The financial turmoil of 2007–2009 resulted in a quick and fundamental change in the way that Basel II was applied to large financial institutions in the United States. Of the original five investment banks that had opted for CSE status with the SEC, three no longer existed as independent entities by 2009: Bear Stearns, Lehman Brothers, and Merrill Lynch. The remaining two, Goldman Sachs and Morgan Stanley, changed their structures to bank holding companies, and they were now under the regulatory auspices of the Federal Reserve. As a result, the SEC Basel II framework was simply no longer relevant and was formally ended by then-Chairman Christopher Cox on September 26, 2008.[24] Chairman Cox maintained that the economic turmoil was not a result of SEC Basel II implementation, but instead that the voluntary opt-in nature of the regulations was to blame.

> As I have reported to the Congress multiple times in recent months, the CSE program was fundamentally flawed from the beginning, because investment banks could opt in or out of supervision voluntarily.[25]

However, there was some speculation and criticism that the SEC had taken a light touch approach to the application of Basel II rules for its five CSEs and that it had, in fact, thereby contributed to the economic crisis. In particular, the high levels of leverage that were permitted by the investment banks were strongly debated, with suggestions that the SEC's CSE rules allowed them to lever up to levels of 30-to-1.[26] The operational risk requirements of Basel II did not seem to receive strong enforcement by the SEC, and operational risk frameworks were put under intense scrutiny once the Federal Reserve moved in as the new regulator for the original CSEs.

Morgan Stanley and Goldman Sachs operated their new bank status under the Basel I framework for some time while they sought to be readmitted to the Basel II club under the Federal Reserve's Basel II regulations. The time taken to meet the Federal Reserve standards does suggest that there may be some truth to the suggestion that their previous Basel II framework under the SEC, including the operational risk requirements, may have been relatively, and inappropriately, light.

Banks that were operating under the Federal Reserve's Basel II framework before the economic crisis continued to pursue their Basel II approval with no major changes. However, they noticed an increased vigilance from their regulator as the emphasis on regulatory stringency was on the upswing, and it was clear that Basel III was coming

U.S. Interagency Guidance on Advanced Measurement Approach

In June 2011, the U.S. regulators issued the "Interagency Guidance on the Advanced Measurement Approaches for Operational Risk."[27] This guidance was agreed to by the Board of Governors of the Federal Reserve System, the FDIC, the OCC, and the OTS.

The guidance had been long awaited and addressed several areas where the range of practices in operational risk had been broad among U.S. banks. While some of the conclusions may have been unpopular, the written guidance pointed toward a clearer path to Basel II AMA approval in the United States. However, confusion continued on the appropriate methods for AMA and pressure mounted to simplify the calculation of operational risk capital.

Dodd-Frank Act

In the United States, regulatory reform progressed along similar lines to those that were proposed by G20. President Barack Obama introduced a guidance document, "A New Foundation: Rebuilding Financial Supervision and Regulation," on June 17, 2009, and 2009 saw many bills introduced that addressed specific aspects of regulatory reform, often overlapping with existing Basel II rules. Davis Polk[28] summarized these as follows:

- The Financial Stability Improvement Act as amended by the House Financial Services Committee through November 6, 2009, or the "House Interim Version."
- The Investor Protection Act, passed by the House Financial Services Committee on November 4, 2009, or the "House Investor Protection bill."
- The Consumer Financial Protection Agency Act, passed by the House Financial Services Committee on October 29, 2009, or the "House CFPA bill."

- The Accountability and Transparency in Rating Agencies Act, passed by the House Financial Services Committee on October 28, 2009, or the "House Rating Agencies bill."
- The Private Fund Investment Advisers Registration Act, passed by the House Financial Services Committee on October 27, 2009, or the "House Private Fund Investment Advisers bill."
- The Derivatives Markets Transparency and Accountability Act, passed by the House Committee on Agriculture on October 21, 2009, or the "Peterson bill."
- The Over-the-Counter Derivatives Markets Act, passed by the House Financial Services Committee on October 15, 2009, or the "Frank OTC bill."
- The Federal Insurance Office Act, introduced by Representative Paul Kanjorski (D-PA) on October 1, 2009, or the "House Insurance bill."
- The Liability for Aiding and Abetting Securities Violations Act, introduced by Senator Arlen Specter (D-PA) on July 30, 2009, or the "Specter bill."
- Treasury Proposals released in the summer of 2009, or the "Treasury proposals."
- The Shareholder Bill of Rights Act, introduced by Senator Charles Schumer (D-NY) on May 19, 2009, or the "Schumer bill."

These all finally culminated in a catch-all bill, the Restoring American Financial Stability Act of 2009, which was introduced into the Senate by Senator Christopher Dodd (D-CT) and into the House of Representatives by Representative Barney Frank (D-MA). It was subsequently renamed the "Dodd-Frank Wall Street Reform and Consumer Protection Act," and President Obama signed the bill into law on July 21, 2010.

The full title of the Act is rather emotive:

> *An Act to promote the financial stability of the United States by improving accountability and transparency in the financial system, to end "too big to fail," to protect the American taxpayer by ending bailouts, to protect consumers from abusive financial services practices, and for other purposes.*

Dodd-Frank addressed some of the Basel III issues and resulted in U.S. regulatory changes that met many of the Financial Stability Board recommendations. The main elements of Dodd-Frank are outlined in the summary released by the Senate Committee on Banking, Housing, and Urban Affairs[29] under the following categories:

- **Consumer Protections with Authority and Independence:** The bill creates "a new independent watchdog, Consumer Financial Protection

Bureau, housed at the Federal Reserve, with the authority to ensure American consumers get the clear, accurate information they need to shop for mortgages, credit cards, and other financial products, and protect them from hidden fees, abusive terms, and deceptive practices."

- **Ends Too Big to Fail:** The bill "ends the possibility that taxpayers will be asked to write a check to bail out financial firms that threaten the economy by: creating a safe way to liquidate failed financial firms; imposing tough new capital and leverage requirements that make it undesirable to get too big; updating the Fed's authority to allow system-wide support but no longer prop up individual firms; and establishing rigorous standards and supervision to protect the economy and American consumers, investors and businesses."
- **Advanced Warning System:** The bill "creates a council to identify and address systemic risks posed by large, complex companies, products, and activities before they threaten the stability of the economy."
- **Transparency and Accountability for Exotic Instruments:** The bill "eliminates loopholes that allow risky and abusive practices to go on unnoticed and unregulated—including loopholes for over-the-counter derivatives, asset-backed securities, hedge funds, mortgage brokers and payday lenders."
- **Federal Bank Supervision:** The bill "streamlines bank supervision to create clarity and accountability and protects the dual banking system that supports community banks."
- **Executive Compensation and Corporate Governance:** The bill "provides shareholders with a say on pay and corporate affairs with a non-binding vote on executive compensation."
- **Protects Investors:** The bill "provides tough new rules for transparency and accountability for credit rating agencies to protect investors and businesses."
- **Enforces Regulations on the Books:** The bill "strengthens oversight and empowers regulators to aggressively pursue financial fraud, conflicts of interest and manipulation of the system that benefit special interests at the expense of American families and businesses."[30]

When President Obama successfully entered his second term, any hopes of a full-scale repeal of Dodd-Frank were put to rest. While some changes were made to some of the elements of the Act, much of the main content moved forward into regulation, albeit at a slower pace than had been originally planned, and has remained in place despite another two presidents having been voted into office since President Obama finished his second term.

BASEL III

The Basel Accords have resulted in global regulatory changes that have reached beyond G10, beyond G20, and into the far reaches of the global financial regulatory environment. Basel I introduced credit risk capital measures, and Basel II provided enhanced risk capital calculation for credit, market, and operational risk. The United States has played a key role on the Basel Committee for Banking Supervision, which designed these accords, and so it is not surprising to find that U.S. regulators have consistently adopted these measures.

The economic crisis highlighted the need for further refinements in the way that banks calculate and hold capital for all risk types, and the importance of sound operational risk management and measurement. In addition, it drew close scrutiny of the methods used to ensure there is robust risk management and healthy liquidity in the bank.

In 2010, the BCBS introduced enhanced capital requirements under Basel III so that banks had to maintain more capital of higher quality to cover unexpected losses. They were clear as to the purpose of the Basel III reforms:

> *The Basel III framework is a central element of the Basel Committee's response to the global financial crisis. It addresses a number of shortcomings in the pre-crisis regulatory framework and provides a foundation for a resilient banking system that will help avoid the build-up of systemic vulnerabilities. The framework will allow the banking system to support the real economy through the economic cycle.*[31]

Minimum Tier 1 capital rose from 4 percent to 6 percent, and at least three-quarters of it had to be of the highest quality (common shares and retained earnings). Global systemically important banks (G-SIBs) were subjected to even higher capital requirements. In other words, the initial approach to the crisis was "hold more capital."

Basel III was originally scheduled for adoption in January 2013, but that deadline was missed by both the EU and the United States, and a delayed and phased implementation was crafted for implementation over the next few years.

Meanwhile, the writing and implementation of rules under Dodd-Frank and similar nation specific rules across the globe continued at a fast pace. While the operational risk framework remained mostly unchanged since Basel II, the plethora of new regulatory requirements and governance enhancements led to increasing complexity in managing the operational risks faced by a bank on a day-to-day basis.

The 2010 focus of Basel III did not address systemic concerns regarding the variability in methods used by the banks to calculate their overall risk-weighted assets (RWAs) nor the apparent disparity between the riskiness of a bank's portfolio and the calculation of its required capital. This remained an area of concern for the BCBS, and they sought to rebuild the credibility of RWAs as an appropriate risk measure and to bring about greater pre-dictability and consistency across the financial system in the calculation of required capital.

In 2017, the BCBS addressed these issues and released finalized Basel III rules regarding standardized approaches for calculating credit risk, market risk, Credit Valuation Adjustment, and operational risk. These guidelines included a simplified approach to calculating operational risk capital. The BCBS sought to ensure greater risk sensitivity and clearer comparisons between banks with these new standards. In addition, new constraints were introduced on the use of internal models, and floor limits were set in order to limit the benefit that a bank could receive from its preferred capital calculation methods. All of these changes meant that the much-maligned Basel II AMA approach was retired, and all four methods of operational risk capital calculation were replaced by a simpler single standardized method that combines a refined measure of gross income with a bank's own internal loss history over 10 years.

In December 2019, BCBS issued new guidance on this simplified standardized calculation of operational risk capital[32] and a final version is due for implementation in January 2023.

In November 2020, BCBS issued a report[33] on the progress of its member nations in the implementation of all of the Basel requirements. In it they acknowledged that implementation had been inconsistent and not all deadlines had been met by all nations. In March 2021 they issued "Revisions to the Principles for the Sound Management of Operational Risk."[34]

These documents now form the basis for the future regulatory expectations for operational risk and provide additional clarity on the management and measurement of this risk.

BCBS recognized the impact of the global COVID-19 pandemic and confirmed that they would extend the deadline for the adoption of the new operational risk capital standard to January 2023.

Both the Basel II and Basel III capital calculation methods are discussed in Chapter 12 and the revised principles will be discussed throughout this book.

KEY POINTS

- The Basel Accords were developed by the Bank of International Settlements (BIS) to ensure capital adequacy.
- Basel II was first published in 2004, and its full title is "International Convergence of Capital Measurement and Capital Standards: A Revised Framework."
- Basel II required operational risk management and measurement for the first time.
- There are three approaches to calculating capital for operational risk under Basel II: the basic approach, the standardized approach, and the advanced measurement approach.
- In 2008, the Federal Reserve, OCC, FDIC, and OTS issued a joint requirement for mandatory Basel II rules for large United States banks and opt-in provisions for noncore banks.
- In 2009 and 2010, the CEBS issued guidance on operational risk management and measurement.
- In 2011, U.S. regulators issued the "Interagency Guidance on the Advanced Measurement Approaches for Operational Risk."
- The United States enacted the Dodd-Frank Wall Street Reform and Consumer Protection Act in July 2010.
- The Act addressed the following areas:
  - Consumer Protections with Authority and Independence
  - Ends Too Big to Fail
  - Advanced Warning System
  - Transparency and Accountability for Exotic Instruments
  - Federal Bank Supervision
  - Executive Compensation and Corporate Governance
  - Protects Investors
  - Enforces Regulations on the Books
- BCBS issued final Basel II rules in 2017 and further guidance on operational risk capital calculation methods in 2019 and revised sound practices for operational risk management in 2021.
- The global pandemic has delayed the full adoption of Basel III.

REVIEW QUESTIONS

1. The full title of Basel II is
   a. "International Convergence of Capital Measurement and Capital Standards: A Revised Framework."
   b. "International Convergence of Capital Accords."

   c. "Accord of the Bank of International Settlements."
   d. "International Convergence of Capital Measurement and Capital Standards."

2. Pillar 1 provides guidance for
   I. Three approaches to credit risk.
   II. Three approaches to operational risk.
   III. Market risk VaR.
   IV. A minimum capital ratio of 8 percent.
   V. Liquidity risk ratios.
   a. I only
   b. I and II only
   c. I, II, and III only
   d. I, II, III, and IV only
   e. All of the above

NOTES

1. "About BIS," n.d., www.bis.org/about/index.htm.
2. "BIS Activities," n.d., www.bis.org/about/member_cb.htm.
3. Central bank and lead financial regulatory representatives from France, Germany, Italy, Japan, the Netherlands, Sweden, Switzerland, the United Kingdom, the United States, and Luxembourg.
4. "Basel Committee Membership," n.d., www.bis.org/bcbs/membership.htm.
5. Bank of International Settlements, Basel Committee, "International Convergence of Capital Measurement and Capital Standards," 1988.
6. Bank of International Settlements, "International Convergence of Capital Measurement and Capital Standard: A Revised Framework," 2004.
7. "Basel Committee Charter," n.d., https://www.bis.org/bcbs/charter.htm.
8. B. J. Balin, "Basel I, Basel II, and Emerging Markets: A Non-Technical Analysis." Washington DC: The Johns Hopkins University School of Advanced International Studies (SAIS), 2008, pp. 3–4.
9. See note 7.
10. "Basel II: Revised International Capital Framework," n.d., www.bis.org/publ/bcbsca.htm.
11. Bank of International Settlements, Basel Committee on Banking Supervision, "International Convergence of Capital Measurement and Capital Standards: A Revised Framework," Comprehensive Version, 2006, section 644.
12. Ibid., p. 144.
13. Ibid., p. 204.
14. Comprising Directive 2006/48/EC and Directive 2006/49/EC.
15. Net Capital Rule Amendments, Securities and Exchange Commission, Release No. 34-49830, 69 *Fed. Reg.* 34427, June 21, 2004.

16. "Risk-Based Capital Standards: Advanced Capital Adequacy," November 2, 2007. Retrieved from www.federalreserve.gov/newsevents/press/bcreg/20071102a.htm.

17. "Supervisory Guidance: Supervisory Review Process of Capital Adequacy (Pillar 2) Related to the Implementation of the Basel II Advanced Capital Framework," 2007.

18. Statement of Christopher Cox, former chairman, U.S. Securities and Exchange Commission before the Committee on Financial Services U.S. House of Representatives, April 20, 2010. Retrieved from www.house.gov/apps/list/hearing/. . .dem/cox_testimony_2010-04-20.pdf.

19. "G20 Must Make Basel II Top Priority: Sources," *Reuters*, April 20, 2010. Retrieved from www.reuters.com/article/idUSTRE63J2QU20100420.

20. "Strengthening the Resilience of the Banking Sector: Consultative Document," Bank of International Settlements, Basel Committee on Banking Supervision, 2009.

21. Ibid.

22. www.eba.europa.eu/documents/Publications/Standards—Guidelines/2010/Management-of-op-risk/CEBS-2010-216-(Guidelines-on-the-management-of-op-.aspx.

23. Retrieved from http://eba.europa.eu/getdoc/0448297d-3f85-4f7d-9fa6-c6ba5f80895a/CEBS-2009_161_rev1_Compendium.aspx.

24. "Chairman Cox Announces End of Consolidated Supervised Entities Program," SEC Press Release, 2008, 230, www.sec.gov/news/press/2008/2008-230.htm.

25. Ibid.

26. P. Madigan, "SEC Adoption of Basel II 'Allowed 30-to-1 leverage,'" *Risk*, October 29, 2009.

27. www.occ.gov/news-issuances/bulletins/2011/bulletin-2011-21a.pdf.

28. Davis Polk, "Summary of the Restoring American Financial Stability Act of 2009, Introduced by Senator Christopher Dodd (D-CT) November 10, 2009." Discussion Draft, 2009.

29. Senate Committee on Banking, Housing, and Urban Affairs, "Summary: Restoring American Financial Stability," 2009.

30. Ibid.

31. Bank of International Settlements, Basel Committee on Banking Supervision, "Finalizing Basel II: In Brief," December 2017, 2, https://www.bis.org/bcbs/publ/d424_inbrief.pdf.

32. Bank of International Settlements, Basel Committee on Banking Supervision, "OPE—Calculation of RWA for Operational Risk, OPE25—Standardized Approach," effective 1 January 2023, https://www.bis.org/basel_framework/chapter/OPE/25.htm?inforce=20230101&published=20200605.

33. Bank of International Settlements, Basel Committee on Banking Supervision, "Implementation of Basel Standards: A Report to G20 Leaders on Implementation of the Basel III Regulatory Reforms," November 2020, https://www.bis.org/bcbs/publ/d510.pdf.

34. Bank of International Settlements, Basel Committee on Banking Supervision, "Revisions to the Principles of the Sound Management of Operational Risk," March 2021, https://www.bis.org/bcbs/publ/d515.htm.

CHAPTER 3

The Operational Risk Framework

This chapter introduces the important elements that are recommended for an operational risk framework. These elements include the foundations of governance, risk appetite, culture and awareness, and policy and procedure; the building blocks of data collection including loss data, risk and control self-assessment, scenario analysis, and key risk indicators; and the final capstones of calculation of capital and reporting.

OVERVIEW OF THE OPERATIONAL RISK FRAMEWORK

As discussed in Chapter 1, an operational risk program should ensure that operational risk is identified, assessed, monitored, controlled, and mitigated.

If a fintech or bank can successfully establish and maintain these elements, then it has the opportunity to avoid unnecessary operational risk and its resulting financial and reputational damage.

The Basel Committee on Banking Supervision's 2021 "Revisions to the Principles for the Sound Management of Operational Risk"[1] provides helpful guidelines for best practices for operational risk departments. When meeting these standards, an operational risk framework needs to be developed that will fit with the culture of the bank or fintech and reflect best practice in the industry.

The main data building blocks of an operational risk framework are:

- Loss data collection.
- Risk and control self-assessment.
- Scenario analysis.
- Key risk indicators.

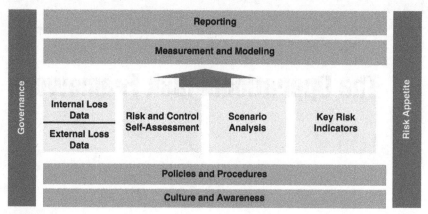

FIGURE 3.1   Operational Risk Framework

The framework must also address governance, provide policies and procedures, drive culture change, and respond to and inform risk appetite. In addition, the framework should feed data into any capital modeling and should feed data and analysis into risk reporting.

Figure 3.1 illustrates a possible framework that includes all of these elements.

Each element is important, but the timing of implementation and the relative weight of each element in the framework will vary depending on the culture of the firm and its regulatory and business drivers. The following chapters will consider each of these elements, their practical application, the tools that are available, and critical factors for their successful implementation.

THE FOUNDATIONS OF THE FRAMEWORK

Two elements drive the design and acceptance of the operational risk framework as a whole, and it is important to start with these. These two elements are *governance* and *culture and awareness*.

Governance

Governance determines the roles and responsibilities of the head of the operational risk function and the team that manages the framework, the committees that oversee and make key decisions about risk management, the operational risk managers in lines of business, and every employee who may encounter operational risk.

In order to develop an operational risk framework that is effective, an appropriate governance structure must be carefully considered at the outset. Governance should also be revisited at least annually, to check whether it is still working as intended. Good governance enables the escalation of risk and ensures that risk transparency is effective through all of the layers of operational risk management that may exist.

Governance holds the whole operational risk framework together. In Chapter 4 we explore the various aspects of governance, including who should own the operational risk function and what the operational risk function should own.

Culture and Awareness

Once governance has been addressed, the next step in developing an operational risk framework is to proactively tackle culture and awareness. While it may be tempting to jump into developing the building blocks of operational risk management, such as loss data collection and risk and control self-assessment, those building blocks will only be successful if sufficient time and energy has been spent on culture and awareness.

The implementation of a successful operational risk framework requires winning over the hearts and minds of the employees of the firm. Spotting operational risks is a developed skill. While the risks exist in all lines of business, it takes the right tone at the top, training, and awareness to identify the risks. Operational risk can arise in any corner of the firm, and it can result in best practice responses, or it may be met with indifference. The response will depend on the work that has been done in the area of culture and awareness. In Chapter 5, we look at various aspects of this essential activity, including training, marketing, and building a brand for the operational risk function.

Policies and Procedures

The next foundational element of the framework is policies and procedures. There was a time, not that long ago, when banks and financial institutions did not take their policy and procedure programs very seriously. Today, that has changed dramatically under the watchful eye of the regulators. Firms are expected to have clear, actionable, and measurable policies and procedures.

Indeed, today all banks pay close attention to writing and actively managing their policies and procedures, and regulators expect a robust policy and procedure framework to be in place. While formal policies and procedures are less well established in fintechs, there is a growing emphasis on these formal documents, and they are often required from investors and third parties during due diligence.

A well-managed policy framework allows lines of business increased flexibility because the rules of the road are clearly articulated and are not ambiguous. Having well-managed policies and procedures gives a financial firm increased autonomy because it is influential in building trust with industry regulators. A good operational risk framework will have well-documented policies and procedures that reflect the requirements of each of the elements.

In Chapter 6, we look at examples of standard policies and procedures and discuss best practices in how to design, implement, maintain, and track these documents.

THE FOUR DATA BUILDING BLOCKS

With governance, culture and awareness, and policy and procedures holding the framework together, we can now turn to the four main pieces of work that are needed in order to have an effective operational risk framework: loss data collection, risk and control self-assessment, scenario analysis, and key risk indicators.

Loss Data Collection

Two types of loss data are key to the framework: internal loss data, which occurs within the firm, and external loss data, which occurs outside the firm.

Internal Loss Data

Operational risk management and measurement require access to data on events that have already occurred in the firm and in the industry, and loss data collection is the first of four activities that form the heart of an operational risk framework. The firm's own data is referred to as *internal loss data*, while industry data is referred to as *external loss data*.

Developing an effective set of internal loss data is often the first major task faced when building out an operational risk framework. Basel III requires a firm to build its capital calculation from its internal loss profile. Therefore, loss data collection needs to be effectively established to ensure that good-quality data is in place.

If loss data collection is started before appropriate governance is established and before culture and awareness have been addressed, then the data collected is likely to be lower quality.

We look into regulatory requirements and best practices in internal loss data collection in Chapter 7.

External Loss Data

Operational risk events that have occurred in the industry (but outside the firm) are very important in understanding the operational risk faced by the firm. Therefore, the collection and analysis of external loss data is a key element in an effective loss data program.

External data help inform risk and control self-assessment and scenario analysis and are often an important component in effective reporting.

We look at sources and uses of external loss data in Chapter 8.

Risk and Control Self-Assessment

The second of the four main building blocks of operational risk management activity is risk and control self-assessment (RCSA). Risks and controls are identified and assessed through RCSA, with a view to controlling and mitigating any unacceptable risks.

While loss data tells us what has already happened, RCSA is designed to help us to understand what additional potential risks we face today. Loss data are backward-looking, but RCSA looks at risk levels now and in the future.

RCSA often becomes the most important part of the framework because it proactively addresses the requirements that we first looked at in Chapter 1. Those requirements are that the operational risk framework should *identify*, *assess*, *control*, and *mitigate* risk.

While loss data allow us to identify and assess risks that have occurred and to consider how to control and mitigate those risks in the future, RCSA allows us to identify all risks, not just those that have already materialized. Loss data is about hindsight. Risk and control self-assessment is about foresight. In Chapter 10, we look at various methodologies and best practices for RCSA.

Scenario Analysis

The third activity in the framework is scenario analysis. Unlike risk and control self-assessment, scenario analysis is only looking for rare, catastrophic risks. It is focused on identifying plausible risks that are so large as to be potentially fatal or severely destructive to a firm.

Scenario analysis stresses the operational risk framework and pushes participants to think outside their comfort zone. RCSA centers on discussions of the risks that are faced and the controls that are in place, whereas scenario analysis requires participants to consider what could happen if there were to be a serious failure of controls or a previously unassessed combination of risks.

Scenario analysis is a challenging area, and was a key element in the Basel II AMA capital calculation approach. Many firms struggled with meeting the AMA regulatory requirements while retaining business value in the process. The simplification of capital calculation in Basel III removed scenario analysis from the calculation, and it is now used as risk management tool rather than as a capital input. We look at alternative approaches to scenario analysis and the uses of scenario analysis in operational risk management and measurement in Chapter 11.

Key Risk Indicators

The final building block of operational risk data gathering are key risk indicators. Operational risk practitioners sometimes use the terms *key risk indicator* and *metric* interchangeably; however, understanding the difference between a metric and a true key risk indicator is important. Metrics provide an important monitoring function across the framework: they can be attached to loss data and to risks or controls in RCSA and can provide useful input to scenario analysis.

A key risk indicator, in comparison, predicts that a risk is changing and allows for proactive intervention. It is difficult to find metrics that are true key risk indicators or that can be combined to form a key risk indicator, because many metrics are simply counting exceptions or measuring performance, rather than measuring an increase or decrease in risk levels. We consider the challenges of developing key risk indicators in Chapter 9, where we also discuss best practices in metrics.

MEASUREMENT AND MODELING

The calculation of operational risk capital is a critical element in the operational risk framework. Under Basel III the operational risk capital requirement is determined by the product of a business indicator component (BIC) and an internal loss multiplier (ILM). The BIC is dependent on the size and complexity of the bank and the ILM is based on the internal loss experience of the bank. However, the original Basel II capital methods are still in place at the time of this writing, and the various capital calculation approaches are discussed in Chapter 12.

REPORTING

All of the above elements feed into operational risk reporting. Without effective reporting, the operational risk framework is a factory that is busy making data widgets that are not used. Reporting gathers all the information that has been collected and analyzed in the loss data program, the RCSA program, the scenario analysis program, the metrics program, and the capital modeling program and puts it to use.

The quality of reporting is critical to the success of an operational risk framework. Reporting that leaves its audience asking "so what?" is of little value. Reporting that asks its audience to think or say or do something is of great value.

In Chapter 13, we explore ways to provide reporting that is not merely data gathering, but instead provides risk analysis and risk transparency and leads to better business decision making.

RISK APPETITE

Finally, the whole framework is held together by risk appetite. It is difficult, but not impossible, to express a risk appetite for operational risk. It often takes time for an operational risk framework to mature to the stage where risk appetite can be effectively discussed and agreed upon.

While governance is the first pillar or support for the framework, risk appetite is its equal partner. Effective governance requires a clear articulation of risk appetite, and risk appetite can be set only when strong governance is in place. In Chapter 14, we explore ways that a risk appetite can be set and applied for operational risk.

KEY POINTS

The main building blocks of an operational risk framework are:

- The foundations
  - Governance
  - Culture and awareness
  - Policy and procedure
- The four data elements
  - Loss data collection, including
    - Internal loss data
    - External loss data
  - Risk and control self-assessment
  - Scenario analysis
  - Key risk indicators

- The key outputs
  - Measurement and modeling
  - Reporting
- The framework operates under the firm's stated risk appetite.

REVIEW QUESTIONS

1. Which of the following is *least* likely to be part of an operational risk framework?
   a. Loss data collection
   b. Risk and control self-assessment
   c. Counterparty credit assessment
   d. Scenario analysis
2. Which of the following is the *best* description of a robust operational risk framework?
   a. It collects all operational risk losses that occur within the firm.
   b. It provides effective tools to identify, assess, control, and mitigate operational risk.
   c. It produces a capital calculation of operational risk.
   d. It is based on a framework that has been successful at another firm.

NOTE

1. Risk Management Group of the Basel Committee on Banking Supervision, "Revisions to the Principles for the Sound Management of Operational Risk," March 2021. Retrieved from www.bis.org/bcbs/publ/d515.pdf.

CHAPTER 4

Operational Risk Governance

This chapter addresses the regulatory requirements for operational risk governance and provides alternative governance approaches that can be adopted. The roles and responsibilities of the first, second, and third lines of defense are outlined, as well as the roles and responsibilities of boards of directors, committees, and senior management. Finally, validation and verification requirements are introduced and explained.

ROLE OF GOVERNANCE

Appropriate governance is essential for effective operational risk management, and the people who are responsible for ownership of the operational risk management program will be unable to make a positive impact without a robust governance structure. An effective governance structure must be implemented to provide oversight of operational risk management and measurement and to ensure an effective route for risk escalation.

Governance holds the framework together, as illustrated in Figure 4.1.

The governance approach adopted by a firm needs to reflect the culture of the firm and must be practical in nature. It is not unusual for the creation of an operational risk function to upset the current overall risk governance framework.

One of the main potential challenges in developing and implementing effective operational risk management is that it touches virtually all activities and functions within an organization. Market, credit, and liquidity risk management all evaluate the outcomes and consequences of transactions and other acts of commerce on profitability and balance sheet management. They do not impact the day-to-day running of most of the organization.

Operational risk management, in contrast, evaluates the outcomes and consequences of the organization's ability to perform and execute those risk

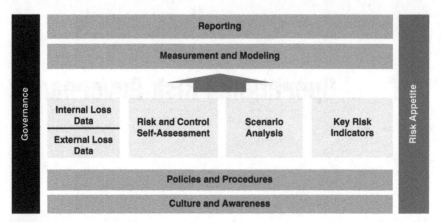

FIGURE 4.1 The Role of Governance in an Operational Risk Framework

management activities as well as all other operations, controls, and business functions on which the organization depends in order to remain viable and in business. This broad scope requires a broad governance framework. The board of directors and senior management treat operational risk management with the same level of stature, independence, and authority as the other core risk management disciplines such as market and credit. This core principle of equal stature has evolved steadily over recent years and has become most clearly articulated in various pronouncements by the Basel Committee on Banking Supervision.

The Basel Committee on Banking Supervision provided the "Principles for Enhancing Corporate Governance"[1] in 2010 and included guidance on the governance of risk, including:

Risk management and internal controls

- *A bank should have a risk management function (including a chief risk officer (CRO) or equivalent for large banks and internationally active banks), a compliance function and an internal audit function, each with sufficient authority, stature, independence, resources and access to the board;*
- *Risks should be identified, assessed and monitored on an ongoing firm-wide and individual entity basis;*
- *An internal controls system which is effective in design and operation should be in place;*
- *The sophistication of a bank's risk management, compliance and internal control infrastructures should keep pace with any changes to its risk profile (including its growth) and to the external risk landscape; and*

■ *Effective risk management requires frank and timely internal communication within the bank about risk, both across the organization and through reporting to the board and senior management.*[2]

Therefore, a precursor for operational risk governance is the adoption of sound risk governance practices generally.

The Basel Committee on Banking Supervision updated its guidance on operational risk governance in its 2021 publication "Revisions to the Principles for Sound Practices for the Management Operational Risk."[3]

Sound internal governance forms the foundation of an effective ORF [operational risk management framework]. Governance of operational risk management has similarities but also differences relative to the management of credit or market risk. Banks' operational risk governance function should be fully integrated into their overall risk management governance structure.[4]

The role of the board and senior management in ensuring good governance is further expanded in Principles 3, 4, and 5 as follows:

Governance

The Board of Directors

Principle 3: The board of directors should approve and periodically review the operational risk management framework and ensure that senior management implements the policies, processes, and systems of the operational risk management framework effectively at all decision levels.

Principle 4: The board of directors should approve and periodically review a risk appetite and tolerance statement for operational risk that articulates the nature, types and levels of operational risk the bank is willing to assume.

Senior Management

Principle 5: Senior management should develop for approval by the board of directors a clear, effective, and robust governance structure with well-defined, transparent, and consistent lines of responsibility. Senior management is responsible for consistently implementing and maintaining throughout the organisation policies, processes and systems for managing operational risk in all of the bank's material products, activities, processes and systems consistent with the bank's risk appetite and tolerance statement.[5]

The importance of ownership of operational risk by the board and by senior management is therefore clear, and the governance framework must reflect that ownership in the reporting structure and in the escalation of risk.

In addition, responsibility for good governance of operational risk lies in three lines of defense. These lines are generally considered to be the business, the corporate operational risk function, and independent review by audit.

While these levels of governance might feel weighty for a fintech, there are benefits to having a path for the escalation of risk. Without a strong path for such escalation operational risks can remain quashed in the corners of the organization, only to finally emerge in a large loss event. Early and effective reporting and escalation are key in effectively mitigating risks and so a governance framework, streamlined to fit with the culture and size of the firm, is a worthwhile investment, even for a smaller organization.

FIRST LINE OF DEFENSE

The first line of defense is the business line. The business owns operational risk and should be managing it as it arises. According to the Basel Committee on Banking Supervision:

> *This means that sound operational risk governance will recognize that business line management is responsible for identifying and managing the risks inherent in the products, activities, processes and systems for which it is accountable.*[6]

Each business line should have an operational risk function in place. The person responsible for operational risk in the business line may have a title such as business risk officer, nonfinancial risk officer, or operational risk manager. They need to maintain independence from the business and so need to have a reporting line that is at the top of the organizational structure. An appropriate reporting line would be to the head of the business or to their chief of staff or chief operating officer.

The expectations of the first line have recently been more clearly outlined as follows:

> *The responsibilities of an effective first line of defence in promoting a sound operational risk management culture should include:*
>
> *a. identifying and assessing the materiality of operational risks inherent in their respective business units through the use of operational risk management tools;*

b. establishing appropriate controls to mitigate inherent operational risks, and assessing the design and effectiveness of these controls through the use of the operational risk management tools;

c. reporting whether the business units lack adequate resources, tools and training to ensure identification and assessment of operational risks;

d. monitoring and reporting the business units' operational risk profiles, and ensuring their adherence to the established operational risk appetite and tolerance statement; and

e. reporting residual operational risks not mitigated by controls, including operational loss events, control deficiencies, process inadequacies, and non-compliance with operational risk tolerances.[7]

Business lines include support functions as well as revenue-generating areas. Therefore, there should be operational risk managers (or their equivalent) in operations, technology, finance, legal, compliance, and human resources as well as in any front office businesses such as fixed income, equities, retail banking, corporate banking, and so on.

The first line of defense operational risk managers might have a direct or dotted reporting line into the second line of defense. The larger and more complex the firm, the more likely it is that the first-line-of-defense operational risk function will be independent from the second-line-of-defense operational risk function.

SECOND LINE OF DEFENSE

The second line of defense is the corporate operational risk function. It is responsible for the development of the operational risk framework and reporting on operational risk matters to the firm's senior management and board of directors. The Basel Committee on Banking Supervision describes the corporate operational risk function, its responsibilities, and its relationship with the business line as follows:

A functionally independent CORF is typically the second line of defence.

> *The responsibilities of an effective second line of defence should include:*

a. developing an independent view regarding business units' (i) identified material operational risks, (ii) design and effectiveness of key controls, and (iii) risk tolerance;

b. challenging the relevance and consistency of the business unit's implementation of the operational risk management tools, measurement activities and reporting systems, and providing evidence of this effective challenge;

c. developing and maintaining operational risk management and measurement policies, standards and guidelines;

d. reviewing and contributing to the monitoring and reporting of the operational risk profile; and

e. designing and providing operational risk training and instilling risk awareness.

The degree of independence of the CORF may differ among banks. At small banks, independence may be achieved through separation of duties and independent review of processes and functions. In larger banks, the CORF should have a reporting structure independent of the risk-generating business units and be responsible for the design, maintenance and ongoing development of the ORMF within the bank. The CORF typically engages relevant corporate control groups (e.g. Compliance, Legal, Finance and IT) to support its assessment of the operational risks and controls. Banks should have a policy which defines clear roles and responsibilities of the CORF, reflective of the size and complexity of the organisation.[8]

In order to meet this standard and to be able to effectively challenge the first line of defense and provide valuable reporting to the top of the house, there are two fundamental governance questions to consider for the second line of defense:

1. Who should own the operational risk function?
2. What should the operational risk function own?

Who Should Own the Operational Risk Function?

While it is critical that the board of directors and senior management demonstrate clear and unequivocal support for operational risk management, it cannot be effectively managed "by committee." Someone in the firm must be specifically accountable for the success of the operational risk function, or, in other words, they must "own" the operational risk function. The corporate operational risk function needs to report upward in such a way that it is endowed with three critical qualities: *independence, importance,* and *relevance.*

When selecting a governance structure for an operational risk function, or when reassessing the current governance of an existing operational risk function, these three qualities should be considered. The governance structure must support the *independence* of the operational risk function, it must bestow stature and *importance* of operational risk management and measurement, and it must demonstrate their *relevance* to the organization. There are various options for the governance of operational risk, and each has practical and strategic advantages and disadvantages.

Option 1: Operational Risk Is Owned by the Chief Risk Officer

This governance approach can be represented by the organization chart in Figure 4.2.

An operational risk function that reports directly to the chief risk officer (CRO) is in the fortunate position of being taken seriously by the rest of the organization. This governance structure best demonstrates the seriousness and commitment with which the board and senior management ensures that the operational risk function is *independent* from both the support and business functions, as it reports directly to the CRO. This reporting line also best reflects the aspirations of many supervisory and regulatory bodies domestically and internationally. In addition, the CRO is generally considered an *important* and highly *relevant* function in any firm, and the operational risk department can inherit these qualities in this governance structure.

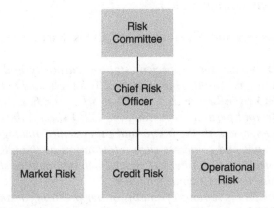

FIGURE 4.2 Example Governance Structure Where Operational Risk Is Owned by the Chief Risk Officer

The establishment of an independent CRO is recommended by the Basel Committee on Banking Supervision in its "Principles for Enhancing Corporate Governance"[9] as follows:

> ### Chief risk officer or equivalent
> *Large banks and internationally active banks, and others depending on their risk profile and local governance requirements, should have an independent senior executive with distinct responsibility for the risk management function and the institution's comprehensive risk management framework across the entire organization. This executive is commonly referred to as the CRO. . . .*

The formal reporting lines and independence of the CRO are further outlined as follows:

> *Formal reporting lines may vary across banks, but regardless of these reporting lines, the independence of the CRO is paramount. While the CRO may report to the CEO or other senior management, the CRO should also report and have direct access to the board and its risk committee without impediment. Also, the CRO should not have any management or financial responsibility in respect of any operational business lines or revenue-generating functions. Interaction between the CRO and the board should occur regularly and be documented adequately. Non-executive board members should have the right to meet regularly—in the absence of senior management—with the CRO.*

The importance and relevance of the CRO is described as follows:

> *The CRO should have sufficient stature, authority and seniority within the organization. This will typically be reflected in the ability of the CRO to influence decisions that affect the bank's exposure to risk. Beyond periodic reporting, the CRO should thus have the ability to engage with the board and other senior management on key risk issues and to access such information as the CRO deems necessary to form his or her judgment. Such interactions should not compromise the CRO's independence.*
> *If the CRO is removed from his or her position for any reason, this should be done with the prior approval of the board and generally should be disclosed publicly. The bank should also discuss the reasons for such removal with its supervisor.*

A head of operational risk who reports to the CRO often enjoys opportunities to sit at the same table as their credit and market risk colleagues. This can help foster an environment where synergies between the risk categories can be identified and can provide the CRO with a more enterprise risk management view. However, there are also potential disadvantages in this governance structure. In practice, operational risk can be overshadowed by market and credit risk if there is only one forum to present all risks at the same time. This can be especially significant if the CRO is from a market or credit risk background. Risk committee meetings can sometimes focus heavily on market and credit risk, to the detriment of operational risk, the latter being relegated to a five-minute briefing at the end of the meeting. A separate dedicated operational risk committee may be needed to overcome this problem. In other words, it may be necessary to augment this governance structure with additional reporting avenues for the operational risk function.

Another potential weakness of this governance structure is the distance it might create between operational risk and its related activities. An effective operational risk function needs to develop strong working relationships with the owners of the existing operational risk activities in the firm. An underlying principle, and a main goal of the Basel standards, is to ensure that operational risk management passes the "use test." This means that the firm's operational risk management policies, procedures, and tool sets are used by the practitioners who execute the day-to-day activities of the firm throughout its business, control, and support functions. These activities include Sarbanes-Oxley activities in the United States, the business continuity planning and information security teams, legal and compliance departments, and other support departments: operations, finance, and information technology. These functions will not report to the CRO, and finding and cultivating these partnerships will require additional effort by the operational risk team.

EXAMPLE

Gamma Bank's management is considering changes in its business environment that might have an impact on all three risk categories. This structure facilitates the discussion in an integrative context, spanning market, credit, and operational risk factors, and encourages transparency and communication between risk disciplines. The close working relationship between the risk functions can support an enterprise risk management (ERM) approach to risk.

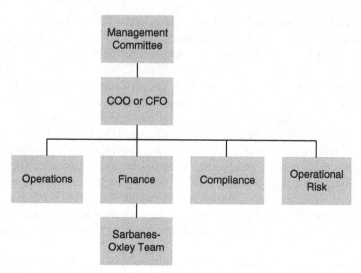

FIGURE 4.3   Example Reporting Structure Where Operational Risk Is Owned by the Chief Operating Officer or the Chief Financial Officer

Option 2: Operational Risk Is Owned by the Chief Operating Officer or the Chief Financial Officer

This governance approach can be represented by the organization chart in Figure 4.3.

In the past, it was common for a firm-wide operational risk department to report to a senior executive such as the chief operating officer (COO), chief financial officer (CFO), or perhaps chief administrative officer (CAO). This structure may be viewed as imbedded in day-to-day operations and therefore not "independent." Consequently, it has been replaced in most firms by a CRO reporting line, but some do still maintain this type of governance structure. This alternative governance structure has its own advantages and disadvantages.

An operational risk function in such a structure has increased opportunities to partner with the other areas that own operational risks, such as legal and compliance, and the Sarbanes-Oxley team. In fact, the COO or CFO might mandate such working relationships.

EXAMPLE

If Gamma Bank's COO oversees both the compliance team and the operational risk team, then they are more likely to insist that there is an effective working relationship between them. This relationship can provide a path through the potential political challenges, such as possible conflicts and overlaps in roles and responsibilities that might otherwise arise.

As a result, such a governance structure raises the opportunity for governance, risk, and control (GRC) initiatives; GRC is discussed in more depth later in Chapter 16.

The role of the COO, CFO, or CAO should provide the operational risk department with a good level of *importance* and *relevance*. However, this structure might weaken the operational risk department's *independence*. Significant levels of operational risk will exist within the departments that lie within the same reporting structure, and this may hinder the impartiality and objectivity of the operational risk department, or at least tarnish the perception of its independence. Therefore, it is essential that in such a governance structure the operational risk department operates under clear policies and procedures that support its independence.

This governance structure also limits the opportunities for strong partnership with the market and credit risk functions and, therefore, provides less opportunity for an ERM approach.

Option 3: Operational Risk Is Owned by the Chief Compliance Officer

This governance approach can be represented by the organization chart in Figure 4.4.

In some firms, generally in smaller and less complex banks and fintechs, the operational risk function reports directly into the compliance department. This is a more unusual arrangement, but for less complex institutions, it has some advantages. There is a clear opportunity to partner closely with

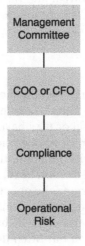

FIGURE 4.4 Example Reporting Structure Where Operational Risk Is Owned by the Chief Compliance Officer

the compliance department and also to leverage the reporting cycles, regular meetings, and existing assessment activities that the compliance department may already have in place. The *independence* of the function can be well maintained in this structure.

The disadvantages of such an approach are that the operational risk function might be perceived to be out of touch with departments that do not usually interact with compliance. Part of the success of operational risk management is self-assessment and self-identification of risk by the day-to-day business, operations, and support practitioners. Self-identification can be inconsistent with the way compliance departments function, and they might be viewed not as a trusted adviser, partner, or risk manager, but rather as a policing function. It may also be harder to demonstrate *importance* and *relevance*. As with the option where the operational risk is owned by the COO or CFO, partnerships with market and credit risk could be more challenging and an ERM approach would be difficult to achieve.

What Should the Operational Risk Function Own?

Once the upward-reporting governance structure has been determined, the next challenge is to determine the appropriate downward-reporting structure for the corporate operational risk function. Who should report to operational risk, or what should operational risk own? There are many potential candidates. Whether a function can effectively report to operational risk will depend on several factors: the upward governance structure; the culture of the firm; the individual personalities involved; and the current maturity of the operational risk function in terms of its importance, relevance, and independence.

The following are areas that could report to a central operational risk function.

Other Operational Risk Teams

Each business unit and support function should have its own first line of defense operational risk team. These teams may have been in place earlier than the corporate level function or may have been implemented as a result of the corporate-level commitment to operational risk management. Unlike a corporate-level operational risk function, these teams can report to their own business head or support function head, as they are generally designed to assist that executive in managing the operational risk in their area.

They might also have a dotted-line relationship with the corporate operational risk team. They certainly will have some reporting responsibilities to the corporate function but often do not report directly to them, having at most a matrix reporting structure where they report to both their own division head and the corporate operational risk head. An example of an appropriate reporting structure is shown in Figure 4.5.

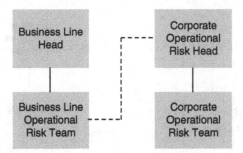

FIGURE 4.5 Operational Risk Team Reporting Structure

Embedded Operational Risk Coordinators or Specialists or Managers

The burden of rolling out an operational risk program usually results in a need for a designated operational risk coordinator, operational risk specialist, or operational risk manager in every department. If that department does not have an operational risk function of its own, then this designated individual provides a contact point for the central operational risk function.

An OR coordinator might be required to spend only a small percentage of their time on operational risk activities, and so may have another day job in which they report directly to a manager in their department. There should be a healthy and regular communication between the OR coordinator and the central operational risk team, as the OR coordinator will be the point person for the operational risk team as the operational risk framework is rolled out across the firm.

Such a reporting structure is represented in Figure 4.6.

It can be useful to have such embedded resources also report to the central operational risk function, in a matrix fashion, but this is not essential. Such a reporting structure is represented in Figure 4.7.

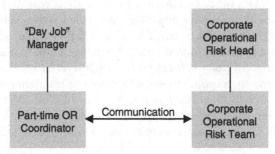

FIGURE 4.6 Operational Risk Coordinator Reporting Structure

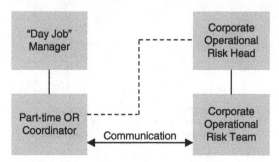

FIGURE 4.7   Operational Risk Coordinator Matrix Reporting Structure

The relationship between the central operational risk function and the OR coordinator can be informal and still be very successful.

Alternatively, there might be an OR coordinator who is working full time on operational risk activities in a particular department, and who reports directly to the central operational risk function. This can disrupt the clear independence between the first and second lines of defense, but it might be sustainable if there are clear segregation of duties in place and policies to enforce them.

An example of the latter is shown in Figure 4.8.

Business Continuity Planning

Business continuity planning (BCP) is often the most well-established pre-existing operational risk function in a firm. BCP generally started life as an information technology function that focused on ensuring that the technology of the firm would continue to function in the case of a disaster. A lot of good BCP work came out of the response of firms to the 9/11 terrorist attack, and many BCP plans were significantly enhanced as a result of lessons learned at that time.

As a result, BCP often focused on disaster recovery plans for technology systems, ensuring that alternate backup sites, data, and systems were available should the main office be compromised for some reason.

Recently, BCP teams have expanded their role to cover other events that might disrupt the business, such as pandemic flu planning. The BCP plans developed for a pandemic raised some new considerations, such as how to ensure business continuity if there were a high level of absenteeism (due to illness) and how to respond to social distancing requirements that might mean that a backup location was not a valid solution (often resulting in an enhanced remote computing contingency plan). These plans have been tested recently as the financial services sector has been challenged by the recent COVID-19 pandemic.

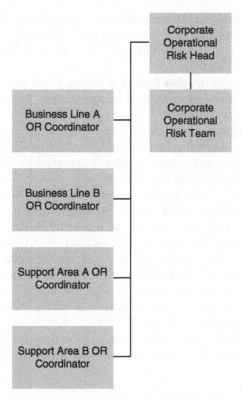

FIGURE 4.8 Embedded Independent Operational Risk Coordinator Reporting Structure

The activities of the BCP team fall squarely within the definition of operational risk, in particular two of the Basel II categories: Damage to Physical Assets and Business Disruption and System Failures.

For this reason, BCP might report to the corporate head of operational risk; this is becoming more and more common in the financial services sector as firms recognize the synergies between the functions.

If there is no direct reporting line from BCP to operational risk, then a strong partnership is essential.

Information Security
The information security function is endowed with the important task of preserving the confidentiality, availability, and integrity of the firm's data, whether it is electronic or otherwise. A failure in this area can result in a serious operational risk event, such as exposing confidential client data,

compromising regulatory data compliance requirements, or the loss of vital financial data. Many information security functions started out in a technology department, where they were focused on protecting the security of the technology systems and data.

However, the information held in a firm is often also held in physical forms (such as paper), and the information security function usually provides policies and procedures for the safeguarding of these records also.

The increasingly complex challenges of managing cyber risk, including hacking and ransom attacks, has elevated the information security function to a broader cyber security function that is governed by its own regulatory requirements and assessment approaches.

In order to effectively provide cyber security for the firm's technical infrastructure and data, it is preferable for the function to sit outside of the technology department, as there may be a conflict between the technology department's needs and the information security department's concerns.

For this reason the information security function is often looking for an independent reporting line, and the operational risk function can provide this for them. Also, as information security risk is a subset of operational risk, it is appropriate to link these functions to ensure they effectively leverage each other's expertise and data.

For these reasons, several banks now have their information security function reporting to the operational risk head or the chief risk officer.

Sarbanes-Oxley Act

The Sarbanes-Oxley Act (SOX) imposed operational risk management requirements regarding the accuracy of financial statements on U.S. publicly traded firms. SOX-related activities are therefore a subset of operational risk. However, the SOX team often started in a separate area of the firm (usually in the finance department) and had specific deadlines and compliance requirements to meet. SOX work might also predate the operational risk function, and the SOX team often exists separately from the operational risk team, with a different reporting line (perhaps to the CFO).

SOX assessments are conducted across the firm, and through these assessments, risks and controls are identified and mitigating actions tracked to ensure compliance with SOX.

This overlaps with the risk assessment activities that will be conducted as part of the operational risk program, and for this reason many firms now have their SOX work incorporated into the operational risk function or have the SOX team report to the operational risk head.

In Chapter 16, we look at the ways that these SOX and operational risk activities can be combined in a GRC approach.

New Business Approval or New Product Approval

Financial firms usually have robust new product approval programs that include policies, procedures, and processes to assess and facilitate the review of new products or businesses before they are launched. These new product approval processes require participants to consider all of the risks of the new product, including operational risk. New product approval provides a forum for discussions around the operational practicalities, accounting and tax practices, legal and regulatory requirements, and any other areas that should be addressed before launch.

The operational risk function sometimes administers the new-product approval process, sometimes they are one of the required signatures for approval, and sometimes they might simply require that all other signatories consider operational risk when giving their sign-off.

Policy Office

Many firms are establishing dedicated policy office functions to centralize and standardize firm-wide policies. The operational risk function will be a critical stakeholder in such a function, as they will be designing, mandating, approving, and monitoring policies that manage operational risk. In some cases, the operational risk function might have responsibility for the policy office, and it is embedded in the operational risk function.

The advantage of such an approach is that the operational risk function will have a strong understanding of risk and control requirements and so can provide a strong hand in the development of appropriate and consistent policies.

In the past few years, we have seen a dramatic increase in regulators' interest in policies and procedures. A central repository and a standard template and approach are not just beneficial but are increasingly necessary in order to manage the myriad of regulatory requests regarding policies.

THIRD LINE OF DEFENSE

The third line of defense provides the final internal checks and balances for the operational risk framework. This third line is the internal audit function.

Audit

It is worth noting that the 2021 "Sound Practices" document expressly forbids first- and second-line operational risk functions from reporting to the audit department.

The third line of defence provides independent assurance to the board of the appropriateness of the bank's ORMF. This function's staff should not be involved in the development, implementation and operation of operational risk management processes by the other two lines of defence.[10] *[emphasis added]*

The document then provides an in-depth description of the independent review responsibilities of the audit function.

An effective independent review should:

a. *review the design and implementation of the operational risk management systems and associated governance processes through the first and second lines of defence (including the independence of the second line of defence);*

b. *review validation processes to ensure they are independent and implemented in a manner consistent with established bank policies;*

c. *ensure that the quantification systems used by the bank are sufficiently robust as (i) they provide assurance of the integrity of inputs, assumptions, processes and methodology and (ii) result in assessments of operational risk that credibly reflect the operational risk profile of the bank;*

d. *ensure that business units' management promptly, accurately and adequately responds to the issues raised, and regularly reports to the board of directors or its relevant committees on pending and closed issues; and*

e. *opine on the overall appropriateness and adequacy of the ORMF and the associated governance processes across the bank. Beyond checking compliance with policies and procedures approved by the board of directors, the independent review should also assess whether the ORMF meets organisational needs and expectations (such as respect of the corporate risk appetite and tolerance, and adjustment of the framework to changing operating circumstances) and complies with statutory and legislative provisions, contractual arrangements, internal rules and ethical conduct.*[11]

The audit function will measure the firm against the operational risk policies and procedures that are in place and will measure the corporate operational risk function against its policies and procedures and its success in designing, maintaining, and monitoring an operational risk framework that meets the firm's regulatory requirements.

Validation

In June 2017, the Basel Committee on Banking Supervision (BCBS) published "Basel III: Finalising post-crisis reforms," which established that capital calculations had to be based on *validated* internal loss data.

> *[Internal loss data] procedures and processes must be subject to validation before the use of the loss data within the operational risk capital requirement measurement methodology, and to regular independent reviews by internal and/or external audit functions.*[12]

This was further clarified in December 2019 when the BCBS issued additional guidance on the appropriate calculation of operational risk capital."[13]

> *The bank's operational risk management processes and assessment system must be subject to validation and regular independent review. These reviews must include both the activities of the business units and of the operational risk management function.*[14]

They also reiterated that independent external validation was also required in order for the regulators to be able to rely on a standardized approach:

> *The bank's operational risk assessment system (including the internal validation processes) must be subject to regular independent review by internal or external auditors and/or supervisors.*[15]

Firms have been struggling with how best to respond to these *validation* requirements as they are not specifically in the hands of audit. Some firms have established a validation function that is independent from the rest of the corporate operational risk function and that validates the quantitative and qualitative elements of the framework.

An annual validation program is now in place in several of the firms that have more mature operational risk frameworks. This annual process may include a comparison of data between work streams, for example, comparing loss data to risk and control assessment, and a review of policies and procedures, for example, reviewing committee activities minutes to ensure compliance.

Some firms are also looking at developing rolling validation programs that continuously examine the accuracy and completeness of data.

RISK COMMITTEES

The risk committee structure that is put in place for the escalation and management of operational risk will reflect the first- and second-line-of-defense governance choices made by the firm.

The 2011 "Sound Practices" document provides the following guidance:

> When designing the operational risk governance structure, a bank should take the following into consideration:
>
> a. Committee structure—Sound industry practice for larger and more complex organizations with a central group function and separate business units is to utilize a board-created enterprise level risk committee for overseeing all risks, to which a management level operational risk committee reports. Depending on the nature, size and complexity of the bank, the enterprise level risk committee may receive input from operational risk committees by country, business or functional area. Smaller and less complex organizations may utilize a flatter organizational structure that oversees operational risk directly within the board's risk management committee;
>
> b. Committee composition—Sound industry practice is for operational risk committees (or the risk committee in smaller banks) to include a combination of members with expertise in business activities and financial, as well as independent risk management. Committee membership can also include independent non-executive board members, which is a requirement in some jurisdictions; and
>
> c. Committee operation—Committee meetings should be held at appropriate frequencies with adequate time and resources to permit productive discussion and decision-making. Records of committee operations should be adequate to permit review and evaluation of committee effectiveness.[16]

This document still stands as guidance for operational risk management, but the BCBS has also published updated general guidance on corporate governance that references the roles and responsibilities of the board risk committee, including its oversight of operational risk:

> 71. A risk committee should:
>
> - be required for systemically important banks and is strongly recommended for other banks based on a bank's size, risk profile or complexity;

- *should be distinct from the audit committee, but may have other related tasks, such as finance;*
- *should have a chair who is an independent director and not the chair of the board or of any other committee;*
- *should include a majority of members who are independent;*
- *should include members who have experience in risk management issues and practices;*
- *should discuss all risk strategies on both an aggregated basis and by type of risk and make recommendations to the board thereon, and on the risk appetite;*
- *is required to review the bank's risk policies at least annually; and*
- *should oversee that management has in place processes to promote the bank's adherence to the approved risk policies.*

72. *The risk committee of the board is responsible for advising the board on the bank's overall current and future risk appetite, overseeing senior management's implementation of the RAS, reporting on the state of risk culture in the bank, and interacting with and overseeing the CRO.*
73. *The committee's work includes oversight of the strategies for capital and liquidity management as well as for all relevant risks of the bank, such as credit, market, operational and reputational risks, to ensure they are consistent with the stated risk appetite.*
74. *The committee should receive regular reporting and communication from the CRO and other relevant functions about the bank's current risk profile, current state of the risk culture, utilisation against the established risk appetite, and limits, limit breaches and mitigation plans (. . .).*
75. *There should be effective communication and coordination between the audit committee and the risk committee to facilitate the exchange of information and effective coverage of all risks, including emerging risks, and any needed adjustments to the risk governance framework of the bank.*[17]

An example of a risk committee structure that would allow for operational risk to be escalated through the organization is shown in Figure 4.9. In this example the business lines have their own operational risk committees, and separate committees exist for operational risk-related functions in the firm.

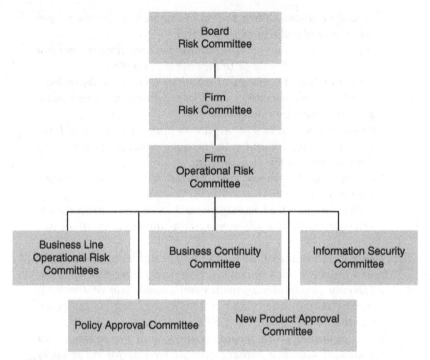

FIGURE 4.9   A Sample Risk Committee Structure

Often, many of these committees have different reporting paths up to the board. In those situations, it is important that operational risks are being consistently represented through the various paths that exist.

The board is required to periodically review and approve the framework, and the committee structure can facilitate that process, for example, by requiring risk committee and then board approval as a final step in the validation procedures.

KEY POINTS

- Boards of directors and senior management have specific accountability for operational risk management, including setting appetite and approving frameworks.
- Good governance requires three lines of defense: the first line is the business, the second line is the corporate operational risk function, and the third line is usually the audit function.

- Validation activities must be put in place to ensure the integrity of the operational risk framework and data.
- A risk committee should be established to facilitate risk escalation and framework approval.
- Firms adopt governance structures that meet their business needs and their regulatory requirements locally and globally.
- There are advantages and disadvantages in each governance approach. Some promote ERM, while others promote GRC strategies.

REVIEW QUESTIONS

1. Which governance structure is most likely to foster an enterprise risk management view?
   a. The operational risk department is part of the compliance department.
   b. The operational risk department reports to the chief risk officer.
   c. The operational risk department reports to the chief financial officer.
   d. The operational risk department reports to the chief operating officer.
2. Which of the following are requirements of a strong governance structure?
   I. There are first, second, and third lines of defense.
   II. The first line of defense is the business line.
   III. The second line of defense is independent from the first line.
   IV. The second line of defense is owned by the audit function.
   V. The third line of defense is owned by the business.
   a. I and II only
   b. I, II, and III only
   c. I, II, and IV only
   d. I, II, and V only

NOTES

1. Basel Committee on Banking Supervision, "Principles for Enhancing Corporate Governance," October 2010, www.bis.org/publ/bcbs176.pdf.
2. Ibid., section 3.
3. Risk Management Group of the Basel Committee on Banking Supervision, "Revision to the Principles of Sound Practices for the Management of Operational Risk," March 2021, www.bis.org/bcbs/publ/d515.pdf.
4. See note 3, section 5.
5. See note 3, sections 24–33.
6. See note 3, section 9.
7. Ibid.

8. See note 3, sections 10 and 11.

9. See note 1, sections 71–74.

10. See note 3, section 12.

11. Ibid.

12. Basel Committee on Banking Supervision, "Basel III: Finalising Post-crisis Reforms," December 2017, section 19, www.bis.org/bcbs/publ/d424.pdf.

13. Basel Committee on Banking Supervision, "OPEC 25 Standardised Approach," December 2019, https://www.bis.org/basel_framework/chapter/OPE/25.htm?tldate=20221231.

14. Ibid., S25.8 (5).

15. Ibid., S25.8 (6).

16. See note 3, section 37.

17. Basel Committee on Banking Supervision, "Corporate Governance Principles for Banks," July 2015, https://www.bis.org/bcbs/publ/d328.pdf.

CHAPTER 5

Culture and Awareness

This chapter explores the challenges of bringing about successful culture change that supports an effective operational risk framework. It considers planning, marketing and communication, training, and sponsorship. It explores the challenges of implementing a framework that works effectively in the digital paradigm and agile approaches that exist today. In addition, this chapter investigates the "use test" requirements of operational risk regulation and explores how activities that change the culture can contribute to meeting the required standards.

WINNING OVER THE FIRM

With a strong governance structure in place, an operational risk function can turn to the important next step: winning over the organization. The time invested in culture and awareness activities is indicative of the likely success of the framework. To be successful, operational risk must be identified, assessed, monitored, controlled, and mitigated across the firm, and this can be achieved only through an energized organizational change program.

The operational risk framework must be designed to reflect the culture of the firm. An approach that is a roaring success in one firm might fall flat in another. Even the best-designed framework needs to be promoted and communicated in order for operational risk management to be adopted and applied throughout the organization. To achieve this, the operational risk function should undertake three important activities—marketing, planning, and training—before it attempts to implement the other elements of the framework.

The role of culture and awareness in underpinning a sound operational risk framework is illustrated in Figure 5.1.

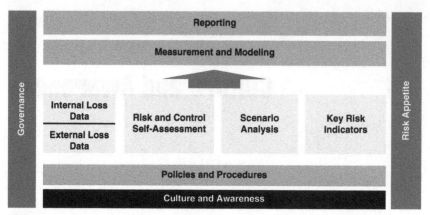

FIGURE 5.1 The Role of Culture and Awareness in an Operational Risk Framework

MARKETING AND COMMUNICATION

Every function in a firm has its own brand, whether it has invested any effort into cultivating that brand or not. Each function has a reputation, either good, bad, or between the two, and this reputation is key to whether the function can achieve its goals. If the operational risk function is seen as a trusted partner, it will be able to progress more quickly toward its goals. If it is an unknown or misunderstood department, then its goals may be frustrated at every turn.

Colleagues, peers, managers, and employees will have formed an opinion of whether this function is one with which they want to work. If they have never heard of the department, there is even more work to do.

Unlike most departments, the operational risk function needs to work with everyone in the firm, as operational risk can arise in every nook and cranny of the organization. To build those working relationships, a firm-wide marketing effort is needed at the launch of the department, and also at every major rollout of the framework.

The firm might have a well-established approach to launching new initiatives, possibly through poster campaigns, e-mail blasts, or town halls. Whatever works well can be leveraged, and if there is nothing to leverage, new approaches can be tried. In fact, new methods of communication tend to draw notice, and so can even be preferable to the standard methods.

In addition to these internal marketing methods, it is important to allow time for face-to-face meeting with all of the key stakeholders. During those meetings it can be helpful to ask, "What are you hoping we will do?" and

"What are you hoping we will not do?" The answers to those two questions provide insight into the current perceptions held about operational risk, both as a function and as a discipline. In addition, the answers to those two questions provide an opportunity to find and leverage mutual goals and aspirations. Armed with the answers to these questions, formal and informal marketing campaigns can be designed to ensure that the following minimal goals are met:

1. The organization knows what operational risk is.
2. People know what to do when they see operational risk.
3. Managers are aware of the benefits of good operational risk management.
4. Managers are aware of the dangers of poor operational risk management.
5. Main supporters are identified and there is a plan for how to leverage that support.
6. Main protagonists are identified, and there is a plan to win them over.

The efforts taken in promoting cultural awareness and developing a relationship with key stakeholders are recouped later in reduced political roadblocks and improved support for operational risk management activities.

A framework that is technically excellent but has little organizational support will never endure and will not succeed in ensuring that operational risks are identified, assessed, controlled, and mitigated. A framework that is built on a bedrock of strong culture and awareness can continue to evolve and mature as experience develops. That development will ensure that risk identification, assessment, control, and mitigation are continuously occurring and improving.

AGILE

It is important for the operational risk function to fit the current culture of the firm. In both fintechs and banks, innovation is a key element of their business strategy, and an operational risk structure that does not support such approaches is unlikely to be effective.

An agile methodology in the technology function will use an iterative approach to development that can be more challenging than a waterfall development approach when it comes to the identification of risks.

A waterfall approach relies on robust business requirements at the beginning of the project, and at that stage it is possible for a new product approval process to identify the potential operational risks in the design.

In contrast, agile development focuses on the fast delivery of a minimum viable product (MVP) rather than a slower delivery of the final complete product.

As the agile approach allows for minimal documentation and optimum iteration during the project, capturing the changing specifications of the product and its associated risks can be very challenging for the risk function.

There are several ways to integrate operational risk into an agile approach. First, if the first line has a strong understanding and ownership of operational risk, then they may be well equipped to identify, assess, monitor, and mitigate risks as they arise at each iteration with coaching from the operational risk team only as needed.

If that maturity is not yet in place in the business, then the operational risk function can embed themselves in the agile process and provide insight and challenge in the daily or weekly stand-up meetings and check-in processes.

Finally, an agile project could be allowed to proceed unchecked with the resulting operational risks assessed at the end, before launch to the customer. Any identified risks would then need to be mitigated and retested before launch.

The operational risk team can also embrace agile methodology in their own processes. I have had some success taking a "sprint" approach to establishing an operational risk program for all critical processes. In several firms we have prepared a list of stories that we wish to complete for each critical process in the firm and then used a Kanban board to track all of the stories to completion during an intense two-week sprint per process. Sample stories for such an approach are:

- Map the process.
- Complete an RCSA.
- Identify all compliance controls.
- Identify all SOX controls.
- Complete a business impact analysis and business continuity plan.
- Identify and validate any models.
- Identify and complete due diligence on any third parties.
- Identify critical applications and assign access appropriately.

By using a two-week sprint and recognizable agile methods, we have been able to meet the business where they are, using language that resonates with them and only impose the risk-build work on them for a two-week period before moving on to the next critical process.

TRAINING

If operational risk is to be managed effectively in every corner of the firm, then it may be beneficial to roll out firm-wide training in addition to a general announcement e-mail or town hall.

There are many ways to deliver effective training, and the type of training should reflect the culture of the firm. Training can be efficiently delivered to all employees using the intranet. If the firm already has an online training program, then an operational risk training module could be added to that. If possible, everyone should be invited to complete the most basic training, with more in-depth training for those who might be involved in specific activities.

A basic training module can facilitate cultural change in the firm, educating employees on the importance of operational risk management, and explaining the role of the operational risk team and any operational risk coordinators, specialists, or managers. There is no need for basic training to be overambitious. It can be short and to the point. For example, the goal of basic training could simply be to make employees aware of operational risk and make sure they know what to do when they see it.

Additional in-person and group training will be needed for the practical implementation of the elements of the framework. For example, before a loss data collection program is launched, it will be necessary to train everyone who will be involved in entering losses. There are many considerations when entering an operational risk loss event, and these are addressed in Chapter 7. Without adequate training, the integrity of the data is likely to be compromised.

Similarly, training will be needed before any risk and control self-assessment (RCSA) activities are launched. There are multiple sources of expertise to assist with the design and roll-out of training. The firm may have its own training and development function that can assist with this or might even manage it entirely.

Possible topics for introductory operational risk awareness training are:

- What is operational risk? (Definition and examples)
- Why should we manage it? (Examples of operational risk events)
- What should I do when I see it?

There are some key success criteria for good training, which should be incorporated into the training design and delivery, including:

- Setting clear learning objectives and being sure to cover them adequately.
- Having realistic expectations of the learning curve of the trainees.
- Providing feedback so that trainees are comfortable that they have mastered the materials.

PLANNING

Planning can make or break an operational risk function. Good planning involves setting clear goals, realistic milestones, and achievable deliverables that add value. Publishing milestones beforehand, and then meeting them on time, builds the positive reputation of the function.

An operational risk framework is a complex and evolving challenge, and to keep its development under control, it is important to apply strong project management skills to the design and implementation of each new element. It is good to plan for short-term and long-term goals so that the function can demonstrate its current successes, as well as its long-term importance to the firm.

Once the elements of an operational risk framework are up and running, they need to be monitored to ensure that they maintain their integrity and do not deteriorate over time. Indeed, an operational risk framework should continue to evolve with experience and in response to feedback from participants, partners, and sponsors. The validation and verification requirements introduced in Chapter 4 are important elements in ensuring that the framework continues to be embedded in the organization and that the quality and integrity of operational risk activities are maintained.

Poor planning can seriously tarnish the image of the department as it can lead to promises that are not kept and deadlines that slip. Every day spent planning is a solid investment in a successful framework and protects the brand of the function within the firm.

MAJOR DELIVERABLES CHECKLIST

In the early stages of an operational risk framework, progress against the deliverables of an implementation plan might be represented in several ways. One method of demonstrating progress is to have a simple checklist of implementation activities completed and pending. For example, the main deliverables that the implementation of an operational risk framework could include are listed next. These deliverables will be further explained in future chapters, but they are included here to provide a useful planning list of the major deliverables of an implementation plan for a new operational risk framework. They are not listed in chronological order, and the order of implementation can depend on the organization and the preferred approach to each area.

Governance

- ☐ First-line-of-defense operational risk managers established:
  - ☐ In all front office areas
  - ☐ In all support areas
- ☐ Second-line-of-defense corporate operational risk function established:
  - ☐ Reporting lines established
  - ☐ Team hired
- ☐ Audit has confirmed ownership of third line of defense.
- ☐ Operational risk committee(s) established.
- ☐ Board has acknowledged review and approval responsibility.
- ☐ Senior management has confirmed ownership of operational risk framework.
- ☐ Validation and verification program has been established.

Culture and Awareness

- ☐ Introductory meetings with senior management team completed.
- ☐ Marketing strategy developed and approved.
- ☐ Marketing activities kicked off (e.g., town hall or e-mail blast).
- ☐ Training strategy developed and approved.
- ☐ Operational risk awareness training delivered.
- ☐ All employees trained.

Policy and Procedures

- ☐ Firm-wide operational risk policy established and approved by board.
- ☐ Loss data procedures established.
- ☐ RCSA procedures established.
- ☐ Scenario analysis procedures established.
- ☐ Metrics or key risk indicator procedures established.
- ☐ Validation and verification procedures established.
- ☐ Modeling procedures established.
- ☐ Reporting procedures established.
- ☐ Taxonomies established:
  - ☐ Risk taxonomy
  - ☐ Control taxonomy
  - ☐ Process taxonomy
  - ☐ Organizational taxonomy

(continued)

(continued)

Loss Data Collection

- ☐ Internal loss data standards established.
- ☐ Internal loss data procedures established.
- ☐ Internal loss data system implemented:
    - ☐ Business requirements gathered
    - ☐ System specifications complete
    - ☐ Development complete
    - ☐ Pilot complete
    - ☐ System rolled out
- ☐ Internal loss data training designed and delivered:
    - ☐ To front office
    - ☐ To support areas

External Loss Data Collection

- ☐ External loss data sources established:
    - ☐ Membership in consortium obtained
    - ☐ Subscription(s) to external data sources established
- ☐ External loss data procedures established.
- ☐ External loss data system developed (if needed).
- ☐ External loss data trained designed and delivered as needed.

Risk and Control Self-Assessment

- ☐ RCSA procedures established.
- ☐ RCSA system implemented:
    - ☐ Business requirements gathered
    - ☐ System specifications complete
    - ☐ Development complete
    - ☐ Pilot complete
    - ☐ System rolled out
- ☐ RCSA training designed and delivered.
- ☐ RCSA calendar established.
- ☐ RCSA program kicked off.
- ☐ RCSA first-run results gathered.
- ☐ RCSA results validated.
- ☐ RCSA mitigation action tracking established.
- ☐ RCSA lessons learned gathered.

Scenario Analysis

☐ Scenario analysis procedures established.
☐ Scenario analysis system implemented:
  ☐ Business requirements gathered
  ☐ System specifications complete
  ☐ Development complete
  ☐ Pilot complete
  ☐ System rolled out
☐ Scenario analysis training designed and delivered.
☐ Scenario analysis calendar established.
☐ Scenario analysis program kicked off.
☐ Scenario analysis first-run results gathered.
☐ Scenario analysis first-run output provided to modeling team.
☐ Scenario analysis first-run results validated.
☐ Scenario analysis mitigation action tracking established.
☐ Scenario analysis lessons learned gathered.

Key Risk Indicators (KRIs) or Metrics

☐ KRI standards established.
☐ KRI procedures established.
☐ KRI system implemented:
  ☐ Business requirements gathered
  ☐ Data sources identified
  ☐ System specifications complete
  ☐ Development complete
  ☐ Pilot complete
  ☐ System rolled out
☐ KRI training designed and delivered.
☐ KRI program kicked off.
☐ KRI first-run results gathered.
☐ KRI results validated.
☐ KRI lessons learned gathered.

Capital Modeling

☐ Operational risk capital modeling approach developed and approved.
☐ Operational risk capital modeling procedures established.
☐ Capital modeling system implemented:

(continued)

(continued)

☐ Business requirements gathered
☐ Data sources identified
☐ System specifications complete
☐ Development complete
☐ Pilot complete
☐ System rolled out
☐ First run of capital model complete.
☐ Capital model validated.

Reporting

☐ Reporting procedures established.
☐ Reporting designed and implemented for the board, for senior management, for the front office, and for support functions including:
☐ Loss data
☐ RCSA
☐ Scenario analysis
☐ KRI
☐ Capital

Risk Appetite

☐ Risk appetite methodology agreed.
☐ Risk appetite incorporated into reporting.
☐ Risk appetite incorporated into policy.
☐ Risk appetite incorporated into training.
☐ Risk appetite incorporated into procedures.

Alternatively, progress against the initial implementation plan may be represented in a milestones project chart as illustrated in Figure 5.2. (This example includes a project line for the development of a global OR system, including a request for information [RFI] and a request for proposal [RFP] from software vendors.)

Once an operational risk framework is implemented, the program should move from a project management phase into a business-as-usual phase. Once a program moves into business as usual, establishing effective tracking and monitoring of repeating deliverables will be important. This

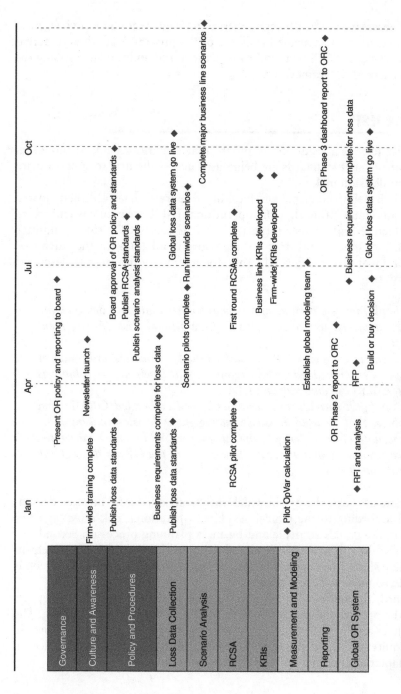

FIGURE 5.2 Sample Project Milestones for an Operational Risk Implementation Plan

will be necessary not just from a practical management point of view, but it will also provide documented evidence of the program's continuous activities. This evidence will be useful to regulators and auditors in assessing the effectiveness of the framework.

THE "USE TEST"

The "use test" is a regulatory standard that requires a bank to show that risk management standards are being used across the firm to support management decision making.

The Basel Committee on Banking Supervision established how a bank can demonstrate that the operational risk framework is embedded and effective and so meets the use test. In June 2011, the Committee published "Operational Risk—Supervisory Guidelines for the Advanced Measurement Approaches." In this document, the use test is described as follows:

> A bank may use various approaches to articulate and demonstrate the integrated use of its ORMF [Operational Risk Management Framework]. . . .
>
> The level to which the broader ORMF processes and practices have been embedded at all organizational levels across a bank is referred to as "embeddedness.". . .
>
> A bank should have sustainable and embedded ORMFs and policies that are used in its risk management decision-making practices, with clear evidence of the integration and linkage between the measurement and management processes of the ORMF through the entire institution.[1]

There are several ways in which this "embeddedness" must be demonstrated according to the Guidelines. First, operational risk must be a key factor in the bank's strategic and business planning processes. Second, the board should approve an operational risk appetite and tolerance statement and there should be controls in place to stay within that appetite (which is considered more fully in Chapter 14).

Third, the business units must be able to demonstrate how they are using the operational risk framework to inform their decision making. The Guidelines also provide details of how reporting can be used to meet the use test requirements, but the important cultural aspects for consideration in this chapter are the first and the third points above.

It is not enough to have a corporate operational risk framework, and it is not enough to have an engaged board of directors. Senior management and the business units must demonstrate that they use their knowledge and awareness of operational risk and appropriate risk measures when making business decisions.

The role of culture and awareness in the framework is vital to meeting this requirement. The business units need to analyze their own operational risk outputs when making decisions. Therefore, operational risk should be under consideration when a business decides to take on a new product, exit a region, expand its workforce, or change its strategy, for example. Operational risk management and measurement need to become an integral part of a business's management practices.

By engaging the business in the early development stages of the operational risk framework, and by training them carefully and comprehensively, the corporate operational risk function can assist the business unit in meeting this regulatory requirement. Simply put, does the business genuinely use operational risk information in its decision making? A well-constructed, well-documented, and well-managed operational risk framework should supply it with the data that it needs to meet this requirement in practice and to be able to demonstrate to a regulator or auditor how it has met this requirement.

The loss data, RCSA, and KRI elements that businesses gather through their first-line-of defense operational risk program can and must be integrated into their day-to-day decision-making processes. Scenario analysis, capital modeling, and firm-wide risks can also provide context for decisions and can be provided to them by the second line of defense, the corporate operational risk function.

The use test is taken seriously by regulators. Often, it results in them going directly to a business unit to see how it is participating in the operational risk framework and to review documented evidence of how it incorporates operational risk considerations into its business decision making. It is no surprise that a regulator is most satisfied if a business can demonstrate that it reached a "no" decision based on an operational risk level that it found unacceptable or a "yes" decision based on careful consideration of the risk metrics and potential risk losses.

The implementation of an operational risk framework is likely to require significant organizational change. This can be achieved through proactive marketing, careful planning, excellent training, and an energized enthusiasm from the operational risk team. The business also needs to fully embrace operational risk management and measurement in order to ensure that it is truly "embedded" in the firm.

KEY POINTS

- The use test requirements mean that the firm must be able to demonstrate that operational risk management and measurement is "embedded."
- "Embeddedness" is considered successful if the business unit is using operational risk as a key input into its decision-making processes, the board is fully engaged, senior management is fully engaged, and reporting is effective.
- Effective internal marketing, planning, and training activities are essential in order to successfully embed an operational risk function in a firm.

REVIEW QUESTION

1. Which of the following are elements of the Basel definition of "embeddedness"?
   I. Operational risk is a key factor in the bank's strategic and business planning processes.
   II. The board has approved the operational risk appetite.
   III. The business units are able to demonstrate how they are using the operational risk framework to inform their decision making.
   a. I and II only
   b. I, II, and III
   c. I and III only
   d. III only

NOTE

1. Basel Committee on Banking Supervision, "Operational Risk—Supervisory Guidelines for the Advanced Measurement Approaches," June 2011, www.bis .org/publ/bcbs196.pdf, sections 17–18.

CHAPTER 6

Policies and Procedures

This chapter explores the important role of strong policies and procedures in an effective operational risk framework. It also considers the role of standards and guidelines documents. Example content is provided for an operational risk policy, as well as samples from procedures, standards, and guidelines.

THE ROLE OF POLICIES, PROCEDURES, GUIDELINES, AND STANDARDS

In recent years, financial services firms have embraced the importance of having clearly articulated and consistently documented policies, procedures, standards, and guidelines. These written documents serve to articulate the firm's interpretation of rules and regulations and their chosen approach to meeting those requirements.

Investors and third parties often request these documents when engaging with a bank or fintech.

It has become clear that it is necessary to have objective goals against which to measure performance. Well-documented policy and procedure documents can help meet this need. Firms have also learned the sometimes painful lesson that good documentation is needed in order to demonstrate that regulatory requirements have been incorporated into the business processes of the firm.

Policies and procedures form an essential foundation for a successful operational risk framework, as is illustrated in Figure 6.1.

As well as continuously improving the content of such documents, many firms have sought efficiency improvements for their documentation. The rapidly increasing level of regulatory scrutiny and the associated increase in

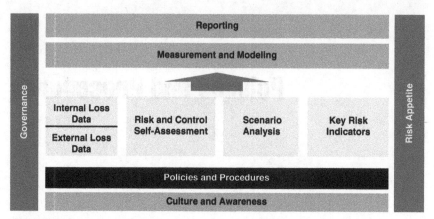

FIGURE 6.1 Policies and Procedures in an Operational Risk Framework

regulatory examinations have made it necessary for firms to streamline and standardize their approach to policies and procedures.

Some firms have developed centralized policy functions and have even written a "policy on policies" that requires standard templates, minimum content, and appropriate approval processes for policies and for procedures. While this may sound overly complex, it can ultimately reduce the effort needed to create and maintain a policy library. With clear guidance on what is, and is not, appropriate in a given document, employees have an easier time creating material that is useful, implementable, and meets both management's and regulator's expectations.

Different firms define the terms *policy* and *procedure* differently and some also have separate *standards* and *guidelines* documents. Whatever approach is taken, it is important for firms to be clear about what they mean by each of these terms.

The Federal Financial Institutions Examination Council (FFIEC) provides useful definitions for policy and for procedure:

> *Policies: Statements, rules or assertions that specify the correct or expected behavior of an entity.*
> *Procedures: A document containing a detailed description of the steps necessary to perform specific operations in conformance with applicable standards. Procedures are defined as part of processes.*
> *Standards: Rules, conditions, or requirements describing the following information for products, systems, services or practices: (i) Classification of components. (ii) Specification of materials, performance, or operations; or (iii) Delineation of procedures.*[1]

Guidelines offer supporting guidance on methods that might be used rather than outlining absolute requirements.

An analogy using cars may be helpful in understanding the differences between these related documents. A policy may state that you must drive safely, including obeying required speed limits. The standards vary from country to country, as the top speed limit is 55 or 65 miles per hour on most highways in America but is 130 kilometers (about 80 miles) per hour on motorways in France. How you accelerate or decelerate is outlined in your car's user manual, which provides the step-by-step instructions for how to use the gas pedal (accelerator) and the brake. When approaching a corner, you may see a chevron sign that indicates that this is a tight corner—this is a guideline, encouraging you to consider lowering your speed, but not requiring it.

Simply put, policy usually outlines *why* something should be done, standards establish *what* specific criteria need to be met, and procedures and guidelines outline *how* it should be done.

The relationship between regulation and the four categories of documentation can be represented as shown in Figure 6.2.

When authoring each document, care needs to be taken to ensure that it meets the requirements contained in documents that lie further up the pyramid.

A firm may combine policies and standards. However, policies generally require senior management approval, and so it can be helpful to keep standards separate so that full senior management approval is not needed if the standards change. A firm might also combine procedures and guidelines and will often incorporate certain principle statements into the policy document.

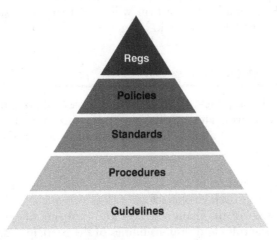

FIGURE 6.2 Policy Documentation Hierarchy

BEST PRACTICES

The high degree of regulatory interest in policies and procedures has led to significant improvements in the authoring of policies and procedures as well as in the associated review and approval processes. These improvements include the use of standard templates, the establishment of an indexed and searchable central repository for the documents, and the implementation of a robust version control process.

Some firms allow regulators direct access to their policy portals, thereby bringing more efficiency and transparency to their relationship. This approach can ease some of the pain of examinations and ensures accuracy and consistency in responses to regulatory requests.

As firms attempt to improve their policy approval processes they sometimes find that they need to adjust their committee structures and governance frameworks as a result. Policies are tightly linked to governance, and when policies are well designed, approved, implemented, and monitored, this provides evidence of strong governance.

The practicalities of publishing policies, standards, procedures, and guidelines will depend on the culture of the firm. If the culture of the firm requires strong consensus, then a lot of work will be needed to ensure that all key stakeholders are engaged in development and implementation. If the culture requires senior management approval for all major documents, then an appropriate and efficient approval workflow must be put in place.

The operational risk framework will need supporting policies, standards, procedures, and guidelines. An audit will measure the firm against this documentation, the regulators will look to them to ensure that the framework is well designed, and the firm will need them to ensure consistent implementation of the framework.

OPERATIONAL RISK POLICY

An operational risk policy is critical to the successful governance of operational risk in a firm. This might be part of an overall risk management policy, or it may stand alone. The policy should be approved by the board and include:

- The firm's definition of operational risk.
- The firm's approach to operational risk governance.
- A description of the main activities and elements of operational risk, including the roles and responsibilities of the participants.

The policy might also include information on each of the elements of the program, or these might be covered in lower-level procedure documents if they are likely to be subject to change. Policy documents usually require a formal sign-off process from the firm's risk committee or similar governance structure, and possibly also from the board. Therefore, the policy should be written at an appropriate level—not so high level that it provides no guidance, and not so low level that it requires formal amendment every time the operational risk framework evolves.

Policies, standards, procedures, and guidelines should cover the minimum requirements for the loss data program, the RCSA program, the scenario analysis program, and the KRI program. There may be additional procedures needed for validation and verification activities and for a capital model. These documents should clearly state the roles and responsibilities of those involved and should not be aspirational. That is to say, if something is not yet in place, it should not be a requirement.

Some regulators are comfortable with the inclusion of certain aspirational aspects as long as there is also a stated plan for how and when that future state will be achieved.

SAMPLE OPERATIONAL RISK POLICY

Figure 6.3 is an example of a possible operational risk policy.

OPERATIONAL RISK POLICY

Drafted: 12/12/20   Revised: 1/3/21   Version: 2.5

Purpose

The management of operational risk is a vital activity within the firm. The firm is subject to Basel II and must therefore implement an operational risk framework that meets the Basel II requirements. In addition, there are strong business drivers for effective operational risk management. This policy outlines a framework that meets both the regulatory and business requirements.

FIGURE 6.3   Sample Operational Risk Policy

FIGURE 6.3 *(continued)*

Definition

The firm's definition of operational risk is "the risk of loss resulting from failed or inadequate people, process, systems, and external events." This definition includes legal risk. This definition excludes strategic and business risk. Reputational risk will also be managed as part of the operational risk framework.

Objectives

The goal of the operational risk management framework is to identify, assess, control, and mitigate operational risk within the firm. A standard operational risk framework is applied across the firm in order to ensure consistency and completeness.

The framework includes the following key elements:

- Governance
- Culture and awareness
- Loss data collection
- Risk and control self-assessment (RCSA)
- Scenario analysis
- Key risk indicators (KRIs)
- Measurement and modeling
- Reporting
- Risk appetite

There are three lines of defense to ensure effective operational risk management. The business units provide the first line of defense, the corporate operational risk department provides the second line of defense, and the audit department provides the third line of defense.

Supporting Documents

Standards, procedures, and guidelines are published for each of the framework elements to support the implementation of this policy.

Scope

This policy applies to all employees of the firm globally, and failure to comply with this policy can result in disciplinary action, including dismissal.

Roles and Responsibilities (Governance)

Board of Directors

The board of directors is responsible for establishing, approving, and periodically reviewing the operational risk framework. The board of directors oversees senior management to ensure that the policies, processes, and systems are implemented effectively at all decision levels.

The board of directors approves and reviews the risk appetite and tolerance statement for operational risk that articulates the nature, types, and levels of operational risk that the bank is willing to assume.

Risk Management Committee

The risk management committee (RMC) develops for approval by the board of directors a clear, effective, and robust governance structure with well-defined, transparent, and consistent lines of responsibility. Senior management is responsible for consistently implementing and maintaining throughout the organization policies, processes, and systems for managing operational risk in all of the bank's material products, activities, processes, and systems consistent with the risk appetite and tolerance.

RMC is responsible for setting the operational risk appetite for the firm and reviewing operational risk reporting and making decisions based on this information. Matters requiring escalation for resolution will be presented to the RMC for their consideration.

RMC is responsible for approving the operational risk policy.

Corporate Operational Risk Department

The operational risk department (CORD) provides the second line of defense. CORD has a reporting structure independent of the risk-generating business lines and is responsible for the design, maintenance, and ongoing development of the operational risk framework within the firm. A key function of CORD is to challenge the business lines' inputs to, and outputs from, the bank's risk management, risk measurement, and reporting systems.

(continued)

FIGURE 6.3   *(continued)*

CORD has the following responsibilities:

- Develop firm-wide strategy for operational risk to meet regulatory and business drivers.
- Design and maintain operational risk framework.
- Provide consolidated reporting to RMC.
- Provide training and awareness activities.
- Coordinate collection and reporting of loss data, and track resolution of mitigating actions.
- Plan and track RCSA activities across the firm and report output to RMC.
- Coordinate design and collection of KRIs.
- Plan and execute scenario analysis activities across the firm.
- Analyze operational risk and present regular reporting on risk profile to RMC.
- Validate operational risk data collected by business units.

Operational Risk Coordinators

The business line is the first line of defense and every business unit must have an operational risk (OR) coordinator identified. The responsibilities of the OR coordinator are:

- Provide main communication contact with CORD.
- Ensure complete and timely reporting of loss data in their area.
- Manage RCSAs in their area.
- Coordinate KRI collection in their area.
- Track action items to completion for their area.
- Assist area in timely completion of all operational risk reporting requirements.
- Coordinate training and awareness activities in their area.
- Provide business heads with operational risk data for consideration in decision making.

All Employees

Every employee in the firm is responsible for effective operational risk management in their activities and for the timely reporting of any operational risk loss events of which they are aware.

Principles

Culture and Awareness

Operational risk training is provided to all employees and to all new hires. The training provides an overview of operational risk and its definition, scope, and importance.

Additional specific training is provided as needed for each element of the operational risk framework. Training is designed and coordinated by CORD.

In addition to training, a newsletter is distributed to all employees once each quarter and a website is accessible on the firm intranet.

Loss Data Collection

Internal Loss Events

Internal loss events are events that occur within the firm and meet the definition of operational risk. Internal loss events are collected in accordance with the operational risk event standards (published separately). Internal loss events are used to assist with the identification, assessment, control, and mitigation of operational risk. Lessons learned from loss events are applied throughout the framework and mitigating actions are tracked by CORD and the OR coordinators to assist with future risk mitigation.

A threshold for loss events is set in the operational risk event standards. All events that are above this threshold must be reported in the loss event database. Additional events may be reported.

External Loss Events

External loss events are those that occur outside the firm. External loss events are used to inform the operational risk framework. In particular, external losses provide an input into the RCSA, scenario analysis, culture and awareness, and reporting elements of the framework. Various sources are used to identify external events, including commercially available databases, news articles, and internet searches.

Risk and Control Self-Assessment

Risk and control self-assessments are used to identify potential operational risks and to provide a scoring for risks and controls in each area. RCSAs are forward-looking and subjective. They are conducted

(continued)

FIGURE 6.3 *(continued)*

on an annual basis in all areas. RCSA outputs are collated and analyzed by ORD and matters requiring escalation are reported to RMC for decision making and/or action.

Scenario Analysis

The purpose of scenario analysis is to identify rare, catastrophic potential events and to estimate the potential financial impact and frequency of such events. Scenario analysis is conducted in selected areas of the firm. CORD facilitates the identification and scoring of scenario analysis.

Key Risk Indicators

KRIs provide a monitoring tool to report on the performance of controls and changes in levels of risk and trends that may inform the operational risk program. CORD may identify key KRIs that must be collected across the firm. The OR coordinators are responsible for ensuring the collection of these KRIs. In addition, unique KRIs may be identified by each area for the purposes of effective operational risk management.

Measurement and Modeling

For the purposes of Basel II, the firm is required to calculate capital for operational risk. The operational risk measurement team is responsible for the development of capital models using the inputs from the operational risk framework. Further information is outlined in the risk modeling policy (published separately).

Reporting

CORD provides reporting to RMC on a quarterly basis. The operational risk report includes the following:

- Internal loss data
- Relevant external loss data
- Action tracking
- RCSA output (when appropriate)
- KRI summary
- Capital requirements (when appropriate)
- Matters requiring decisions or escalation
- Analysis of current operational risk profile

Risk Appetite

Operational risk appetite is set by RMC and the board.

It is anticipated that the operational risk framework will continue to evolve as experience develops. As the framework matures, the elements of the framework will inform the firm of the current risk profile and will allow for refinement of the setting of future risk appetite. The strategy and objectives of the operational risk framework will be continually reviewed and revised to ensure effective identification, assessment, control, and mitigation of operational risk.

Approval

This policy will be reviewed and approved annually by RMC and the board.

SAMPLE STANDARDS, PROCEDURES, AND GUIDELINES

The following extracts provide examples of the type of wording that might be found in governance documents for loss data collection, including a standards document, a procedures document, and a guidelines document.

Extract from a Loss Data Standards Document

Operational Risk Event Minimum Data Requirements

When reporting an operational risk event, the reporter must provide the following minimum data in a timely manner:

- Date reported
- Date event occurred
- Name of reporter
- Reporting department
- Name of event
- Description of event:
  - The description must be sufficient that a person from a different area can understand what occurred. The use of shorthand, jargon, and acronyms should be avoided. The name of a client or individual should not be included.
  - The description should not apportion blame for the event, but should provide a factual recounting of what occurred.

- Involved departments: Include all departments that were involved in the event.
- Business line: Regardless of where the error occurred, all events must be allocated to a revenue area.
- Amount of direct loss.
- Amount of indirect loss: Indirect losses include legal fees, consulting fees, and the like.
- Recovery to date.
- Other impacts: Where appropriate, select additional nonfinancial impacts from reputational, client, regulatory, and life safety.
- Event category: Select from event categories as established in the Risk Taxonomy Standards.
- Event subcategory: Select from event subcategories as established in the Risk Taxonomy Standards.
- Cause: Select from people, process, systems, and external events.
- Action: A mitigating action must be identified, or it must be stated that no mitigating action will be taken and a reason must be given.

Extract from a Loss Data Procedures Document

Data Collection

On identification of an operational risk event, the identifying person will immediately inform the business unit operational risk coordinator. The operational risk coordinator will determine whether the event is one that meets the definition of operational risk and, if so, will enter the event into the loss data system including all data elements as outlined in the Loss Data Standards.

Extract from a Loss Data Guidelines Document

Training

To ensure timely identification and entry of loss events, it is recommended that all employees in a business unit receive operational risk management training annually.

Linkage between Documents

As can be seen from these examples, careful drafting of these documents can allow for updates to the standards, procedures, or guidelines without requiring additional changes to the related documents.

In these examples, the exact data requirements are set in the standards, the method of collecting the data is provided in the procedures, and opportunities for quality improvement are recommended in the guidelines. However, it is common for standards to be combined with policy or with procedures and for guidelines to be incorporated into procedures.

As the operational risk framework evolves through experience, regular updates to the documents are likely. It is therefore important to ensure that the update and approval process is designed to be as efficient as possible within the culture of the firm.

KEY POINTS

- An operational risk policy should include:
  - The firm's definition of operational risk
  - The governance of operational risk including who owns it, what it owns, and how issues are escalated
  - The main activities/elements that are managed by the operational risk function
- An operational risk policy should be realistic and not aspirational.
- Each element of the framework must have written policies and procedures against which the firm is audited by its internal audit department.
- Standards provide detailed measures of what criteria must be met by the procedures.
- Procedures outline how activities should be undertaken, with step-to-step tasks explained.
- Guidelines are nonmandatory in nature and provide support for the procedures and further details as needed.

REVIEW QUESTION

1. Which of the following best describes an aspect of a good policy document?
   a. Content requires continuous updating.
   b. Detailed steps and activities are outlined.
   c. It is approved by a senior management committee on an annual basis.
   d. It represents the future state goal for best practices.

NOTE

1. https://ithandbook.ffiec.gov/glossary.aspx.

CHAPTER 7

Internal Operational Risk Event Loss Data

This chapter explores the collection of operational risk event loss data. It explores the reasons for data collection and the methods used. The seven Basel operational risk categories and the Basel business line categories are described and their use in the framework is discussed. Operational risk event data standards are introduced, along with examples of regulatory expectations and best practices for the many elements of an operational risk event data collection process.

OPERATIONAL RISK EVENT DATA

Once governance, culture, awareness, and initial policies and procedures are in place, the four core elements of the operational risk program can be designed and launched. These four elements are:

1. Operational risk event (internal loss) data.
2. Risk and control self-assessments (RCSAs).
3. Scenario analysis.
4. Key risk indicators (KRIs).

The first of these is referred to as internal loss data in the Basel regulatory guidance, but is better named "operational risk event data," as it refers not just to losses, but to a broader category of operational risk events.

A robust operational risk framework includes consideration of both internal and external operational risk events. Internal events are those that have happened in or to the firm. External events are those that have happened not in or to the firm but elsewhere in the industry.

INTERNAL LOSS DATA OR INTERNAL OPERATIONAL RISK EVENTS

Loss data is a key element in the operational risk framework, as is illustrated in Figure 7.1. Firms have found that collecting and analyzing operational risk events, or loss data, provides a valuable insight into the current operational risk exposure of the firm. Until these data are collected, there can be a mistaken perception that operational risk is not a real concern. Once internal loss data start to come in, there is often a new appreciation of the importance of managing this category of risk.

Many loss data programs are started as a result of a realization that you cannot manage what you cannot measure. Others are started as a result of specific regulatory requirements, such as Basel II.

The Basel Committee on Banking Supervision (BCBS) reinforced the importance of effective management of operational risk event data in its March 2021 guidance "Revisions to the Principles for the Sound Management of Operational Risk":

> *Operational risk event data—Banks often maintain a comprehensive operational risk event dataset that collects all material events experienced by the bank and serves as basis for operational risk assessments. The event dataset typically includes internal loss data, near misses, and, when feasible, external operational loss event data (as external data is informative of risks that common across the industry). Event data is typically classified according to a taxonomy defined in the ORMF policies and consistently applied across the*

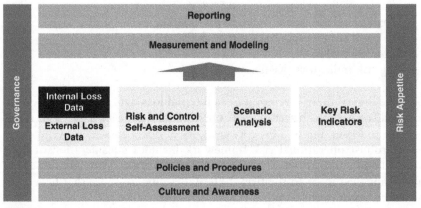

FIGURE 7.1 Internal Loss Data in an Operational Risk Framework

bank. Event data typically include the date of the event (occurrence date, discovery date and accounting date) and, in the case of loss events, financial impact. When other root cause information for events is available, ideally it can also be included in the operational risk dataset. When feasible, banks are encouraged to also seek to gather external operational risk event data and use this data in their internal analysis, as it is often informative of risks that are common across the industry.[1]

When collecting operational risk event data, it is important to consider many aspects of the program, including who, what, where, when, and why. We will start with "why?"

Why Collect Operational Risk Event Data?

The design of an operational risk event database will be driven by the purpose of the program. There are several possible purposes for implementing an operational risk event collection program, and most firms have more than one in mind. When designing operational risk event collection policies, procedures, standards, and guidelines, a firm should consider which of the following reasons apply:

- They are collecting data for capital modeling purposes.
- They wish to use events to help identify control weaknesses.
- They wish to kick off risk mitigation activities when events occur.
- They wish to evaluate risk events and outcomes.
- They wish to use events to help them understand their current operational risk exposure and any areas of excessive risk.
- They wish to use event collection as a way to embed the operational risk discipline.

Each purpose will result in different design elements in the program and will impact the policies and procedures that are developed around loss data. An effective loss data, or operational risk event, program will be designed to reflect the specific purposes and culture of the firm. It will also be accompanied by a strong training program to maximize participation.

The audit department should audit the departments of the firm against the operational risk event data policies, procedures, and standards.

It is pragmatic to expect the initial quality of the database to be somewhat disappointing. It takes some time for culture change to take effect and for a significant number of operational risk events to be captured as intended.

Who Should Collect the Operational Risk Event Data?

Who will be responsible for reporting operational risk-related events in the firm? Responsibility must be clear in order to ensure good participation. The operational risk policy might assign responsibility, or it might be outlined in a separate operational risk event policy or procedure document.

The firm might designate a particular representative in each department to ensure that all events are collected for their department. For example, an operational risk coordinator, specialist, or manager for each department might be tasked with ensuring that all events are entered into the operational risk event database. This empowers them to seek out and report events that might otherwise languish unreported. It also ensures that someone owns the data-reporting responsibility.

Some departments will be in a position to identify events that did not occur in their area but that are captured by their controls. For example, the operations or finance departments may catch events during reconciliation activities.

It may be prudent, therefore, to endow these departments with additional responsibilities to inform the operational risk department of likely events that they come across in their day-to-day activities. Finance may also be involved in reconciling operational risk events to the general ledger if that is one of the goals of the loss data capture program in that firm. However, some firms do not attempt to reconcile loss events to the general ledger.

It can be helpful to adopt an "if you see it, you must report it" policy; or perhaps, more practically, an "if you see it, you must ensure that someone reports it" policy. This is reminiscent of the antiterrorism posters in the subways of New York City after 9/11 (as illustrated in Figure 7.2) and may form the basis of a strong marketing campaign to ensure good participation in operational risk event collection.

This helps to ensure that an event does not remain unreported when several people are aware of it but they all believe it is someone else's responsibility to report it.

```
if you
SEE
something
SAY
something
```

FIGURE 7.2 Loss Data Marketing Poster

Reporting of events should not be associated with fault, but rather should be associated with effective operational risk management. An open access database allows all employees at a firm to enter an event. However, if it is not practical to allow everyone to be able to report an event, then there needs to be a policy or procedure that allows for anyone to pass an event to a designated operational risk event reporter.

If there is an open access database approach, then it may be prudent to allow only very minimal data to be entered, with more being gathered by someone who has been trained in loss data collection. This will help to avoid some of the dangers of poor reporting. These dangers are covered later in this chapter.

What Should Be Collected in the Operational Risk Event Data Program?

Any event that meets a firm's definition of operational risk should be captured in the operational risk event data database, subject to any conditions that are outlined in the loss data or operational risk event policy.

There are several useful pieces of information that should (or must, if under Basel II) be captured for each event. First, it is important to assign an event to one, and only one, appropriate risk category. Risk categories are provided by Basel II, and many firms adopt these at the highest level and then customize lower levels to better match their firm's culture and products.

RISK EVENT CATEGORIES

Every event should be mapped to the risk event categories being used at the firm. These risk categories should be clearly outlined in the policies, procedures, standards, or guidelines that have been published in the firm for operational risk management.

Basel II provides a useful set of seven categories, which most firms have adopted or adapted to meet their own reporting needs. Basel II describes the seven categories as shown in Table 7.1.

There is a somewhat confusing mixture of events and causes in this list of seven (for example, fraud *causes* a loss, but damage to physical assets might *be* the actual loss). However, despite this, these seven categories have lived on successfully since they were first published in the Basel II document.

The categories are remarkably resilient and remain the standard high-level groupings in the financial services industry. They also continue to work well in other, nonfinancial, industries and at this highest level, they effectively capture all types of operational risk events.

TABLE 7.1   Basel II Operational Risk Event Categories

Event-Type Category (Level 1)	Definition
Internal Fraud	Losses due to acts of a type intended to defraud, misappropriate property, or circumvent regulations, the law, or company policy, excluding diversity/discrimination events, which involves at least one internal party
External Fraud	Losses due to acts of a type intended to defraud, misappropriate property, or circumvent the law, by a third party
Employment Practices and Workplace Safety	Losses arising from acts inconsistent with employment, health, or safety laws or agreements, from payment of personal injury claims, or from diversity/discrimination events
Clients, Products, and Business Practices	Losses arising from an unintentional or negligent failure to meet a professional obligation to specific clients (including fiduciary and suitability requirements), or from the nature or design of a product
Damage to Physical Assets	Losses arising from loss or damage to physical assets from natural disaster or other events
Business Disruption and System Failures	Losses arising from disruption of business or system failures
Execution, Delivery, and Process Management	Losses from failed transaction processing or process management, from relations with trade counterparties and vendors

Source: Based on Bank for International Settlements, Annex 9, "International Convergence of Capital Measurement and Capital Standards: A Revised Framework," 2004.

The severity and frequency of losses can be quite different in the different categories. For example, events are more frequent in the last category—Execution, Delivery, and Process Management—as this category captures lots of small errors. In contrast, events in the Clients, Products, and Business Practices category tend to be rarer but can be very large when they occur (for example, class action lawsuits).

For this reason, the modeling of loss data can be quite different in each category and so it is important to ensure that an event is placed in the correct category.

Having said that, it can still be argued that consistency is more important than accuracy. In other words, as long as similar events are always categorized in the same way, then operational risk management can be effective. In order to ensure this consistency, it is necessary to go down to a lower level of categorization. Let us consider each category from Table 7.1 in turn.

Internal Fraud

Losses due to acts of a type intended to defraud, misappropriate property, or circumvent regulations, the law, or company policy, excluding diversity/ discrimination events, which involves at least one internal party.

Internal Fraud captures any event where there has been intentional wrongful behavior by an employee of the firm. In Annex 9 of the Basel II document, this category is further explained at a lower level, Level 2.

At Level 2, Internal Fraud is broken down into two subcategories: Unauthorized Activity, and Theft and Fraud. Basel II provides Level 3 examples to illustrate these subcategories, as shown in Table 7.2.

TABLE 7.2   Internal Fraud Subcategories

Categories (Level 2)	Activity Examples (Level 3)
Unauthorized Activity	Transactions not reported (intentional)
	Transaction type unauthorized (w/monetary loss)
	Mismarking of position (intentional)
Theft and Fraud	Fraud/credit fraud/worthless deposits
	Theft/extortion/embezzlement/robbery
	Misappropriation of assets
	Malicious destruction of assets
	Forgery
	Check kiting
	Smuggling
	Account takeover/impersonation/etc.
	Tax noncompliance/evasion (willful)
	Bribes/kickbacks
	Insider trading (not on firm's account)

Source: Based on Bank for International Settlements, Annex 9, "International Convergence of Capital Measurement and Capital Standards: A Revised Framework," 2004.

From these second and third levels, it becomes clear that insider trading and unauthorized trading are captured under this category. It is also clear that unintentional acts are not captured here. In fact, you will see similar activities fall under Execution, Delivery, and Process Management or under Clients, Products, and Business Practices when they are unintentional mistakes.

Capturing operational risk events that have a fraud element is likely to be very sensitive. This category and the External Fraud category often require legal review before being entered into a database. They might also have only minimal information entered in order to ensure confidentiality.

External Fraud

Losses due to acts of a type intended to defraud, misappropriate property, or circumvent the law, by a third party.

External Fraud captures all events where there has been fraud, with no collusion or participation from an internal employee.

At Level 2, External Fraud is broken down into two subcategories: Theft and Fraud and Systems Security. Basel II provides Level 3 examples to illustrate these subcategories, as shown in Table 7.3.

From these second and third levels, we can see that one of the most high-profile operational risks is captured here: cyber security. In 2004, the Basel Committee was unaware just how dangerous cyber-attacks would become for the financial services industry, but they did have the foresight to include it as a Level 3 example in their risk categories. In the past few years, the volume, sophistication, and effectiveness of cyber-attacks have increased dramatically.

TABLE 7.3   External Fraud Subcategories

Categories (Level 2)	Activity Examples (Level 3)
Theft and Fraud	Theft/robbery
	Forgery
	Check kiting
Systems Security	Hacking damage
	Theft of information (w/monetary loss)

Source: Based on Bank for International Settlements, Annex 9, "International Convergence of Capital Measurement and Capital Standards: A Revised Framework," 2004.

As a result, this risk category is currently enjoying intense scrutiny. The proliferation of politically motivated attacks such as events involving WikiLeaks and Anonymous are of high concern. In addition, the threat of ransom attacks by organized criminal groups and the rise of cyber terrorism are significant concerns that are consistently highlighted by governments and regulators.

Traditional external fraud is also captured here, and theft and forgery are examples of criminal events that are captured in operational risk event databases.

Employment Practices and Workplace Safety

Losses arising from acts inconsistent with employment, health, or safety laws or agreements, from payment of personal injury claims, or from diversity/ discrimination events.

The Employment Practices and Workplace Safety category captures losses that result from harm suffered by employees, either due to workplace accident or due to mistreatment by the firm.

At Level 2, Employment Practices and Workplace Safety is broken down into three subcategories: Employee Relations, Safe Environment, and Diversity and Discrimination. Basel II provides Level 3 examples to illustrate these subcategories, as shown in Table 7.4.

Events that are captured in this category might be highly sensitive, and some firms have a policy that allows only the human resources department to enter events in this category.

TABLE 7.4 Employment Practices and Workplace Safety Subcategories

Categories (Level 2)	Activity Examples (Level 3)
Employee Relations	Compensation, benefit, termination issues Organized labor activity
Safe Environment	General liability (slip and fall, etc.) Employee health and safety rules events Workers' compensation
Diversity and Discrimination	All discrimination types

Source: Based on Bank for International Settlements, Annex 9, "International Convergence of Capital Measurement and Capital Standards: A Revised Framework," 2004.

Workers' compensation items are captured in this category, and it can be helpful to set up an automatic link with any workers' compensation database so that such data can be automatically linked or reconciled.

Discriminatory actions are likely to be kept confidential and will often have only minimal information entered for that reason.

There is sometimes confusion regarding termination payments. If someone is compensated beyond the usual termination notice period due to grievances, should such a payment be considered an operational risk event? Different firms treat these sensitive cases differently. Going back to the definition of operational risk, it should certainly be entered if, but only if, there is a loss resulting from failed or inadequate processes, people, systems, or external events. Consistency is key here. Whatever approach a firm decides to adopt, a clear standard needs to be established and consistently applied.

Clients, Products, and Business Practices

Losses arising from an unintentional or negligent failure to meet a professional obligation to specific clients (including fiduciary and suitability requirements), or from the nature or design of a product.

This category has some of the largest events, as large legal losses are often captured here. A class action lawsuit that alleges client misselling will fall into this category, as will any large litigation concerning a badly flawed financial product.

At Level 2 there are many subcategories for Clients, Products, and Business Practices: Suitability, Disclosure, and Fiduciary; Improper Business or Market Practices; Product Flaws; Selection, Sponsorship, and Exposure; and Advisory Activities. Basel II provides Level 3 examples to illustrate these subcategories, as shown in Table 7.5.

You will notice that the Level 3 examples present a disturbing list of the worst things that can go wrong for a financial institution, from model error to money laundering. Criminal activity by the firm may be captured in this category along with regulatory breaches. Regulatory fines and legal penalties often dominate this category. In fact, some are tempted to rename this category "Legal Events." However, legal events can certainly arise in other categories, as we have just seen in the Employment Practices and Workplace Safety category.

Clients, Products, and Business Practices events often have a serious reputational impact as well as a financial cost. Items in this category are most likely to get negative press coverage, and the legal department is usually (painfully) aware of these events.

TABLE 7.5 Client, Products, and Business Practices Subcategories

Categories (Level 2)	Activity Examples (Level 3)
Suitability, Disclosure, and Fiduciary	Fiduciary breaches/guideline violations Suitability/disclosure issues (KYC, etc.) Retail customer disclosure violations Breach of privacy Aggressive sales Account churning Misuse of confidential information Lender liability
Improper Business or Market Practices	Antitrust Improper trade/market practices Market manipulation Insider trading (on firm's account) Unlicensed activity Money laundering
Product Flaws	Product defects (unauthorized, etc.) Model errors
Selection, Sponsorship, and Exposure	Failure to investigate client per guidelines Exceeding client exposure limits
Advisory Activities	Disputes over performance of advisory activities

Source: Based on Bank for International Settlements, Annex 9, "International Convergence of Capital Measurement and Capital Standards: A Revised Framework," 2004.

It is important to clearly establish and maintain a process for ensuring that events that are being considered by legal are also being captured in the operational risk database. Regulators are now asking for legal reserves to be captured along with realized losses. For this reason, it can be beneficial to have an automated link between any legal database and the operational risk database, to ensure accurate and timely reporting and to reconcile the two sources.

Damage to Physical Assets

Losses arising from loss or damage to physical assets from natural disaster or other events.

Damage to Physical Assets can occur for a variety of reasons. There is only one Level 2 subcategory provided by Basel II—Disasters and Other Events—and little further explanation in Level 3, as seen in Table 7.6.

Most events in this category will be covered, at least in part, by insurance. However, the original loss should still be captured, and regulators allow only a small amount of insurance recovery to be considered. The reason for this is clear: it might take more than a year to receive an insurance recovery, and during that period the firm needs to be able to demonstrate that is has enough capital to cover the loss. We consider insurance further in Chapter 12.

Business Disruption and System Failures

Losses arising from disruption of business or system failures.

There is only one Level 2 subcategory for Business Disruption and System Failures: Systems. Basel II provides Level 3 examples of the systems to be considered, as shown in Table 7.7.

It is often hard to put a value on losses in this category. While the impact of a major network or telecommunications outage can be serious, it is often

TABLE 7.6 Damage to Physical Assets Subcategories

Categories (Level 2)	Activity Examples (Level 3)
Disasters and Other Events	Natural disaster losses
	Human losses from external sources (terrorism, vandalism)

Source: Based on Bank for International Settlements, Annex 9, "International Convergence of Capital Measurement and Capital Standards: A Revised Framework," 2004.

TABLE 7.7 Business Disruption and System Failures Subcategories

Categories (Level 2)	Activity Examples (Level 3)
Systems	Hardware
	Software
	Telecommunications
	Utility outage/disruptions

Source: Based on Bank for International Settlements, Annex 9, "International Convergence of Capital Measurement and Capital Standards: A Revised Framework," 2004.

best measured in lost opportunities rather than in direct losses. An operational risk event database might be designed to capture both the opportunity costs as well as direct costs, but many firms do not take that extra step.

Losses in this category are also often challenging in that they need to be assigned to a particular business line, but the impact may be firm-wide. If that is the case, then an allocation methodology needs to be established, and this is discussed further later in this chapter.

In the past few years, we have seen many wide-scale power outages as a result of extreme weather as well as examples of simple human error and equipment errors.

Extreme weather may well cause damage to physical assets as well as business disruption. For example, in the United States alone, the past 10 years have seen multiple severe weather-related events. Since Hurricane Sandy hit the eastern states in the autumn of 2012, there have been multiple record-setting hurricanes, including Harvey, Irma, and Maria in 2017 and Dorian in 2019. The United States has also experienced catastrophic tornados, devastating winter blizzards, damaging flooding, and widely destructive forest fires.

These patterns of extreme and disruptive weather have been seen across the globe.

The resulting physical damage in all of these events was severe, and there were major disruptions to telecommunications and utilities. It can be seen from this example that one cause can produce multiple operational risk events that sit in different risk categories.

Execution, Delivery, and Process Management

Losses from failed transaction processing or process management, from relations with trade counterparties and vendors.

The majority of operational risk events occur in the Execution, Delivery, and Process Management category. The frequency of events is usually relatively high compared to other categories. However, many of the events may be small, and so the severity might be relatively low compared to other categories.

There are many Level 2 subcategories: Transaction Capture, Execution, and Maintenance; Monitoring and Reporting; Customer Intake and Documentation; Customer/Client Account Management; Trade Counterparties; and Vendors and Suppliers. Basel II provides Level 3 examples, as shown in Table 7.8.

As can be seen, the list of examples is comprehensive. Anything that goes wrong somewhere in the process of executing a trade, onboarding a client, creating regulatory reports, or dealing with third parties will be

TABLE 7.8 Execution, Delivery, and Process Management Subcategories

Categories (Level 2)	Activity Examples (Level 3)
Transaction Capture, Execution, and Maintenance	Miscommunication
	Data entry, maintenance, or loading error
	Missed deadline or responsibility
	Model/system misoperation
	Accounting error/entity attribution error
	Other task misperformance
	Delivery failure
	Collateral management failure
	Reference data maintenance
Monitoring and Reporting	Failed mandatory reporting obligation
	Inaccurate external report (loss incurred)
Customer Intake and Documentation	Client permissions/disclaimers missing
	Legal documents missing/incomplete
Customer/Client Account Management	Unapproved access given to accounts
	Incorrect client records (loss incurred)
	Negligent loss or damage of client assets
Trade Counterparties	Nonclient counterparty misperformance
	Miscellaneous nonclient counterparty disputes
Vendors and Suppliers	Outsourcing
	Vendor disputes

Source: Based on Bank for International Settlements, Annex 9, "International Convergence of Capital Measurement and Capital Standards: A Revised Framework," 2004.

captured in this category. Many support functions are designed to manage controls to prevent these types of errors, so you may find that your operations, controllers, and technology departments already capture information on events that occur in the category.

USING THE BASEL RISK CATEGORIES

The Basel risk categories must be used to report operational risk events for firms that are required to meet the Basel regulations. However, they can also be used effectively in other ways. Most firms use the same categorization taxonomies for their risk and control self-assessment (RCSA) programs as they do for their operational risk event data. They may also align any key risk indicators (KRIs) and any scenario analysis work with the same categories.

While the seven Level 1 categories are mandatory for capital calculation and loss data capture by a Basel firm, the second and third levels are often adapted to better suit those firms.

The Basel risk categories are used to capture a risk event, not a cause. This does result in some confusion, as the wording used by the Basel Committee does suggest "cause" in some cases. However, when designing a risk categorization taxonomy for a firm, it is important to be clear about the difference between risk impacts and causes.

These risk categories are helpful buckets in which to gather operational risk event data, and the categorization scheme that is used in the loss data program should be applied across the operational risk framework.

If a different set of Level 1 categories is used in a firm, then a behind-the-scenes mapping to the seven Basel categories is needed for Basel firms.

Banks and fintechs that do not have Basel II requirements often find these categories a helpful starting place for the development of their own risk classification system.

MINIMUM OPERATIONAL RISK EVENT DATA STANDARDS

It is important to have a clear policy and standards on the minimum reporting requirements for operational risk event data. The event data standards should contain minimum reporting criteria as mandated by any relevant regulation and any data requirements that have been selected to facilitate strong operational risk management practices at the firm.

When looking for guidance on how to establish an internal loss data program with appropriate rigor, it may be helpful to refer to the guidance issued by BCBS in the original Basel II requirements and reinforced in the most recent guidance for the new Standardized Approach to capital modeling. This new capital approach relies heavily on internal loss data and, at the time of this writing, is scheduled to become mandated in January 2023.[2]

Examples of minimum criteria considerations include the following elements.

Comprehensive

> *The operational risk event data program must be comprehensive and capture all material activities and exposures from all appropriate subsystems and geographic locations.*[3]

Practically speaking, it can be extremely difficult to ensure that every nook and cranny of the organization is participating effectively in the operational risk event data collection program. As a result, it is important that the operational risk department regularly reviews the business structure of the firm to ensure that new acquisitions, mergers, or business changes are reflected in the coverage of the operational risk data program.

Threshold

The operational risk data program must include all material losses that are above a de minimis gross loss threshold, for example, €20,000.

There should be a threshold over which events *must* be entered. Setting a threshold will depend on the risk appetite of the firm and any regulatory requirements that it needs to meet. Recent Basel guidance suggests that a threshold of €20,000 would be appropriate, but even Basel II firms have selected different thresholds: from zero to $100,000. In recent years, regulatory pressure has been downward, and most firms are now requiring mandatory reporting of all events over €10,000 or $10,000. However, the most recent guidance suggests that a national regulator might allow larger banks to set a threshold of €100,000 for the purposes of including their losses in the new Standardized Approach capital calculation.[4]

Fintechs do not have a regulatory mandated threshold and so should select one that meets their own risk appetite.

A zero threshold will set a high reporting burden on the firm. Every error that is a result of inadequate or failed processes, people, and systems or from external events will have to be captured. Taken literally, this would mean that a pencil stolen from the supply cabinet would be an event that needs to be entered in the operational risk event database.

In practice, firms that have a zero threshold apply it only to areas of the firm where it is practical to collect that data. For example, if they have a data feed for all trading errors, then it might not be burdensome to capture them all, however small.

Some departments may want to capture all losses, regardless of the threshold. For example, an operations department may want to track every error, or a finance department might want to track every time there is a wire transfer error, whatever the size.

However, there will be other requirements around each event in addition to the amount, and these may be unnecessary details for smaller losses and might be excluded from the reporting requirements. A firm that has a zero threshold for operational risk event reporting is therefore likely to have a higher threshold for full details to be mandatory.

Many firms do indeed have varying reporting thresholds for different departments, but there must also be a minimum corporate threshold, over which an operational risk event must be reported and will be included in the firm's program and in any operational risk capital calculation.

Amount

Each operational risk event data entry must include the loss amount.

This can be the source of some contention and may need intervention from the operational risk department, or a dedicated controller, as there may be some confusion over the exact amount lost. Some firms reconcile their operational risk events to their general ledger; others do not. The actual gross loss amount will often be different from the net loss amount or the loss after all recoveries. Both the gross and net amounts should be captured.

There may be conflicting views as to how much was actually lost. For example, a trade error that results in a loss can give rise to disagreements regarding the time and price at which the resulting loss should be calculated. A hedging error might produce a loss, but it may be unclear exactly what loss was realized.

In addition to ensuring that the correct amount of loss is entered, there are considerations as to which losses should be included in the loss data system. In June 2011, the BCBS issued "Operational Risk—Supervisory Guidelines for the Advanced Measurement Approaches" in which they offered further guidance on how to determine the correct gross amount.

> *Measures of the gross loss amount*
> *There are different ways to measure the gross loss amount:*
>
> a. *Mark-to-market: the economic impact of an operational risk loss is usually the same as the accounting impact when an operational risk loss affects assets or accounts treated on a mark-to-market basis. In such cases, the gross loss amount is the loss or adjustment as recognized in the comprehensive statement of income.*
> b. *Replacement cost: the economic impact of an operational risk loss usually differs from the accounting impact when losses affect assets or accounts that are not maintained on a mark-to-market basis such as property, plant, equipment or intangible assets. The gross loss amount is the replacement cost of the item. Replacement cost means the cost to replace an item or to restore it to its pre-loss condition.[5]*

The Committee also provided guidance on what should be included in a gross loss amount:

The following specific items should be included in gross loss computation.

a. *Direct charges (including impairments) to the statement on comprehensive income and write-downs due to operational risk events.*
b. *Costs incurred as a consequence of the event that should include external expenses with a direct link to the operational risk event (e.g., legal expenses directly related to the event and fees paid to advisors, attorneys or suppliers) and costs of repair or replacement, to restore the position that was prevailing before the operational risk event.*
c. *Provisions ("reserves"); the potential operational loss impact is reflected in the comprehensive income statement and should be taken into account in the gross loss amount.*
d. *Pending losses stem from operational risk events with a definitive financial impact, which are temporarily booked in transitory and/or suspense accounts and are not yet reflected in the statement of comprehensive income. For instance, in some countries, the impact of some events (e.g., legal events, damage to physical assets) may be known and clearly identifiable before these events are recognized through the establishment of a reserve. Moreover, the way this reserve is established (e.g., the date of recognition) can vary across institutions or countries. "Pending losses," that are recognized to have a relevant impact, should be included in the scope of operational risk loss within a time period commensurate to the size and age of the pending item; this can be done through the recognition of their actual amount in the loss database or pertinent scenario analysis.*[6]

Until the publication of these guidelines there was a wide range of practice regarding the definition of "gross" and "net" loss. The Committee went further and provided clarification of what should *not* be included in the gross amount:

The following specific items should be excluded from the gross loss computation. It should not be considered to be an exhaustive list:

a. *Costs of general maintenance contracts on property, plant or equipment;*

   b. *Internal or external expenditures to enhance the business after the operational risk event: upgrades, improvements, risk assessment initiatives and enhancements;*
   c. *Insurance premiums.*[7]

National regulators applied their interpretation of this guidance to all of their AMA banks. As has been noted earlier, even financial institutions that were not technically required to adopt AMA practices were generally advised by their regulators that AMA standards were "best practices" and therefore should be adopted anyway.

For the upcoming new Standardized Approach, further guidance has been provided:

> *Gross loss is a loss before recoveries of any type. Net loss is defined as the loss after taking into account the impact of recoveries. The recovery is an independent occurrence, related to the original loss event, separate in time, in which funds or inflows of economic benefits are received from a third party.*
>
> *22. Banks must be able to identify the gross loss amounts, non-insurance recoveries, and insurance recoveries for all operational loss events. Banks should use losses net of recoveries (including insurance recoveries) in the loss dataset. However, recoveries can be used to reduce losses only after the bank receives payment . . .*
>
> *23. The following items must be included in the gross loss computation of the loss data set:*
>
> **a.** *Direct charges, including impairments and settlements, to the bank's P&L accounts and write-downs due to the operational risk event;*
> **b.** *Costs incurred as a consequence of the event including external expenses with a direct link to the operational risk event (e.g. legal expenses directly related to the event and fees paid to advisors, attorneys or suppliers) and costs of repair or replacement, incurred to restore the position that was prevailing before the operational risk event;*
> **c.** *Provisions or reserves accounted for in the P&L against the potential operational loss impact;*
> **d.** *Losses stemming from operational risk events with a definitive financial impact, which are temporarily booked in transitory and/or suspense accounts and are not yet reflected in the P&L ("pending losses"). Material pending losses should be included in the*

loss data set within a time period commensurate with the size and age of the pending item; and

e. *Negative economic impacts booked in a financial accounting period, due to operational risk events impacting the cash flows or financial statements of previous financial accounting periods (timing losses"). Material "timing losses" should be included in the loss data set when they are due to operational risk events that span more than one financial accounting period and give rise to legal risk.*

24. *The following items should be excluded from the gross loss computation of the loss data set:*

a. *Costs of general maintenance contracts on property, plant or equipment;*

b. *Internal or external expenditures to enhance the business after the operational risk losses: upgrades, improvements, risk assessment initiatives and enhancements; and*

c. *Insurance premiums.*[8]

We consider several of these elements later in this chapter.

Indirect Costs

In addition to the direct financial impact of the loss, there may be other indirect costs, such as resulting legal fees or the costs to fix the control failure that caused the loss. In the preceding guidelines, these indirect costs are referred to as "costs incurred as a consequence of the event."

The inclusion of associated legal fees in the gross amount can have a large impact on the loss data. Legal fees can be extremely high and may be incurred over several years. This raises the question of how to treat an event that crosses the reporting threshold only because of the associated costs incurred. The operational risk event data policy and standards of a firm need to clearly articulate whether such items are exempt because the initial loss was under the threshold, or whether they become reportable as soon as the associated costs take it over the threshold. In the latter case, there needs to be a mechanism for tracking events that are too small now, but have the potential to be large later due to legal costs. The reporting timing issues that can result are discussed later under the date consideration.

A firm's operational risk event data policy, procedures, and standards must clearly state whether these indirect costs must be captured, and if they are, then the methods to be used to calculate them.

The latest guidance specifically includes these indirect costs:

23. The following items must be included in the gross loss compu-
tation of the loss data set: . . .

b. Costs incurred as a consequence of the event including exter-
nal expenses with a direct link to the operational risk event (e.g.
legal expenses directly related to the event and fees paid to advi-
sors, attorneys or suppliers) and costs of repair or replacement,
incurred to restore the position that was prevailing before the
operational risk event;[9]

Gains, Near-Misses, and Opportunity Costs

Most operational risk event data programs also collect gains that are realized due to operational risk events. For example, a trade error might be
followed by a market move that results in an inadvertent gain to the firm.

Near-misses are also valuable opportunities to manage operational risk
proactively. An event might produce a loss under the threshold or no loss at
all but indicate an unmitigated operational risk.

Similarly, opportunity costs or lost revenue might result from an event,
even though there is no direct loss. For example, if a trading system fails
and no trades can be made for a day, then that day's revenue has been lost.

The event itself is still a concern to the firm as it indicates that a control
failed or a process is flawed, and the next time the market could move in the
other direction, causing a loss.

For this reason, gains, near-misses, and opportunity costs are valuable
additions to the operational risk event database, and often a loss database is
named to reflect this. For example, it might be called the "operational risk
event database" rather than an "internal loss database" to more accurately
reflect its purpose and content.

The AMA Guidelines reinforce this:

Some items are important for risk management although they may
be beyond the scope required for quantification. In particular, the
items below can be useful for promptly detecting failures and errors
in processes or internal control systems. These items may also be
useful inputs for scenario analysis.

a. "Near-miss events": operational risk events that do not lead to
a loss. For example, an IT disruption in the trading room just
outside trading hours.

b. "Operational risk gain events": operational risk events that gen-
erate a gain.

  c. *"Opportunity costs/lost revenues"*: *operational risk events that prevent undetermined future business from being conducted (e.g., unbudgeted staff costs, forgone revenue and project costs related to improving processes).*[10]

Accounting Adjustments or Timing Events

Some operational risk event databases include accounting adjustments as well as actual losses. For example, if the accounting treatment that has been used by a firm is declared incorrect by a regulator, then the books and records of the firm need to be adjusted. This can result in significant downward adjustments even though no payment has actually been made to correct the error.

Some firms use the operational risk event database to track such events and include balance sheet or profit and loss adjustments as loss events. The threshold for these events is often much higher than the minimum threshold for a direct financial loss, and they might be excluded from any capital calculations.

There is some discussion as to whether these are actual losses or "timing events" or "accounting adjustments." The operational risk event data standards in the firm's policy must clearly outline whether such events should be included and the criteria that should be applied to them.

The AMA Guidelines consider these items as follows:

Timing losses are defined as the negative economic impacts booked in an accounting period, due to operational risk events impacting the cash flows or financial statements of previous accounting periods. Timing impacts typically relate to the occurrence of operational risk events that result in the temporary distortion of an institution's financial accounts (e.g., revenue overstatement, accounting errors and mark-to-market errors). While these events do not represent a true financial impact on the institution (net impact over time is zero), if the error continues across two or more accounting periods, it may represent a material misrepresentation of the institution's financial statements. Material "timing losses" due to operational risk events that span two or more accounting periods should be included, i.e., full amount that includes make-up payments as well as penalties and interest, in the scope of operational risk loss when they give rise to legal events.[11]

As outlined earlier in this chapter, the guidance issued for the use of internal losses in the calculation of the new Standardized Approach from

January 2023 has clarified that these types of losses must be included when they span more than one financial period.

> 23. *The following items must be included in the gross loss compu-tation of the loss data set: . . .*
>
> e. *Negative economic impacts booked in a financial accounting period, due to operational risk events impacting the cash flows or financial statements of previous financial accounting periods (tim-ing losses"). Material "timing losses" should be included in the loss data set when they are due to operational risk events that span more than one financial accounting period and give rise to legal risk.*[12]

Recoveries

Each operational risk event data entry must include any recoveries against the gross loss amount.

This can cause some confusion, as is best illustrated with an exam-ple. If a wire transfer is sent to the wrong party and the amount is above the threshold, then this would be an operational risk event that must be reported. However, if the amount is quickly returned by the erroneous party, some firms consider this to be a "near miss" and do not consider it a realized event. Other firms consider this a gross loss, with a recovery equal to the gross loss and therefore with a net loss of zero. The treatment of such events must be clearly established in the operational risk event data policy in order to avoid confusion and inconsistency.

The AMA Guidelines acknowledged this range of practice and con-firmed that if the recovery is rapid, then the event can be considered a near-miss rather than a loss event.[13]

For both recoveries and timing events, the AMA Guidelines state that "the inclusion or exclusion of the . . . items depends on their nature and materiality."[14]

Date

Each loss data entry must include the date of the event.

Perhaps surprisingly, this can be a difficult piece of data to nail down. For example, if the loss is the result of several consecutive control failings, then is the date of the event the date that the first control failing occurred, or the date that the last control failing occurred? Or is the correct date the date the loss hit the accounts? Or is it the date that it was detected? The date requirements must therefore be clearly defined in the operational risk event data policy or standards.

The recent guidance for the new Standardized Approach provides the following requirements for the collection of date information:

> *Aside from information on gross loss amounts, the bank must collect information about the reference dates of operational risk events, including*
>
> - *the date when the event happened or first began ("date of occurrence"), where available;*
> - *the date on which the bank became aware of the event ("date of discovery"); and*
> - *the date (or dates) when a loss event results in a loss, reserve or provision against a loss being recognised in the bank's profit and loss (P&L) accounts ("date of accounting").*[15]

So, for the future calculation of operational risk capital, it will be necessary to collect at least the date of occurrence, date of discovery, and date of accounting for each event.

Date Challenges for Legal Events

Reserves   Regulatory guidance in some jurisdictions requires that legal reserves for operational risk events should be collected in the database at the time of reserve. For some years the industry has been arguing that this might amount to double counting. The strongest argument was: Why collect loss data to calculate capital to cover something that is already being reserved for? Another concern was the possibility that information would be discoverable and could compromise the bank or lead to further litigation. However, most firms have procedures in place that protect the confidentiality of such matters by providing only minimum information in the database.

Despite these arguments, regulators have determined that it is better to include all known losses as promptly as possible, and they point out that holding a reserve is not double counting capital, as the event would only be one data point in the operational risk capital calculation.

The latest guidance includes reserves and provisions in the definition of gross losses and provides guidance on the date that should be used to capture those losses:

> *23. The following items must be included in the gross loss computation of the loss data set: . . .*
>
> *c. Provisions or reserves accounted for in the P&L against the potential operational loss impact; . . .*

25. Banks must use the date of accounting for building the loss data set. The bank must use a date no later than the date of accounting for including losses related to legal events in the loss data set. For legal loss events, the date of accounting is the date when a legal reserve is established for the probable estimated loss in the P&L.[16]

Legal Fees Date issues can arise when legal fees are collected, as these fees continue to accrue over time. Some firms have adopted an approach where a legal event is entered as a loss only once it is "final." "Final" might be determined as when a final settlement had been reached or a case closed with no further appeals anticipated. The legal fees accrued up to that date could then be entered as a final amount.

However, some cases span several years, and if a legal reserve has been taken, there may be an expectation that associated fees are being collected on a regular basis. The AMA Guidelines provide an excellent example of the complexities that can arise with dating legal events:

Bank X is named in an investor lawsuit claiming inadequate and misleading disclosure of mortgage-related losses on 4 May 2006 (discovery date). The suit asks for monetary damages for investment losses in the amount €5 billion. At the discovery date, when the bank was served with a potential exposure of €5 billion, legal counsel indicated that the suit had no merit, and that the likelihood of loss is remote. On 15 November 2008, following a review of internal documents/discovery the bank's legal counsel recommends that the "least cost" would be to settle the case for €1 billion. As a result, the bank takes a reserve for that amount. The case is settled two years later (settlement date) for €2 billion.

At the reserve date, the exposure of €1 billion is reasonably probable and it has been reasonably estimated. Supervisors expect the reserve amount of €1 billion to be reflected as a direct input into the AMA model. However, between the discovery date and the reserve date, legal counsel updates the probability that some settlement would be paid. During that time period the bank should consider reflecting this exposure in the capital calculation, for instance by a scenario analysis.

Between the reserve date and settlement date, the exposure may increase or decrease based on the outcome of settlement negotiations. In this example, the settlement amount increased to €2 billion, so during the period between the reserve date and settlement date that bank should reflect the increased exposure in its' AMA capital requirement estimation process. Alternatively, if the exposure declined to €500 million, the bank should reflect the decreased exposure in its AMA capital requirement estimation process. However, if the bank paid a settlement as a provisional execution following a court decision, only to have the decision/ settlement overturned or reduced, the bank should reflect the paid amount as its gross loss with any reduction reflected as a recovery.[17]

The Guidelines recommend that the event be included in the operational risk event database at the date of reserve, that any changes to exposure be captured in the capital modeling through alternative methods, such as scenario analysis, and that there should be a robust process to update the amount between the reserve date and the final settlement date.[18]

Once the simplified Standardized Approach to capital calculation is in effect, this will be somewhat simplified.

Description and Causes

For effective operational risk management, each operational risk data entry should include descriptive information about the drivers or causes of the loss event.

The most sensitive information about the event will often be in the description of the drivers and causes.

A firm's operational risk data standards may include a list of possible causes to select from—often related to the firm's operational risk definition. For example, the cause might be selected from people, process, systems, or external event. Alternatively, there may be a more sophisticated list of causes to select from that are specific to the firm, or to a department in the firm.

It is always politically challenging to memorialize fault or blame, and so care must be taken in providing clear guidelines on what should (and should not) be included in a description. Good training must be provided on these guidelines. Some firms are concerned enough about this information to engage their legal departments in reviewing and editing the entries where necessary, so as to avoid inadvertently exposing the firm to legal risk through inappropriate wording.

The Operational Riskdata eXchange Association (ORX) is a not-for-profit industry association dedicated to advancing the measurement and management of operational risk in the global financial services industry. The ORX database collects operational risk event data from a consortium of banks, and it is discussed more fully in Chapter 8. For events over $10 million the member banks are required to select a cause for the event. ORX provides a helpful taxonomy of causes as shown in Table 7.9.

TABLE 7.9   Level 1 and Level 2 Causes Taxonomy in ORX

Level 1	Level 2
Employees	Accidental causes (people)
	Lack of adequate training/competency
	Insufficient resourcing level
	Ineffective roles and responsibilities
	Miscommunication
	Ineffective culture
	Malice
Process Failure	Procedure/process design failure
	Procedure/process implementation failure
	Change/projects mismanagement
	Governance failure
External	Natural disaster
	Malice
	Terrorism/external attacks (excluding cyber-attacks)
	Environment (excluding natural disaster)
	Geopolitical/economic/social instability
	Regulatory and legislative environment
Systems	Functionality issues
	Performance/capacity issues
	Lack of maintenance/unsupported legacy
	Unavailability
	Inadequate testing/development
	Release/deployment issues
	Misconfiguration
	Inadequate data storage/retention and destruction management
	Exploitation of IT security vulnerability
	Technology-related planning issues

Source: ORX Reference Taxonomy for Operational and Non-Financial Risk—Causes & Impacts. Summary Report, November 2020, https://managingrisktogether.orx. org/operational-risk-reference-taxonomy/orx-cause-impact-reference-taxonomy.

As there may well be more than one cause, ORX allows its members to select up to three causes. In the same way, many firms' operational risk event data standards allow for several causes to be selected for a single event. They also provide lower-level descriptions and examples that can be found in their standards document and are easily accessible online.

Criteria for Allocation to Business Line

There must be documented, objective criteria for allocating losses to specified business lines. The purpose for this allocation is twofold. First, if a firm is currently applying the Advanced Measurement Approach (or the future-state Standardized Approach) for capital calculation, then the location of the event may directly impact the capital calculation. Second, it is helpful to be able to demonstrate which business areas are generating operational risk events, so that the firm can understand the relative operational risk profiles of each business area.

Every event needs an owner, or in other words, it must be determined which front office area suffered the loss. This can cause some tension in cases where, for example, the cause of the loss occurs in a department outside the front office, but the impact is placed on the profit-and-loss account of the business area. For this reason, it is helpful to have clear, objective criteria, including a limited list of business areas to select from when identifying where the loss hit the firm's accounts.

The latest Basel guidance describes business line categorization, as shown in Table 7.10.

The organizational structure of a firm might well not fit neatly into this categorization structure, and most firms have developed a mapping behind the scenes. This mapping allows them to collect data in a way that makes sense to their firm, but also allows them to group data appropriately for regulatory reporting as needed.

Criteria for Allocation to Central and Supporting Functions

If an event occurs in a central function and impacts the whole firm or several business lines, such as a network outage, then the operational risk event data policy should clearly outline how any resulting loss is allocated to each business line. Basel II originally outlined this requirement for operational risk event collection as follows:

> *A bank must develop specific criteria for assigning loss data arising from an event in a centralized function (e.g. an information technology department) or an activity that spans more than one business line, as well as from related events over time.*[19]

The most recent Bank for International Settlements (BIS) guidance on operational risk capital also provides guidance on how to relate a supporting

TABLE 7.10 Basel II Business Line Categories

Level 1	Level 2	Activity Groups
Corporate Finance	Corporate finance Municipal/government finance Merchant banking Advisory services	Mergers and acquisitions, underwriting, privatizations, securitization, research, debt (government, high yield), equity, syndications, initial public offerings, secondary private placements
Trading and Sales	Sales Market-making Proprietary positions Treasury	Fixed income, equity, foreign exchanges, commodities, credit, funding, own position securities, lending and repos, brokerage, debt, prime brokerage
Retail Banking	Retail banking	Retail lending and deposits, banking services, trust and estates
	Private banking	Private lending and deposits, banking services, trust and estate, investment advice
	Card services	Merchant/commercial/corporate cards, private labels, and retail
Commercial Banking	Commercial banking	Project finance, real estate, export finance, trade finance, factoring, leasing, lending, guarantees, bills of exchange
Payment and Settlement	External clients	Payments and collections, funds transfer, clearing and settlement
Agency Services	Custody	Escrow, depository receipts, securities lending (customers), corporate actions
	Corporate agency Corporate trust	Issuer and payer agents
Asset Management	Discretionary fund management	Pooled, segregated, retail, institutional, closed, open, private equity
	Non-discretionary fund management	Pooled, segregated, retail, institutional, closed, open
Retail Brokerage	Retail brokerage	Execution and full service

Source: Bank for International Settlements (BIS), 2021, "OPE – Calculation of Operational Risk, OPE 25 Standardized Approach," section 25.16, https://www.bis.org/basel_framework/chapter/OPE/25.htm.

function to the Basel categories of business lines for the purpose of assigning revenue.

> *Any banking or non-banking activity which cannot be readily mapped into the business line framework, but which represents an ancillary function to an activity included in the framework, must be allocated to the business line it supports. If more than one business line is supported through the ancillary activity, an objective mapping criteria must be used.*[20]

All Impacted Departments

It is often helpful to specify in the operational risk event data criteria that all departments that are involved in the event must be identified as the event is entered. This helps to ensure good communication around the event. Many events impact several areas, and the operational risk event data system often needs strong workflow components to facilitate entries and discussions by multiple parties.

Boundary Events Identified

Credit risk–related operational risk events and market risk–related operational risk events should be collected and flagged as boundary events. When using operational risk event data as an input into a capital calculation, credit risk boundary events can be excluded from the calculation, but market risk events must be included. An example of a boundary credit risk/operational risk event is where a counterparty fails and the collateral that was supposed to have been collected has failed to be requested, leading to an avoidable financial loss.

An example of a boundary market risk/operational risk event is where a trade error occurs and the market moves dramatically in a direction that increases the loss.

It is generally accepted that credit risk/operational risk boundary events are captured in credit risk capital calculations, and so can be excluded from any operational risk capital calculations. In contrast, market risk/operational risk boundary events are not captured in market risk capital calculations, and so should be included in operational risk capital calculations.

If an operational risk event database is being used to calculate operational risk capital, then these boundary events need to be carefully tagged to ensure that they are appropriately included or excluded from the operational risk calculation.

Action Items

As losses are gathered, there should also be identified mitigating actions, either to ensure the recovery of the funds or to support the prevention of future similar events. Actions should include an owner and due date for each task, and should be tracked to completion. From a practical point of view, having good action-tracking processes in place is necessary to ensure that actions do not sit ignored in the event database, but are being actively pursued in order to mitigate the operational risk that has been identified by the event.

Nonfinancial Impacts

In addition to the financial impact of the event, there may be other impacts that can be gathered as part of the operational risk event data collection program. While it may be difficult to put a value on impacts such as reputational damage, a firm's event data standards might include a field for a qualitative or free prose assessment of any reputational impact.

WHERE SHOULD OPERATIONAL RISK EVENT DATA BE COLLECTED?

Most firms have implemented robust technology systems to manage their operational risk event data. This allows them to effectively manage the multiple data standards and complex workflow requirements of the program.

While most operational risk event databases started life as simple spreadsheets, it became quickly evident that a more sophisticated approach would be needed. Some firms have developed in-house solutions, and some have purchased off-the-shelf solutions. In the past 15 years, off-the-shelf solutions have proliferated and improved. The implementation of a new operational risk event database should certainly be preceded by an assessment of the advantages and disadvantages of building a system in-house versus purchasing one readymade.

Operational risk event databases are sometimes stand-alone elements in an operational risk framework, and sometimes they are integrated into the other elements of the program—sharing data with RCSA systems, KRI systems, scenario analysis, and capital calculation systems.

Many firms are investigating the best way to integrate their operational risk systems to best support excellent operational risk identification, assessment, monitoring, and mitigation.

For example, JPMorgan Chase's annual report in 2008 described their integrated operational risk system, Phoenix, as follows:

> *The Firm's operational risk framework is supported by Phoenix, an internally designed operational risk software tool. Phoenix integrates the individual components of the operational risk management framework into a unified, web-based tool. Phoenix enhances the capture, reporting and analysis of operational risk data by enabling risk identification, measurement, monitoring, reporting and analysis to be done in an integrated manner, thereby enabling efficiencies in the Firm's monitoring and management of its operational risk.*[21]

By 2021, however, they were using a third party–supplied system that addressed multiple elements of their operational risk program, including operational risk event losses.

WHEN SHOULD OPERATIONAL RISK EVENT DATA BE COLLECTED?

Operational risk event reporting is most effective when there is prompt and accurate reporting of events and tracking of remediation activities. For this reason, many firms adopt standards that require timely reporting of an event, sometimes in an initial draft form, and timely maintenance of the event record to reflect new or more accurate information.

The final sign-off on an event might occur much later, once all parties are comfortable that the record is accurate. Depending on the culture of the firm, an event might remain out of sight of the central operational risk function until the business line or department involved is ready to sign off and pass it on. Some of the reluctance to enter draft data can be alleviated through robust security features in the system, to prevent general viewing of an item until it is final. Some firms decide to restrict viewing access of events to certain departments; others take a more transparent approach and allow viewing access broadly to support risk management awareness.

HOW SHOULD OPERATIONAL RISK EVENT DATA BE COLLECTED?

The workflow for loss data collection will depend on each firm's policies and procedures regarding who, what, where, and when data is collected.

One example of a possible operational risk event data collection process for the initial reporter of the event is provided in Figure 7.3. The workflow shows the progress of the event from the identification to reporting and the role of the corporate operational risk function (CORF). The complete workflow for all parties involved would be more complex and may vary from department to department and region to region within a firm.

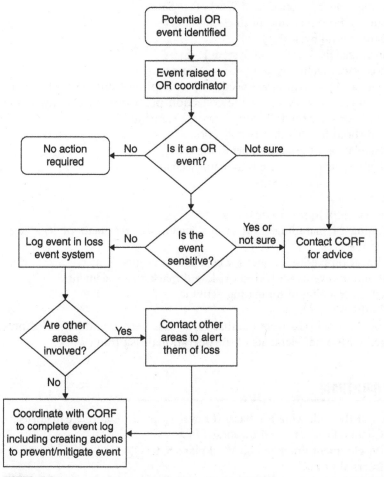

FIGURE 7.3 Simple Operational Risk Event Workflow for the Initial Reporter of an Event

KEY POINTS

- Internal loss data collection is often required for regulatory compliance, but it also provides valuable business benefits as it allows a firm to learn from past events.
- Losses should be categorized into appropriate risk types, and the Basel II categories are:
  - Internal Fraud
  - External Fraud
  - Employment Practices and Workplace Safety
  - Clients, Products, and Business Practices
  - Damage to Physical Assets
  - Business Disruption and System Failures
  - Execution, Delivery, and Process Management
- Policies and procedures are needed to set minimum criteria for loss data collection and to establish the collection process methodology. These need to consider the following key data elements:
  - Threshold for mandatory collection
  - Calculation of gross and net amounts
  - Gains, near-misses, and opportunity costs
  - Accounting adjustments
  - Recoveries
  - Selection of appropriate dates
  - Timing of including legal events, including treatment of legal fees and reserves
  - Allocation methodologies for centralized events
  - Boundary events with credit risk and market risk elements
  - Action tracking of mitigating activities
  - Nonfinancial impacts
- An operational risk event database system is needed and might be integrated with other elements of the operational risk framework.

REVIEW QUESTIONS

1. Which of the following are Basel II Level 1 operational risk categories?
   - I. Clients, Products, and Business Practices
   - II. Employment Practice and Workplace Safety
   - III. Internal Fraud
   - IV. Damage to Systems
   - V. Unauthorized Trading

a. I only
b. I and II only
c. I, II, and III only
d. I, II, III, and IV only
e. All of the above

A U.S. bank's operational risk department has established an operational risk event data system, which is accessible on the intranet by all employees and requires the completion of several fields, some of which are mandatory. All operational risk loss events over $10,000 must be entered into the system. An employee in the trade support department has discovered that an error has been made by a trader. The trader has written a buy order on his blotter, but has entered a sell order into the trading systems. This has resulted in a loss of $150,000.

Using the information above, answer questions 2 through 4.

2. The event should be mapped to which of the following Level 1 Basel II categories?
   a. Trading Error
   b. Execution, Delivery, and Process Management
   c. Business Disruption and System Failure
   d. Transaction Capture, Execution, and Maintenance
   e. Data Entry, Maintenance, or Loading Error
3. Why should the trade support employee enter the event into the database? Select the best answer.
   a. Because the trader should be free to focus on making a profit for the firm
   b. Because it might not have been the trader's fault
   c. Because the trade support employee is in the back office
   d. Because $150,000 is over the threshold
   e. Because every employee is responsible for reporting operational risk events
4. The trade support employee decides not to enter the data into the event database and does not inform anyone of the error. What is the most serious consequence of this action? Select the best answer.
   a. He is risking being fired for breaching company policy.
   b. The trader cannot learn from his mistake.
   c. Audit will issue an audit point if the omission is discovered.
   d. Effective operational risk management in the firm is undermined.
   e. The firm might fail its Basel II examination.

NOTES

1. https://www.bis.org/bcbs/publ/d515.htm.
2. Bank for International Settlements, Basel Committee on Banking Supervision, "Basel III–Finalizing Post Crisis Reforms," December 2017, 128, https://www .bis.org/bcbs/publ/d424.htm.
3. Ibid., 131.
4. Ibid.
5. www.bis.org/publ/bcbs196.pdf, section 88.
6. Ibid., section 85.
7. Ibid., section 86.
8. See note 2, 132.
9. Ibid.
10. Ibid., section 89.
11. Ibid., section 87(a).
12. See note 2, p. 132.
13. Ibid., section 87(b), which states: "Rapidly recovered loss events are operational risk events that lead to losses recognized in financial statements that are recovered over a short period. For instance, a large internal loss is rapidly recovered when a bank transfers money to a wrong party but recovers all or part of the loss soon thereafter. A bank may consider this to be a gross loss and a recovery. However, when the recovery is made rapidly, the bank may consider that only the loss net of the rapid recovery constitutes an actual loss. When the rapid recovery is full, the event is considered to be a 'near miss.'" It should be noted that the new guidance for the Standardized Approach stays silent on near misses and simply allows for the collection of net losses—suggesting that the net loss would be zero when a full recovery is quickly made.
14. Ibid., section 87.
15. See note 2, 131.
16 See note 2, 132.
17. Ibid., section 135.
18. Ibid., section 134.
19. Bank for International Settlements, "International Convergence of Capital Measurement and Capital Standards: A Revised Framework," 2004, section 673.
20. See note 19, section 25.17.
21. JPMorgan Chase & Co. Annual Report, 2008, 166.

CHAPTER 8

External Loss Data

In this chapter, we consider the use of external loss data in the operational risk framework. In addition to the events that have occurred within a firm, the operational risk department will look at those that have occurred outside the firm. These events can offer valuable insight into the operational risks faced at the firm, and may also provide input into any operational risk capital calculation. External data is also a required element in an Advanced Measurement Approach (AMA) capital calculation and in the new Standardized Approach. The use of external data in capital calculations is considered further in Chapter 12.

EXTERNAL OPERATIONAL RISK EVENT DATA

External events are useful in many areas of the firm's operational risk framework. They can help inform the risk and control self-assessment activities, they can provide sample input for scenario analysis, and they might be used to develop key risk indicators that monitor the changing business environment.

The role of external data in the operational risk framework is illustrated in Figure 8.1.

External events are often of real interest to senior management, as major news headlines are often associated with operational risk. External data is therefore a key element in the development of a strong operational risk culture and a firm-wide awareness of the importance of effective operational risk management. When events occur in the industry among peers and competitors, it helps to underscore the importance of effective operational risk management and mitigation.

An example of an operational risk event that had a huge impact on the discipline was the $7 billion unauthorized trading scandal at Société

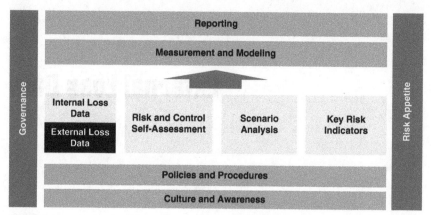

FIGURE 8.1   The Role of External Loss Data in the Operational Risk Framework

Générale in 2006, which is discussed later in this chapter. This was an internal loss data event for Société Générale, but for the rest of the industry it was a very large external event that underscored the size of losses that can be experienced as a result of operational risk. This event is often considered a watershed moment in the development of the operational risk discipline.

Despite the lessons learned from that event, the industry saw another huge unauthorized trading event at UBS in 2011. This led financial firms to revisit what they had learned from Société Générale just five years earlier and to reassess the way that they respond to large external events to ensure that the lessons have truly been learned. It took large events for the financial services sector to embrace the necessary controls to prevent large unauthorized trading losses. The UBS event is discussed in more depth in Chapter 18.

Chapter 18 considers several more recent operational risk case studies. Each of those cases offer important external data points for the firms that were not involved (and painful internal loss data points for those that were).

SOURCES OF EXTERNAL LOSS EVENT DATA

There are many good online sources of operational risk event data in the form of news articles, journals, and e-mail update services. Some operational risk system vendors also have external databases that they make available on a subscription basis. For example, SAS offers an external database to its technology users, and IBM offers a subscription service called IBM FIRST Risk Case Studies®.[1] There are also member consortiums of operational risk losses such as The Operational Riskdata eXchange Association (ORX), which is discussed further in the next section.

External events are a valuable source of operational risk information on an individual event basis and also as a benchmarking tool. Comparing internal loss patterns to external loss patterns can provide insight into whether the losses in a firm reflect the usual losses in their industry.

Subscription Databases

These databases include descriptions and analyses of operational risk events that are gleaned from legal and regulatory sources and from news articles. They provide helpful data to assist with mapping the events to the appropriate business lines, risk categories, and causes. The mission of these external databases is to collect tail losses and so to provide examples of potential large exposures.

The data also provide insight into the types of events that have occurred in the industry, but that a firm may not yet have experienced itself.

Consortium Data

In addition to subscription-based external data services, there are consortium-based operational risk event services that provide central data repositories and benchmarking services to their members. ORX provides such a service to its 81 members.

ORX gathers operational risk event data from its banking members and produces benchmarking information. It applies quality assurance standards around the receipt and delivery of data to promote members' anonymity and to provide consistency in definitions.

Unlike news-based subscription services, ORX data does not suffer from the availability bias that skews subscription data, which relies on public sources of data. In contrast, *all* operational risk events that occur in the member institutions are provided anonymously into the database.

However, the ORX data relate only to a subset of financial services, those member banks that provide data to ORX.

ORX publishes reports that summarize the data. Table 8.1 is derived from ORX data and illustrates the number of losses and the amount of losses in euros for each business line and each risk category for the period of 2015–2020.

ORX uses slightly different business lines than the Basel business line categories, as they split out Retail Banking into two groups: Retail Banking and Private Banking. They also rename Payment and Settlement as Clearing and capture Corporate Items in a separate category. Also, instead of Damage to Physical Assets (DPA) and Business Disruptions and System Failure (BDSF) risk types, they use Disasters and Public Safety (DPS) and Technology and Infrastructure Failure (TIF) when categorizing losses.

TABLE 8.1 Number and Amount of Losses (in Euros) by Business Line and Risk Category between 2015 and 2020

		Client, Product & Business Practices (CPBP)	Disasters & Public Safety (DPS)	Employment Practices and Workplace Safety (EPWS)	Execution, Delivery, and Process Management (EDPM)	External Fraud (EF)	Internal Fraud (IF)	Technology & Infrastructure Failure (TIF)	Total of Number of Losses/ Total Amount of Losses (M)
Trading and Investment	Corporate Finance	382 / € 671.8	15 / € 12.3	186 / € 90.9	940 / € 409.7	157 / € 572.8	28 / € 69.7	66 / € 55.5	1,774 / € 1,882.7
	Trading and Sales	2,375 / € 15,592.0	37 / € 10.7	772 / € 310.2	18,176 / € 11,085.9	247 / € 315.3	75 / € 815.1	2,094 / € 3,924.1	23,776 / € 32,053.3
Banking	Retail Banking	37,984 / € 23,388.9	2,519 / € 635.2	30,394 / € 2,919.6	47,846 / € 12,249.1	107,289 / € 6,934.7	4,210 / € 919.9	2,169 / € 1,079.3	232,411 / € 48,126.7
	Private Banking	3,139 / € 2,285.7	32 / € 4.7	1,469 / € 187.5	4,493 / € 1,374.8	1,638 / € 304.2	148 / € 188.6	165 / € 45.8	11,084 / € 4,391.3
	Commercial Banking	7,660 / € 5,584.1	216 / € 327.6	1,844 / € 217.3	13,343 / € 5,799.8	8,670 / € 5,791.8	281 / € 167.3	638 / € 613.2	32,652 / € 18,501.1
	Clearing	214 / € 152.0	18 / € 4.4	270 / € 21.9	2,253 / € 954.4	1,776 / € 147.1	30 / € 11.4	194 / € 527.7	4,755 / € 1,818.9
Other	Agency Services	404 / € 1,083.3	28 / € 8.0	621 / € 72.5	5,274 / € 2,006.4	59 / € 34.3	6 / € 1.9	286 / € 59.3	6,678 / € 3,265.7
	Asset Management	905 / € 892.2	8 / € 1.8	295 / € 60.6	3,500 / € 808.7	106 / € 54.9	23 / € 57.5	151 / € 29.5	4,988 / € 1,905.2
	Retail Brokerage	6,396 / € 2,258.5	19 / € 4.1	1,407 / € 537.3	4,099 / € 491.2	1,092 / € 124.2	395 / € 264.6	191 / € 76.5	13,599 / € 3,756.4
	Corporate Items	22,771 / € 8,264.8	1,471 / € 939.8	14,266 / € 1,421.6	7,517 / € 4,767.5	1,868 / € 431.8	174 / € 173.2	314 / € 1,429.3	48,381 / € 17,428.0
Total Number of Losses / Total Amount of Losses		82,230 / € 60,173.3	4,363 / € 1,948.6	51,524 / € 5,839.4	107,441 / € 39,947.5	122,902 / € 14,711.1	5,370 / € 2,669.2	6,268 / € 7,840.2	380,098 / € 133,129.3

To date, ORX has gathered more than 800,000 events that have cost their consortium members over €500 billion. The cost of operational risk is abundantly clear. This table shows that ORX business line data is dominated by Retail Banking events, both in size of losses and frequency of events.

To further understand the relative impact to the different businesses and from the different risk categories, it is helpful to take another look at this data in percentage format, as shown in Table 8.2.

From Table 8.2 we can see that over 61 percent of the total number of events is generated in the Retail Banking business area and most of those are in the External Fraud category.

Retail Banking also has a large share of the total costs of events, with over 36 percent of the total losses. Trading and Sales has more than 24 percent of losses, and Commercial Banking and Corporate Items follow, with about 14 percent and 13 percent, respectively.

It is clear that External Fraud and Execution, Delivery, and Process Management produce the greatest number of events, between them accounting for more than 60 percent of the number of events and 40 percent of the total costs.

Clients, Products, and Business Practices accounts for a little under 21 percent of the events but carries more than 45 percent of the total loss amount. This demonstrates that for the member banks of ORX, Clients, Products, and Business Practices events tend to be larger events. It is for this reason that many firms carefully investigate this category in scenario analysis to attempt to identify potential "fat-tail" events—that is, events that are infrequent but very large.

The data can also be used to visually represent the relative levels of operational risk in each business line, as shown in Figure 8.2.

Figure 8.2 clearly illustrates the relatively high levels of operational risk that exist today in the Retail Banking sector.

CHALLENGES OF EXTERNAL DATA

Many operational risk functions use ORX or IBM FIRST or other provider data and then supplement these data with their own research by subscribing to online news feeds and relevant industry journals.

However, these data must be used with caution. There are several challenges with external data.

First, if the external data are gathered from news sources, then they are subject to a bias in reporting. Only events that are interesting to the press are reported in the press, resulting in a bias in favor of illegal and dramatic events over errors. For example, a large fraud will receive intensive coverage,

TABLE 8.2 The Percentage Contribution to Number of Events and Amount of Losses by Business Line and Risk Category between 2015 and 2020

		Client, Product & Business Practices (CPBP)	Disasters & Public Safety (DPS)	Employment Practices and Workplace Safety (EPWS)	Execution, Delivery, and Process Management (EDPM)	External Fraud (EF)	Internal Fraud (IF)	Technology & Infrastructure Failure (TIF)	Total of Number of Losses/ Total Amount of Losses (M)
Trading and Investment	Corporate Finance	0.5% / 1.1%	0.3% / 0.6%	0.4% / 1.6%	0.9% / 1.0%	0.1% / 3.9%	0.5% / 2.6%	1.1% / 0.7%	0.5% / 1.4%
	Trading and Sales	2.9% / 25.9%	0.8% / 0.5%	1.5% / 5.3%	16.9% / 27.8%	0.2% / 2.1%	1.4% / 30.5%	33.4% / 50.1%	6.3% / 24.1%
Banking	Retail Banking	46.2% / 38.9%	57.7% / 32.6%	59.0% / 50.0%	44.5% / 30.7%	87.3% / 47.1%	78.4% / 34.5%	34.6% / 13.8%	61.1% / 36.2%
	Private Banking	3.8% / 3.8%	0.7% / 0.2%	2.9% / 3.2%	4.2% / 3.4%	1.3% / 2.1%	2.8% / 7.1%	2.6% / 0.6%	2.9% / 3.3%
	Commercial Banking	9.3% / 9.3%	5.0% / 16.8%	3.6% / 3.7%	12.4% / 14.5%	7.1% / 39.4%	5.2% / 6.3%	10.2% / 7.8%	8.6% / 13.9%
	Clearing	0.3% / 0.3%	0.4% / 0.2%	0.5% / 0.4%	2.1% / 2.4%	1.4% / 1.0%	0.6% / 0.4%	3.1% / 6.7%	1.3% / 1.4%
Other	Agency Services	0.5% / 1.8%	0.6% / 0.4%	1.2% / 1.2%	4.9% / 5.0%	0.0% / 0.2%	0.1% / 0.1%	4.6% / 0.8%	1.8% / 2.5%
	Asset Management	1.1% / 1.5%	0.2% / 0.1%	0.6% / 1.0%	3.3% / 2.0%	0.1% / 0.4%	0.4% / 2.2%	2.4% / 0.4%	1.3% / 1.4%
	Retail Brokerage	7.8% / 3.8%	0.4% / 0.2%	2.7% / 9.2%	3.8% / 1.2%	0.9% / 0.8%	7.4% / 9.9%	3.0% / 1.0%	3.6% / 2.8%
	Corporate Items	27.7% / 13.7%	33.7% / 48.2%	27.7% / 24.3%	7.0% / 11.9%	1.5% / 2.9%	3.2% / 6.5%	5.0% / 18.2%	12.7% / 13.1%
Total Number of Losses		21.6%	1.1%	13.6%	28.3%	32.3%	1.4%	1.6%	100%
Total Amount of Losses		45.2%	1.5%	4.4%	30.0%	11.1%	2.0%	5.9%	100%

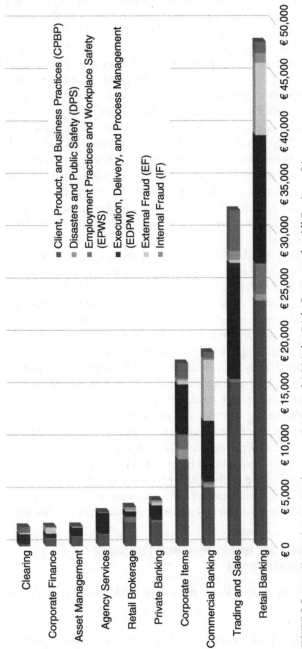

FIGURE 8.2 Dollar Value Losses between 2015 and 2020, by Risk Category for All Business Lines

while a major systems outage might not make it into any press report. It is also unlikely that a major gain will make the press in the same way that a major loss would, although the same lessons could be learned in both cases.

Second, it can be difficult to determine whether an event is relevant. The fact that a firm has the same business line does not mean it could have the same event occur, as it may have a different product or a stronger (or weaker) control environment. Indeed, many external events might be ignored simply because they "could not happen here" for one or many reasons. The best use of external data is not to use it to try to spot an exact event that should be avoided, but rather to determine the types of errors and control failings that can occur so as to avoid similar (rather than identical) losses.

An external event may have direct relevance regardless of the exact details. For example, the Société Générale event (which is considered in detail later) led to many firms overhauling their fraud controls, regardless of whether they had any traders working on the exact same desks as Société Générale's Jérôme Kerviel.

Third, the use of benchmarked data relies on the quality of the underlying data, and there may be a chance that the comparisons made are not accurate due to a different interpretation of the underlying definitions.

However, if all of these challenges are acknowledged, then external data have a very valuable role to play in operational risk management. They provide insight into lessons that can be learned prior to an event occurring at the firm. They demonstrate that the size of an event may be beyond the initial estimation made by the firm. They provide context and highlight trends in the industry.

Internal and external operational risk events provide a rich source of data on what has already gone wrong. It is possible to use these data to implement mitigating controls to prevent future repetitions of the same events. Moreover, operational risk event data provide a valuable input into the other elements of the operational risk framework that will be designed to predict potential events that have not yet occurred.

Loss data provide useful examples for risk and control self-assessment and scenario analysis discussions and analysis, as well as key risk indicators (KRIs) that can indicate trends of losses and control weaknesses.

Société Générale and the External Event That Shook the Operational Risk World

This event was originally reported in IBM FIRST Risk Case Studies as follows:

> *In what the* Wall Street Journal *(1/24/2008) called a "singular feat in the world of finance" Societe Generale announced a €4.9 billion*

(USD $7.2 billion) loss on January 24, 2008, arising from the mis-deeds of a single rogue trader. The bank characterized the largest rogue trading event to date as involving "elaborate fictitious trans-actions" that allowed Jerome Kerviel to circumvent its internal con-trols. The trades involved the arbitrage of "plain vanilla" stock-index futures. Mr. Kerviel had previously worked in a back office function and learned how to circumvent the bank's systems. Although he was initially characterized by the governor of the Bank of France as a "computer genius" later he was described as an unexceptional employee who worked very hard to conceal unauthorized trading positions, which SocGen estimated to have a value of €50 billion ($73.26 billion). The French Finance Ministry said that Kerviel's rogue trading started in 2005; he was allegedly given a warning at the time concerning trading above prescribed limits. In addition to the €4.9 billion trading loss, the French Banking Commission levied a €4 million fine against Societe Generale on July 4, 2008, bringing the total loss amount to €4,904,000,000. On October 5, 2010, a court in Paris sentenced Mr. Kerviel to three years' imprisonment, plus a two year suspended sentence and ordered him to repay €4.9 billion ($6.7 billion) to his employer.[2]

On October 24, 2012, a French appeals court upheld Kerviel's fraud conviction and lifetime trading ban.

This external event galvanized the operational risk world, as it clearly demonstrated the dangers that exist in unmitigated operational risk. In 2008, many firms were still engaged in developing their early operational risk frameworks and were often focused on first-run delivery of new report-ing, new loss data tools, and new adaptations to their RCSA and scenario analysis programs. The regulatory requirements were paramount in many programs, with the business benefits being developed as rapidly as possible, but sometimes lagging behind the urgent regulatory pressures.

However, when the news hit of Kerviel's audacious activities and their multibillion-dollar impact on his firm, many heads of operational risk found themselves in front of their executive management being asked the urgent question: "Could that happen here?"

This was a classic large operational risk event in that it resulted from numerous control failings. Kerviel's job was to make arbitrage trades that would result in small gains, but he began taking unauthorized "directional" positions starting in 2005, and these grew in size until he was discovered in January 2008.

Reports on the events suggest that Kerviel may have been more motivated by a sense of pride than an attempt to defraud the firm. His unauthorized activities did not result in secret transfers into his bank account; they resulted in huge positions at the bank.

At one point, Kerviel's activities allegedly resulted in gains for the firm that have been estimated to have been as high as €1 billion in 2007. It has been suggested that he realized that these gains were too large to explain, and so he pursued a strategy to reduce them. That strategy, it is alleged, resulted in losses of €1.5 billion by February 2008. The adverse market conditions that existed when Société Générale discovered the unauthorized trading and unwound the positions resulted in the loss growing to €4.9 billion.

This is an extreme example of how an operational risk event can be exacerbated by a market risk event.

IBM FIRST Risk Case Studies provides an in-depth prose analysis of the event based on extensive press reviews. The highlights of the many contributing factors that are alleged can be summarized as follows:

1. Kerviel engaged in extensive unauthorized activities in order to demonstrate his prowess as a trader rather than to defraud the bank.
2. He was insufficiently supervised and at times had no supervisor at all.
3. He had worked in the middle and back offices prior to becoming a trader and used his knowledge of those controls to ensure that his activities were not detected.
4. He gained password access to back office systems that allowed him to manipulate data and approve his own trades.

It is alleged that many red flags were raised but were ignored or were dismissed as unimportant.

> The head of the Bank of France, Christian Noyer, said that Mr. Kerviel managed to breach "five levels of controls." The controls were identified in the earlier Mission Green report[3] and included cancelled or modified transactions; transactions with deferred dates; technical (internal) counterparties; nominal (non-netted exposures) and intramonth cash flows. In addition, the second and more detailed Mission Green report[4] identified a host of supervisory lapses, organizational gaps, and warning signs that were never heeded.[5]

It is alleged that there were numerous other red flags that were not heeded including:

1. Kerviel requested an unusually high bonus due to his above-market returns.
2. He frequently breached limits, and despite being reprimanded for this in the past, was able to continue to do so.

3. Concerns were raised by EUREX regarding his trading volume but were dropped after a response from Kerviel satisfied their concerns.
4. At least 75 compliance alerts were raised but were dismissed when Kerviel supplied minimal, and sometimes forged, documentation to explain his unusual activity.
5. Kerviel never took his vacation time, allowing him to be on-site to continue to maintain and conceal his unauthorized activities.
6. The bank had to rely on manual processing due to inadequate technology to support the increasing volumes in the market.
7. Net cash flows were monitored, whereas monitoring of nominal flows might have revealed the unauthorized activity.

IBM FIRST Risk Case Studies categorized this event, as shown in Table 8.3.

TABLE 8.3 Classification in IBM FIRST Risk Case Studies

Entity Type	Financial Services/Banking/Commercial/Full-Service Bank
Business Unit Type	Trading and Sales (BIS)/Trading
Service/Product Offering Type	Derivatives, structured products, and commodities/derivative products/futures and options/equity index futures
Contributory/ Control Factors	Corporate Governance/General Corporate Governance Issues, Corporate/Market Conditions/Corporate and Market Conditions, Employee Action/Inaction/Employee Misdeeds, Employee Action/Inaction/Employee Omissions, Lack of Control/Failure to Question Above-Market Returns, Lack of Control/Failure to Reconcile Daily Cash Flows, Lack of Control/Failure to Test for Data Accuracy, Lack of Control/ Lack of Internal Controls, Lack of Control/Lax Security, Lack of Control/Rules, Regulations, and Compliance Issues, Management Action/Inaction/Lack Management Escalation Process, Management Action/Inaction/Undertook Excessive Risks,Omissions/Failure to Set or Enforce Proper Limits, Omissions/Failure to Supervise Employees, Omissions/ Inadequate Due Diligence Efforts, Omissions/Omissions and Lapses, Organizational Structure/Inadequate Organizational Structures, Organizational Structure/Organizational Gap(s), Strategy Flaw/Inadequate Technology Planning Process, Organizational Structure/Organizational Structure—General, Lack of Control/Lack of Internal Controls—General, Management Action/Inaction/Undertook Excessive Risks, Omissions/Omissions—General

(Continued)

TABLE 8.3 *(Continued)*

Loss Impact	Direct Loss/Regulatory/Compliance/Taxation Penalty (BIS)/ Fines/Penalties, Direct Loss/Write-Down (BIS)/Write-Downs, Indirect Loss/Management Remediation, Indirect Loss/ Ratings Agency Downgrade/Ratings Watch, Indirect Loss/ Related Market Risk Losses, Indirect Loss/Reputational (Nonmonetary), Indirect Loss/Share Price
Loss Detection Sources	Whistle Blowing/Employee Originated
Market Focus	Institutional Services
Event Trigger	People Risk Class/Trading Misdeeds/Unauthorized Trading/ Activity above Limits/Unauthorized Trading—Proprietary Accounts
Basel Levels I and II	Internal Fraud/Unauthorized Activity/Trans type unauthorized (w/monetary loss)
Basel Business Line	Investment Banking/Trading and Sales/Proprietary Positions
Entity Type	Financial Services/Banking/Commercial/Full-Service Bank
Business Unit Type	Trading and Sales (BIS)/Trading

ORX also provides a news service, and they categorized this event as shown in Figure 8.3.

The industry responded to this event with energy. Operational risk teams met with senior management, as executive teams and boards asked whether such an event could happen at their firm. Perhaps for the first time, the possible size of an operational risk event was fully appreciated, and the operational risk function had an opportunity to demonstrate its relevance and importance.

FIGURE 8.3 ORX Classification of the Société Générale Event

Fraud risk assessments were conducted in many firms, and numerous control improvements were implemented. Mandatory vacation policies were written and enforced. Passwords were disabled for employees who had moved to new roles. Supervisory oversight was reviewed.

Industry forums were held as operational risk managers compared notes on how best to minimize the risk that such an event could happen in the industry again. As an external data point, the event galvanized many aspects of operational risk frameworks across the industry and also paved the way for how to respond to future serious events.

Work plans were drawn up to evaluate the current state of the controls that had failed at Société Générale and to kick off work to remediate any control gaps that might be uncovered. RCSAs and scenario analysis were updated in the unauthorized trading aspects of internal fraud. Working groups were formed, board packs prepared, and external event tracking was enhanced. As IBM FIRST Risk Cases notes in its longer description of the event:

> *The AFP press agency reported (October 8, 2010) that Société Générale's own efforts to enhance its internal controls in the wake of the event were estimated to have cost the bank at least 150 million euros over a three-year period.*

The Société Générale event shocked the financial services industry, and turned the spotlight on to operational risk. However, only three years later another startlingly similar event occurred at UBS, and since the financial crisis, we have seen several very large events occur; these incidents are discussed in the case studies in Chapter 18.

KEY POINTS

- Loss events that have occurred outside the firm can provide valuable insight into potential catastrophic events, as well as opportunities to benchmark internal data against the industry.
- Subscription databases use legal, regulatory, and press reports of events to provide analysis and categorization of operational risk events.
- Consortium databases collect data from members and share trends and benchmarking information with members.
- The methods of collection can produce biases in data that must be considered when analyzing external sources of data.

REVIEW QUESTION

1. Which of the following statements best describes the value of using external database sources?
   a. Consortium data provide a full data set for a bank to use for benchmarking.
   b. Subscription data sources provide a full data set for a bank to use for benchmarking.
   c. A combination of subscription and consortium data provides a full data set for a bank to use for benchmarking.
   d. Consortium and subscription data provide helpful information on external loss data trends that can help inform a bank's operational risk framework.

NOTES

1. IBM FIRST Risk Case Studies. Property of IBM. 5725-H59 © Copyright IBM Corp. and others 1992, 2021, IBM, the IBM logo, ibm.com.
2. Excerpted and reproduced with permission of IBM FIRST Risk Case Studies (see note 1).
3. Investigatory report published on February 20, 2008, by Société Générale.
4. Investigatory report published in May 2008 by Société Générale.
5. IBM FIRST Risk Case Report.

CHAPTER 9

Key Risk Indicators

This chapter explores the benefits and challenges of the use of metrics in the operational risk (OR) framework. Metrics can provide the business environment and internal control factors (BEICF) needed for an AMA capital approach, but more importantly, they can provide insight into the changing operational risk environment.

KEY RISK INDICATORS

Key risk indicators, or KRIs, are used in the operational risk framework to keep a finger on the pulse of the changing risk environment. External risk factors, internal risk factors, and the control environment can be monitored using metrics.

In Basel II, there is a requirement for Advanced Measurement Approach (AMA) banks to collect BEICF for use in the capital model. These BEICF have proved elusive and capital models have struggled with how to incorporate them. The use of BEICF in capital modeling is discussed later in Chapter 12.

However, it is common sense that monitoring our environment and our controls will lead to better operational risk management, regardless of their use in the capital model, and all firms attempt to develop a key risk indicator (KRI) structure of some kind. Some are highly sophisticated; some are simple.

In fintechs it is common for the strategic business plan to be monitored by objectives and key results (OKRs), and aligning operational risk KRIs to these OKRs is an effective way to embed a strong risk culture.

KRIs are an important pillar in the operational risk framework, as illustrated in Figure 9.1.

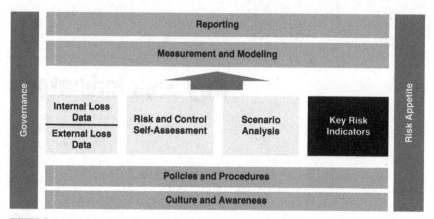

FIGURE 9.1 Key Risk Indicators in the Operational Risk Framework

At its most complex, a metrics or KRI program can lead to the danger of frisking the ant while the elephant walks by—that is to say, we can become so focused on detailed data that we miss the major looming operational risk that is not being captured in our metrics systems.

The challenge is to identify a suitable metric that is truly measuring risk. Most metrics simply count something and should not be confused with a true KRI.

For this reason, it may be safer to refer to gathered metrics as "indicators" rather than KRIs until they have proven their worth. For example, the number of failed trades per day is a metric. This metric alone does not indicate rising or falling risk levels unless it is combined with other related metrics, such as volume. In contrast, an indicator that measures the percentage of failed trades in the total volume of trades is a more helpful indicator and might be a true KRI.

There are many types of indicators, and each has its own strengths and weaknesses and can be used effectively in the right place.

When considering the role of KRIs in the operational risk framework, it is important to remember that they provide input into the framework. They are not the end; they are simply one of the means to the end. There is a danger in relying too heavily on metrics in that we can become overconfident that we are collecting all of the right data, and that a green dashboard of metrics means everything is fine and operational risk is under control. Conversely, we may panic over a red dashboard when all that has happened is that we set our thresholds too low.

An analogy may be helpful. If managing operational risk is like driving a car, then KRIs are the dashboard of the car. No one would be foolish enough to drive without a dashboard, as it tells us important information such as our speed, our fuel levels, and whether we have any issues such as overheating or running low on oil.

But we do not drive with our heads down, looking at the dashboard of our cars. We look ahead at the road to see where we are going and what is coming over the horizon. We learn to drive, and we drive safely and carefully.

To take the analogy one step further, sometimes, through no fault of our own, we get crashed into by a truck. That is why we have insurance, and that is why we calculate and hold operational risk capital. We hold capital for the rare catastrophic events that can occur, either through our own reckless behavior or through no fault of our own.

It is important to have a good functioning dashboard and to rely on it appropriately and build out the rest of the framework that you need in order to "drive safely."

Key Performance Indicators

Key performance indicators, or KPIs, measure how well something is performing, or how efficient it is. For example, the average time taken to resolve a help desk request would be a KPI. KPIs are used extensively in sales to track which sales area is performing best or which sales method is producing the best results. They are also effective tools to measure the efficiency of process and an operations function will usually have a dashboard of KPIs for that purpose.

Key Control Indicators

Key controls indicators, or KCIs, measure how effectively a control is working. For example, the number of viruses caught in a virus protection screen is a KCI. The number of viruses that got past the virus protection is also a KCI.

Metric Types

Whether a metric is a KPI or a KCI, it may be one of three types of metric: an exception monitor, a lagging indicator, or a leading indicator.

Exception Monitoring

Exception monitoring indicators raise a flag when an exception occurs. For example, if a report fails to print, then this could produce a "yes" flag for a "Report Print Failure" indicator. Another example might be where a new product has been launched without the proper approvals. This could raise a red flag in the new-product approval process. More important, exception monitoring can raise red flags in urgent situations to ensure remediation.

Exceptions are easily understood as they have a binary outcome. They typically produce ad-hoc reporting to alert managers to the issue that has arisen.

Lagging Indicators

Lagging indicators track past activity and look for trends over time. Lagging indicators can be very useful but have limitations, as they can only show us what has already happened, not what is going to happen. As we all know, past performance is not necessarily an indication of future performance. However, analyzing trends can be helpful in the formation of strategy and in identifying changing risk profiles.

A KCI that is showing a constant deterioration of a control will allow for decisions to be made to alleviate any rising risk. Lagging indicators are the most common metrics in most reporting packs, and management is generally very comfortable interpreting them.

Perhaps the strongest lagging indicator in the operational risk framework is operational event data. The losses that were suffered in the past can be analyzed for trends and patterns.

However, as mentioned earlier, lagging indicators can give a false sense of urgency or complacency if they are not carefully designed and managed. Lagging indicators are often found in regular monthly and quarterly reporting decks.

Leading Indicators

A true KRI will be a leading indicator. Leading indicators attempt to predict points of emerging risk. They are rare. An example of a leading indicator might be customer complaints. A high number of customer complaints might correlate with the size and number of class action lawsuits that a retail firm faces. If so, then the number of customer complaints is a leading indicator for legal risk.

Perhaps we can go further back the chain of causation. If it can be shown that a drop of more than 30 percent in the asset value in a customer account produces a significant increase in complaints, then a drop in asset value in an account becomes a leading indicator for legal risk.

If strong leading indicators can be found, they allow for preventive measures to be taken. In this example, whenever an account drops more than 30 percent, there could be a process in place to ensure that the customer is called within one day to discuss their needs and any changes they might wish to make.

Leading, lagging, and exception indicators are often monitored by line managers as part of ensuring efficiency and excellence in their processes. The operational risk framework can look for such indicators, link them to risks through the risk and control self-assessment (RCSA) process, and then produce a dashboard of operational risk-relevant indicators for tracking.

SELECTING KRIS

The indicators selected by a firm to monitor its risk may be KPIs or KCIs or combinations of the two. There are many challenges in finding appropriate KRIs for the operational risk framework. Metrics that are valuable for the day-to-day running of a department might be inappropriate or insufficient for operational risk management.

Many operational risk functions are faced with a sea of metric data when they first request KRIs.

These metrics needed to be filtered and enhanced in order to find the most appropriate indicators. It is helpful to complete the RCSA program before seeking KRIs so that the search can be narrowed down to only those metrics that are relevant to the risks that have been identified in the RCSA.

The RCSA will assist the operational risk manager in identifying which are the high risks and which risks are currently low but are in danger of increasing if the control environment deteriorates. The manager can then explore which controls are contributing to the risk rating and how those controls might be monitored by a KRI.

Having identified the areas of interest, the manager can set about developing a metric and hopefully one that is a KRI. They will often need to work with managers in other departments in order to establish ownership and find a reliable source for the data. They will also need to ensure that the quality of the metric is validated.

Once the risks that need to be monitored are identified, SMART principles can be applied in the selection or creation of an appropriate KRI. SMART principles suggest that a KRI should be:

Specific

Measurable

Attainable

Relevant

Timely

In practice, it is difficult to find indicators that meet all of these criteria, and it may be necessary to use proxy indicators temporarily, or even permanently.

Having established what data needs to be collected, the operational risk manager must then put in place thresholds and appropriate reporting scales and processes.

THRESHOLDS

The thresholds that are set for a metric are critical. Once thresholds are set, they are unlikely to be changed for some time and so they need to be set at the correct point.

Picking a threshold for a metric might produce an outcome that gives a high, medium, or low risk score. For example, if a firm's system has been shown to become unstable above 1 million trades, then a metric that tracks the number of trades in a day might have three thresholds set, as shown below.

Example of Thresholds for a Trade Volume Metric

Metric	Low Risk	Medium Risk	High Risk
Daily trade volume	<500,000	500,001–1,000,000	>1,000,000

This is a purely subjective and qualitative approach and can work well for many metrics as it is based on the management experience within the firm.

However, a more scientific approach can be helpful. If you have a data set for the metric that spans a good period of time, then you can apply statistical analysis to that data set and determine the properties of those data. By establishing the mean and the standard deviation, it is possible to apply a consistent threshold approach to all metrics.

For example, the operational risk function might establish in the KRI standards that a standard deviation in a metric above 0.5 should result in a medium risk rating and a standard deviation above 1 should result in a high risk rating. This assumes that the metrics are set up appropriately so that increases or decreases are appropriately tracked where they may indicate increased risk.

KRI STANDARDS

Each KRI must be monitored, and the minimum standards for KRIs should be set by the operational risk department. Gathering KRIs can be a manually intensive task, and many firms have implemented technology systems to extract metrics automatically where possible and to house metrics for analysis.

For each KRI, certain criteria need to be set, including:

- Name of the indicator.
- Risk that it is being monitored against.
- Method of calculation.
- Owner of the KRI.
- Red flag threshold, or red, amber, green or high, medium, low thresholds.
- Reporting period.

KRI CHALLENGES

The biggest challenge with KRIs is finding the right one. There is no consensus on which KRIs should be collected, although some best practice is starting to emerge. It is also often practically challenging to collect data that might be very helpful in managing operational risk. Einstein put it best when he said: "Not everything that can be counted counts, and not everything that counts can be counted."[1]

Industry collaboration has led to some recommendations from the American Banking Association and from the Risk Management Association (RMA) on appropriate KRIs. However, these recommended KRIs number in the hundreds or even thousands, and every firm is seeking the magical minimum number of KRIs that can indicate the operational risk health of the firm.

Firms are participating in collaborative exercises with these and other organizations to compare metrics and seek out possible benchmarking opportunities.

Without industry benchmarking, a firm's KRI can be compared only to itself. This can result in a false sense of security in an indicator that is remaining stable but that may in fact indicate that the control being monitored is operating at below industry standard.

As mentioned earlier, it is good practice to link KRIs to risks and controls that have been identified in the RCSA process and are known to be key to operational risk management. A complete KRI program also requires constant validation and feedback and strong standards.

METRICS EXAMPLES

KRIs could be developed based on the following examples of indicators that can be helpful in an operational risk program.

People Metrics

Some common examples of people metrics are provided in Table 9.1.

TABLE 9.1 Sample People Metrics

Metric	Description	Possible Parameters
Staff turnover	A simple metric that tracks the number of staff leaving and joining.	Number of leavers; number of joiners.
Regretted losses	The number of staff who have left the firm not due to downsizing or firing.	Percentage of workforce; percentage of total leavers.
Reason for leaving	Human resources generally tracks the reasons for leaving, and capturing that information may give an indication of morale and other people issues.	Categories could be: compensation, lack of training, lack of opportunities for advancement.
Educational levels	Highest level of education for each employee.	High school, bachelor's, MA, PhD.
Professional level	Professional exams taken and passed.	For example, Series 7, CPEs, CLEs, etc.
Training days	May indicate the level of expertise in the firm and may relate to morale and reasons for leaving.	Average number of days per employee; number of days per department/ business unit.
Staff morale	Firm-wide surveys can provide information that can assist with measuring the morale in the firm.	Average morale score; high and low scores; departmental/business unit comparisons; year-on-year comparisons.
Compensation	Benchmarking compensation can help ensure salaries are competitive.	Comparison with industry benchmarks.

Compliance Metrics

Some common examples of compliance metrics are provided in Table 9.2.

TABLE 9.2 Sample Compliance Metrics

Metric	Description	Possible Parameters
Number of action letters from regulator	Regulators provide investigation notices that require a response by the firm.	Number of letters, number of letters resolved without issue, number of letters requiring remediating actions.
Regulatory fines	This is a subset of loss data that may provide insight into the compliance health of the firm.	Number of fines, dollar value of fines, total dollars in fines this month/quarter/year.
Frequency of compliance reviews	Compliance desk reviews are mandatory in some areas.	Frequency or length of time since last review, by division, desk, etc.
Number of open compliance issues	Remediating actions are often required by compliance departments.	Number of actions open, number of actions late, number of high-priority actions open, etc.
Time taken to complete AML	Measures how promptly anti–money laundering checks are made.	Days/hours from request to completion.
Number of new products traded without new-product approval	Products that miss this process may expose the firm to elevated operational risk (as well as market and credit risk).	Number of new products approved by month; number of products identified that missed NPA process.
Number of complaints	Customer complaints regarding the clarity and fairness of products may indicate compliance risk.	Number of customer complaints related to alleged unfair, deceptive or abusive practices.

Technology and Infrastructure Metrics

Some common examples of technology and infrastructure metrics are provided in Table 9.3.

TABLE 9.3 Samples of Technology and Infrastructure Metrics

Metric	Description	Possible Parameters
Average time to resolve support requests	Time between initial request and response or final resolution.	Days/hours/minutes to respond; days/hours/minutes to resolve.
Number of support requests	Number of requests received by the help desk, or production support areas. May indicate issues with the systems. Should be compared to number of support staff and response times.	Number of requests total; number of requests per area; number of requests per time of day, week, month.
Network downtime	Measures resiliency of the network.	Days/hours/minutes down; by process/department/system, etc.
Hardware failure	Measures failed hardware.	Number of incidents; time to resolution or replacement.
Number of software patches	Measures quality of systems and workload of IT.	Number of patches by process/department/system.
Number of security breaches	Number of virus/hacker attacks may indicate the stability of the systems and security confidence.	Number of total attacks; number of attacks caught at firewall; number of attacks penetrating security.
System capacity	Measures the redundancy in the systems to ensure they can handle peak requirements.	Percentage of average system capacity per month; percentage of peak system capacity per month.
Password exceptions	Measures how often password attempts are made to monitor security breach attempts.	Number of password breaches; number of authorize exceptions to password resets.
Telecoms failure	Measures failed telecommunications infrastructure.	Number of incidents; time to resolution or replacement.

TABLE 9.4 Sample Business Continuity Metrics

Metric	Description	Possible Parameters
Number of completed business continuity plans	Tracks how many plans are in place, but does not evaluate their quality. Quality may be scored by BCP team.	Number of plans; number of plans scoring as "high"; date since last plan update.
Date since last BCP test	Tracks the age of BCP testing to ensure it does not get stale.	Days/months since last test by process/system/department/location.

Business Continuity Metrics

Some common examples of business continuity metrics are provided in Table 9.4.

Client Metrics

Some common examples of client metrics are provided in Table 9.5.

TABLE 9.5 Sample Client Metrics

Metric	Description	Possible Parameters
Number of client complaints	Customer satisfaction changes may provide insight into changes in employee practice, product issues, client profile changes.	Number of complaints; types of complaints; by department/region/product.
Number of new accounts opened	The number of accounts opened may indicate resources constraints.	Number of accounts opened; number of accounts opened with missing data.
Number of client records complete	Measures how many clients have completed reference records. This measure can be used for EDPM, CPBP, and fraud risks.	Percentage of client records that are incomplete.

Trade Execution and Process Management Metrics

Some common examples of trade execution and process management metrics are provided in Table 9.6.

Financial Statement Metrics

Some common examples of financial statement metrics are provided in Table 9.7.

TABLE 9.6 Sample Execution and Process Management Metrics

Metric	Description	Possible Parameters
Volume of transactions	All transactional measures require further insight than mere volumes. They can be considered in relation to each other, e.g., number of fails as percentage of total volume.	Total number of transactions; number per desk/product/department; compared to last day/week/month.
Number of fails		Total number of fails number per desk/product/department; compared to last day/week/month; compared to total volume.
Number of cancel and corrects		Total number of cancel; percentage of corrects; number per desk/product/department; compared to last day/week/month; compared to total volume.
Number of manual wire transfers	An increase in manual wire transfers might increase errors.	Total number or comparison with last week/month; number of erroneous wire transfers per total number of manual transfers.
Downtime of external feeds	Loss of external feeds may affect performance and increase errors.	Days/hours/minutes downtime of each external feed.

TABLE 9.7 Sample Financial Statement Metrics

Basic Indicator	Description	Possible Parameters
Percentage of SOX controls tested	SOX controls provide evidence that the financials are correct.	Total number tested; percentage tested; percentage tested and failed.
Number of errors in financial statements	The number of erroneous entries and fixes.	Number of entries; percentage of entries requiring fixes; number of fixes; number of unreconciled entries.
Percentage of SOX controls tested	SOX controls provide evidence that the financials are correct.	Total number tested; percentage tested; percentage tested and failed.

KEY POINTS

- KRIs are used to monitor changing risk levels, and true KRIs are difficult to identify.
- Metrics may provide the business environment and internal control factors that are required for an Advanced Measurement Approach capital model under Basel II.
- There are many types of metrics, including exception monitoring, performance indicators and control indicators.
- A metric might be a lagging, leading, or exception metric.
- SMART principles suggest that a KRI should be specific, measurable, attainable, relevant, and timely.
- It is important to ensure that thresholds are carefully set and monitored.

REVIEW QUESTION

1. An indicator that measures the average time taken to resolve a help desk request would best be described as a
   a. key risk indicator.
   b. key performance indicator.
   c. key control indicator.
   d. simple metric.

NOTE

1. Quote has been attributed to Albert Einstein (1879–1955), but it has also been attributed to William Bruce Cameron's 1963 text, *Informal Sociology: A Casual Introduction to Sociological Thinking*.

CHAPTER 10

Risk and Control Self-Assessments

This chapter explores the role of risk and control self-assessment (RCSA) in the operational risk framework. Various RCSA methods are described and compared, and several scoring methodologies are discussed. RCSA challenges and best practices are explained, and the practical considerations that can help ensure the success of an RCSA program are outlined.

THE ROLE OF ASSESSMENTS

Risk and control self-assessments play a vital role in the operational risk framework.

While operational risk event databases are effective in responding to past events, additional elements are needed in order to identify, assess, monitor, control, and mitigate events that have not yet occurred. A well-designed RCSA program provides insight into risks that exist in the firm, regardless of whether they have occurred before. The RCSA program fits into the operational risk framework as illustrated in Figure 10.1. While loss data allows us to look back at what has already happened, RCSA gives a tool to look forward at what might happen in the future. RCSA results often provide the best leading indicators of where risk needs to be mitigated.

Even if these risks are well understood by their owners, there is rarely a tool outside the operational risk framework that provides consistency and transparency in reporting, mitigating, and escalating these risks. For this reason, risk and control assessments are often the most enthusiastically adopted elements of the program, as they can quickly add value by providing a way for a department to articulate its risks.

However, they are also often the most troublesome elements, as finding the right way to manage the assessments that fits the culture of the firm,

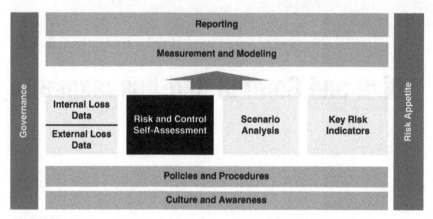

FIGURE 10.1   Risk and Control Self-Assessment in the Operational Risk Framework

meets regulatory requirements, and meets the goals of identifying, assessing, and controlling operational risk can be very difficult.

Many firms have experienced putting tremendous effort into rolling out RCSA programs only to find that they do not meet their needs and have to be redesigned and rolled out again. In fact, many firms have been through RCSA redesigns a few times already and may now be looking yet again at how to get this right.

The challenge is that the effort needed to populate the RCSA with valuable and accurate information can sometimes exceed the business benefit garnered from that information. The business benefit is being able to see your risks with transparency and make informed decisions about them.

The business benefits of an RCSA program are clear, but there may also be regulatory requirements that can be met through RCSAs. For example, Basel II firms that are taking an advanced approach to capital calculation have to show that they are including business environment and internal control factors in their calculation. These factors should reflect an understanding of the underlying business risk factors that are relevant to the firm and the effectiveness of the internal control environment in managing and mitigating those risks. Key risk indicators (KRIs) can be used to track those indicators, as discussed in Chapter 9. However, RCSA is best suited to identify which indicators are relevant and worthy of monitoring.

In the section on business environment internal control factors (BEICF), Basel II provides a good definition of RCSAs that can be applied to assessments undertaken in any operational risk framework:

> . . . *a bank's firm-wide risk assessment methodology must capture key business environment and internal control factors that can*

change its operational risk profile. These factors will make a bank's risk assessments more forward-looking, more directly reflect the quality of the bank's control and operating environments, help align capital assessments with risk management objectives, and recognize both improvements and deterioration in operational risk profiles in a more immediate fashion.[1]

RCSAs are used by Basel II Advanced Measurement Approach (AMA) firms to gather these factors, and there is further discussion in Chapter 12 on how these are then incorporated into the capital calculation. Newer and more simplified capital calculations are slated for implementation soon, but the value of a good RCSA program remains. The same methodologies are applicable to all firms as, regardless of regulatory requirements, the firm needs tools to allow it to meet the operational risk management goal of "recognizing both improvements and deterioration in operational risk profiles" to inform its decision making.

Risk and control self-assessment is a term that can refer to many different types of assessment. It should be clearly differentiated from control assessments and from risk and control assessments, neither of which have the "self" assessment characteristic.

Control Assessments

A simple control assessment is one that tests a control's effectiveness against set criteria and issues a pass/fail or level of effectiveness score. A control assessment is often done *to* the department by a third party, perhaps audit, compliance, or the Sarbanes-Oxley team.

Control assessment can produce output that is very useful to the RCSA program. For example, it may provide effectiveness scores for controls that can be leveraged in the RCSA program. Indeed, where a control has been assigned a score in a control assessment it is preferable to avoid reassessing that control. However, while this seems sensible, in practical terms it can prove difficult to leverage scores from other assessment programs unless the firm has adopted a standard taxonomy for controls, processes, and organizational structure. Without such taxonomies, mapping results from one assessment to another can be difficult.

Risk and Control Assessments

A risk and control assessment is similar to a control assessment, in that it is applied to an area by a third party. However, these do include a risk assessment in addition to a control assessment and so will incorporate several of the elements of the RCSA that will be further described below. As with control assessment, the results of these might be leveraged for the RCSA.

RCSAs

A risk and control *self*-assessment (RCSA) is distinguished from a control assessment and from a risk and control assessment by its subjective nature. While often facilitated by an operational risk manager, an RCSA is conducted by the department or business unit, and the scoring of risks and controls reflects not the view of a third party, but the view of the department or business itself.

It is the subjective perspective of the RCSA that presents both its biggest advantages and its strongest challenges.

The advantage of such an approach is that it further embeds the culture of operational risk management. Each department takes ownership of its own risks and controls and assesses the risks that may exist in its area. Empowered with this assessment the department can then prioritize mitigating actions and escalate risks that require higher authority for remediation.

The challenge of such an approach is that a subjective view can be considered as less accurate than an objective view, and there may be some skepticism over the scoring in the assessment. In practice, a well-designed RCSA program can produce accurate and transparent operational risk reporting that can be used effectively in the firm. It is important to never lose sight of the subjective nature of this element, however, and to be diligent in applying standards and strong facilitation throughout.

RCSAs should be included in the audit cycle, with each department audited as to its participation in the RCSA program and the reasonableness of their scoring. For example, loss data should be compared to RCSA scores as a check. If losses are high in an area that has been scored as low risk in the RCSA, that would raise a serious question as to the quality of the self-assessment and might result in an audit point. This has been raised by the regulators in recent years under their validation and verification requirements that were discussed in Chapter 4. There are now regulatory requirements that demand that RCSA and loss data be routinely compared to ensure that the RCSAs are reflecting the loss experience of the firm.

RCSA METHODS

There are several RCSA methods, and each has its own advantages and disadvantages. The main methods to consider are the questionnaire approach, the workshop approach, and the hybrid approach.

Questionnaire Approach

The questionnaire-based approach uses a template to present standard risk and control questions to participants. The content of the questionnaire is designed by the operational risk team, usually after intensive discussions across the firm. Each risk category or business process is analyzed and a list of related risks is prepared. For each risk, expected controls are identified.

The questionnaire is usually distributed to a nominated party in each department, who completes the questionnaire, providing self-assessed scores for each expected control, and risk levels (for example, high, medium, or low) and probabilities for each risk.

The level of complexity of questionnaire-based RCSAs' content and workflow varies enormously. Some questionnaire RCSAs ask participants to score just the controls (and in this case might be better named a control self-assessment or CSA). Others have several rounds of completion, the first being risk and control identification, the second being control effectiveness scoring by the control owners, and the last being residual risk scoring by the risk owners.

There are several advantages of a questionnaire-based RCSA method. The use of standard risks and controls makes it easier to consolidate reporting and identify cross-firm themes and trends. Also, the use of standard risks and controls ensures that a consistent approach is being taken across the firm and ensures that risks and controls that have been identified by the operational risk department are considered by every department.

These characteristics make a questionnaire-based RCSA particularly well suited to a firm that has multiple similar activities. For example, a bank that has many branches that offer the same products and services would be well served by a questionnaire-based RCSA. A fintech that has back office processes that are completed in multiple locations would benefit from this type of approach. The results can be collected electronically and the responses compared to identify themes, trends, and areas of potential control weakness or elevated risk.

Another advantage is that this method can take advantage of technology to distribute and collect questionnaires. Many software providers have entered this space with tools that provide good workflow functionality. Where firms have found that these off-the-shelf solutions do not meet their needs, they have developed their own RCSA workflow tools, with varying degrees of success.

There are also disadvantages to the questionnaire-based RCSA. If a firm does not have standard branches or repeated processes, then a standard RCSA might be more frustrating than it is helpful. The assessed business areas may push back on a questionnaire that contains many risk and control areas that are not relevant to them.

Another disadvantage of the questionnaire-based approach is that it is usually sent to specific nominated parties for completion. For this reason, careful facilitation is required to ensure that a departmental view, not just one person's opinion, is being expressed in the assessment.

An additional potential weakness in the questionnaire-based approach is that the original design might be missing a key risk or control, and participants might not have an opportunity to, or may be reluctant to, raise new items.

In fact, a general challenge in any questionnaire-based task is that it can result in a "check all" mentality, where the participants simply check the boxes that are likely to result in the least follow-up work or that express an average score or the middle ground.

A questionnaire-based method is efficient and is highly effective in the right environment, but the supporting training and facilitation should not be underestimated in order to ensure that any disadvantages have been effectively overcome.

Workshop Approach

A workshop method RCSA is discussed in a group setting, with facilitation from the operational risk department. Each risk is discussed, and related controls are scored for effectiveness. Once the controls have been scored, the residual risk is scored, often on a high-medium-low scale, along with related probabilities. Alternatively, the exposure might be expressed in financial terms. Some workshops also collect other impact data, such as possible client impact, legal or regulatory impact, reputational impact, and life safety impact.

Workshops often run for two to three hours, and perhaps more than one session is needed for each RCSA. As such, they are time consuming for all involved and require a strong commitment from both the participants and the facilitators.

Preparation for the workshop is usually extensive, involving the review of past losses, audit, compliance, and Sarbanes-Oxley reports and interviews with business managers and support areas. There are several advantages to a workshop-based RCSA. Perhaps mostly importantly, it provides a forum for an in-depth discussion of the operational risks in the firm. For this reason, it can be effective in embedding operational risk management.

The group approach to scoring ensures that there has been full participation in the scoring, rather than a single view. However, reaching a true consensus can be challenging and requires strong facilitation skills.

The workshop session often results in new risks and controls being identified and so contributes to the richness of the operational risk framework.

Workshop-based approaches are generally more appropriate for firms that do not have consistent branches or processes, and that need more flexibility than can be offered in a questionnaire-based approach. For example, a financial services firm that does not have retail branches, but has fixed income, equity, and asset management divisions, might be better suited to a workshop-based approach so that the unique risks and controls in each area can be appropriately assessed.

However, as with the questionnaire approach, there are several disadvantages to the workshop approach. The flexibility can also result in inconsistency as risks and controls might be newly raised in several areas, perhaps with different terminology. Also, consolidating the results can be challenging as each workshop output might look very different to the others.

Another disadvantage is that the rollout of a workshop-based approach is extremely burdensome on the operational risk department and on the firm. Many people will be involved in the sessions and the preparation and facilitation can use up a large proportion of an operational risk department's resources.

Hybrid RCSA Methods

As the operational risk framework matures and evolves, RCSA design will also mature and evolve. In the meantime, some firms use both the questionnaire and workshop approaches in order to get the most out of their RCSA program. For example, a firm that used the workshop approach in its first year might then use the output from that workshop to design a questionnaire approach for the subsequent years.

Alternatively, a firm might alternate questionnaire and workshop approaches in order to ensure that new risks and controls are identified and that a full discussion of operational risk is undertaken on a regular basis.

A firm might implement a sophisticated RCSA technology system that supports a flexible and collaborative approach and so decide not to hold workshop RCSAs anymore.

A firm might adopt a questionnaire approach but set certain triggers that will result in a workshop being held for a particular risk category. For example, a trigger might arise if losses escalate in a particular risk category or process, or if a major external event occurs that suggests that a reassessment of that risk would be prudent.

RCSA SCORING METHODS

There are many different ways to produce scores from RCSAs. Most RCSAs require some score of the likely impact and probability of an event occurring.

TABLE 10.1   Scoring Control Design and Performance

	Low	Medium	High
Design	The design provides only limited protection when used correctly.	The design provides some protection when used correctly.	The design provides excellent protection when used correctly.
Performance	The control is rarely performed.	The control is sometimes performed.	The control is always performed.

Some also require control effectiveness scores that might be entered directly or calculated from control design and performance scores. Some RCSAs might require scores for nonfinancial impacts such as reputational damages, client loss, legal or regulatory exposures, or even life safety impacts.

Scoring Control Effectiveness

A firm that has a Sarbanes-Oxley program in place might well have a control effectiveness scoring methodology in place. This might be leveraged for control scoring requirements in an RCSA. If there is no control scoring method in place, then one can be developed that assesses both the design and the performance of the control. One example of such a scoring method could be as shown in Table 10.1.

The design and performance scores for each control might then be combined to produce an overall effectiveness score as in Figure 10.2.

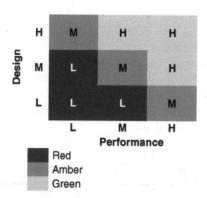

FIGURE 10.2   Control Effectiveness Scoring Matrix

In this example scale, a control that is well designed (H) but poorly performing (L) would have an overall control effectiveness score of low. Often, a red-amber-green, or RAG, rating will be used in assessments. In this example, controls that had an overall low effectiveness would produce a red result. The use of RAG ratings to visually highlight areas of concern can be very effective, but can also produce a strong reaction and so need to be used with caution.

An alternative control scoring method would be to have a list of control attributes for control design and have the overall design calculated or subjectively summarized based on those criteria. For example, a preventive control might be considered to be a stronger safeguard than a detective control and might help raise the score of that control. Similarly, an automated control would be considered stronger than a manual control.

It may also be possible to score control performance using key performance or key control indicators. As the RCSA matures, more and more key performance indicators (KPIs) and key control indicators (KCIs) will be identified, and these can be incorporated into the RCSA to provide more objective scoring for the controls where possible.

Each firm will determine its own appropriate control scoring method. Controls might be scored individually or as a group for each risk.

Risk Impact Scores

Some RCSAs simply require a financial impact score, for example, the maximum loss, the maximum plausible loss, or the likely loss amount.

Other RCSAs also require a score for other impact types on a scale that is provided. For example, a sample scale that provides high, medium, and low scores for several impact types is provided in Table 10.2.

The impact is usually scored on a residual scale that is the likely impact after all the controls are in place, or after the control effectiveness scores have been determined. Some RCSAs also score the inherent impact; that is the likely impact before controls are considered and this inherent impact score is sometimes used to prioritize the assessment of risks that have a high inherent impact. The inherent impact can be helpful in understanding the relative value of controls. However, some firms do not collect inherent values and focus only on risks that have a high residual impact.

Probability or Frequency

An RCSA might require a probability score in terms of the likelihood that the risk event could happen in the next 12 months. For example, if the event is likely to happen five times in the next 12 months, the probability would

TABLE 10.2 A Risk Impact Scoring Scale That Includes Nonfinancial Impact Categories

Impact Type	Low	Medium	High
Financial	Less than $100,000.	Between $100,000 and $1 million.	Over $1 million.
Reputational	Negative reputational impact is local.	Negative reputational impact is regional.	Negative reputational impact is global.
Legal or Regulatory	Breach of contractual or regulatory obligations, with no costs.	Breach of contractual or regulatory obligations with some costs or censure.	Breach of contractual or regulatory obligations leading to major litigation, fines, or severe censure.
Clients	Minor service failure to noncritical clients.	Minor service failure to critical client(s) or moderate service failure to noncritical clients.	Moderate service failure to critical clients or major service failure to noncritical clients.
Life Safety	An employee is slightly injured or ill.	More than one employee is injured or ill.	Serious injury or loss of life.

be 5. If it is likely to happen only once in the next 10 years, then the probability would be 0.1.

Alternatively, the probability or frequency might simply be scored as high, medium, or low as shown in Table 10.3.

Risk Severity

Once the impact and frequency have been scored, some RCSAs combine these to give an overall risk severity score. This might be calculated using a combination of the scores as in Figure 10.3.

TABLE 10.3 Sample Scoring Method for Frequency or Probability

	Low	Medium	High
Length of time between events	>5 years	Between 1 and 5 years	<1 year

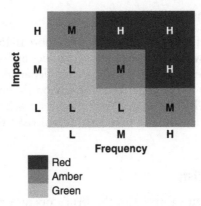

FIGURE 10.3   Risk Severity Scoring Matrix

Using this methodology, a score of low (L) for impact and high (H) for frequency would give an overall risk severity of medium (M). Once again, a RAG rating that indicates high scores as red, medium scores as amber, and low scores as green can be a powerful tool and should be used with caution.

Scoring scales need to be adapted to meet the risk appetites of the firm. One scoring method might be effective in one firm, but inappropriate in another. For this reason, scoring methods vary greatly from firm to firm.

RCSA BEST PRACTICES

There are several key elements to a successful RCSA program, regardless of approach taken. When designing and implementing an RCSA, it is prudent to consider the following elements.

Interview Participants Beforehand

To ensure that the RCSA is well designed and reflects the business processes and associated risks and controls in each department, it is important to spend time interviewing participants, stakeholders, and support functions prior to launching the RCSA.

Review Available Background Data from Other Functions

There will be valuable information available for preparation purposes in recent audit reports, compliance reviews, independent testing results, KPIs and KCIs, and Sarbanes-Oxley assessments. A review of these documents can provide insight into existing and recently remediated operational risks.

Review Past RCSAs and Related RCSAs

Once the RCSA program has been running for more than a year, past RCSAs should be reviewed when a department is conducting its next RCSA. There should also be a review of related RCSAs from departments that either provide support services to the department or rely on support from the department. These related RCSAs may have raised risks where the controls are owned by this department, and may have raised risks that the department needs to be aware of.

Review Internal Loss Data

Events that have been captured in the firm's operational risk event database provide a valuable backdrop, and help to identify the risks and control weaknesses that need to be addressed in the RCSA. They also demonstrate the possible impact and frequency of risk events and so can be used to validate assessments made during the RCSA.

Review of External Events

External events are also helpful in informing the discussions around potential risks. The RCSA is designed to consider all possible risks, not just those that have already occurred in the firm, but this can be a difficult task and examples of events in the industry are useful for this purpose.

Carefully Select and Train Participants

The RCSA participant(s) should be selected with care and trained in the RCSA method beforehand. It is helpful to include representatives from areas that support the department that is completing its RCSA, as they will have a (sometimes surprising) view on the effectiveness of the controls that they own. Ensure that control owners participate in scoring their own controls.

It can be helpful to have the head of the department included if it is a workshop-style RCSA, but only if their presence will not intimidate the other participants and so skew the results to just one view.

Document Results

The RCSA output should be consistently and carefully documented with an emphasis on providing evidential support for conclusions and scores whenever possible. Every detail of the discussions need not, and indeed probably should not, be recorded. However, the output must be captured in a way that can be reviewed, analyzed, and acted upon. This might mean that the results are put into a system or simply recorded in a spreadsheet or document, depending on the RCSA method used.

Regulatory expectations regarding the documentation of RCSA results have risen over the past few years and a subjective score is often not considered to be sufficient by the regulator. For this reason, many firms have been looking to adopt more objective control scoring methods and have been applying taxonomies for processes, risks, and controls. This is discussed further in this chapter under "Ensure Completeness Using Taxonomies."

Score Appropriately

The RCSA scoring methodology should be appropriate for the firm and each firm should consider whether it might be beneficial to its operational risk management goals to include nonfinancial impacts such as reputational, legal, regulatory, client, and life safety, where appropriate.

Identify Mitigating Actions

An RCSA is incomplete without the identification of any actions that have been agreed upon during the assessment. These actions will be undertaken to lower any unacceptable risk levels, either by improving, changing, or adding a control. Generally, a high risk will need to be mitigated, unless the risk is accepted without mitigation. If the risk is accepted, then this should be clearly stated in the assessment. Action items need to be tracked in the operational risk framework, through to their completion. If a high risk is not going to be mitigated then there needs to be a transparent risk acceptance process to log that decision.

Implement Appropriate Technology

RCSA technology should be used appropriately to manage the process and to report on the outcome. An RCSA tool should support the methodology and provide access to reporting and analysis of the assessments.

Ensure Completeness Using Taxonomies

RCSAs should cover the entire firm and be complete and comprehensive; indeed, national regulatory standards often require this. In recent years, firms have taken this to heart and have been using several methods to demonstrate this.

First, it is important to show that all material areas of the firm have been covered. This can be done by using the organizational hierarchy and checking that all aspects of the hierarchy have participated in an RCSA.

Second, firms are now moving toward developing standard process taxonomies. These process taxonomies can be used by every area in the firm to identify processes that they undertake and to ensure that all of those processes are included in their RCSA program.

Third, firms are also moving to developing risk taxonomies. These taxonomies are often built out of the Basel II seven operational risk categories of Internal Fraud; External Fraud; Employment Practices and Workplace Safety; Clients, Products, and Business Practices; Damage to Physical Assets; Business Disruption and System Failures; and Execution, Delivery, and Process Management. It has proven helpful for many firms to develop their own risk taxonomy down to a Level 3 categorization.

Fourth, firms have moved toward developing control or control-type taxonomies.

Finally, all of these elements can be brought together to ensure completeness in the following way. The corporate operational risk function can work with the businesses and support functions to determine which of the risks in the risk taxonomy could arise in each process. They can also determine which of the control types in the control taxonomy could mitigate the risks in the risk taxonomy.

Armed with this information, an RCSA can be designed that captures all the departments, all the processes in each department, all the risks associated with those processes, and all the expected control types that can mitigate those risks.

This is, not surprisingly, a huge undertaking. Developing the taxonomies alone can require heroic efforts and collaboration across the firms. Even once the taxonomies have been agreed on, the size of RCSA that might result could be burdensome, and this will mean that a triaging or prioritization procedure will likely be needed. This procedure will need to be well documented and defensible if it is not going to undermine the goal of demonstrating completeness.

Finally, the maintenance of such taxonomies is a large and constant undertaking and needs to be owned by a function that has the capacity and authority to maintain it.

If such taxonomies and their mapping relationships are adopted across the firm by audit, compliance, technology risk, and other assessment functions, then the benefits may well outweigh the burden as they will all then be able to leverage each other's work.

Themes Identified

The whole RCSA program should be reviewed for the identification of firm wide themes that may require escalation. One of the important roles of the operational risk function is to take a step back from the details of the individual RCSAs and deduce where there are firm-wide themes that might need to be addressed. Several local solutions might be less effective than a firm-wide strategy to mitigate a particular risk.

For example, if several areas identified that they had difficulty training their staff in a timely way, and that this was impacting several risk scores, then the appropriate solution might be for the firm to improve its corporate training and development programs rather than addressing the training differently in each location.

Leverage Existing Assessments

Risks and controls may have been assessed as part of other programs in the firm, such as business continuity planning or Sarbanes-Oxley. If so, these assessments should be used in the operational risk RCSA, and every effort should be made to avoid repeating an assessment of a risk or of a control. This is important in order to protect the integrity of both the original assessment and the operational risk RCSA. Conflicting scores can cause serious problems, and it is frustrating for all involved if the work is merely repetitive. This is discussed in more depth in Chapter 16, under "Governance, Risk, and Compliance."

Schedule Appropriately

Many firms conduct RCSAs on an annual basis. However, each firm should select an appropriate scheduling interval, and this might be monthly, quarterly, annually, or ad hoc in response to a certain trigger event.

The schedule should ensure that the information is not stale and that the burden of collecting the assessment does not outweigh the benefit in responding to the assessments with timely mitigation. Reporting on the remediation efforts generated by RCSA activity should occur more frequently, probably monthly, in order to ensure that risks are being mitigated as expected.

Risk and control self-assessments have a unique and powerful role to play in an effective operational risk program. The risk and control scores that are gathered during the RCSA are vital to meeting the goals of identifying, assessing, monitoring, controlling, and mitigating operational risk.

RCSAs ensure that there is proactive risk management across the firm, to supplement the reactive risk management that occurs in response to loss events. The challenges with RCSAs are keeping them current, designing them to be relevant and valuable to participants and to senior management, and ensuring that they produce tracked actions.

It is worth spending time planning and piloting RCSA methods before use, and it is important to allow these methods to evolve as experience develops and as the operational risk management function matures.

Backtest or Validate Results

Regulatory expectations now require the validation of RCSA results. The simplest validation method is to compare loss data results with RCSA scores. If loss data suggest that an area produces significant losses in a particular risk category, but the RCSA is indicating low risk severity in that same area, then this should raise concerns. Such contradictions should lead to a review of the RCSA and the justification for the scoring in the RCSA. Backtesting and validation can (and should) be independently undertaken by the second line of defense: the corporate-level operational risk function.

KEY POINTS

- RCSAs provide an opportunity to look forward and consider what could occur in the future, whereas loss data focus on what has already occurred in the past.
- RCSAs come in many different forms and an appropriate method needs to be developed at each firm to meet its particular regulatory and business needs.
- RCSAs can be used to collect scores for the effectiveness of controls, the potential size and probability of a risk event's occurring, and the overall risk severity associated with a potential event.
- Workshop method RCSAs focus on group scoring and discussion while questionnaire method RCSAs often use standard templates and automated delivery methods.
- The qualitative nature of many RCSA methods raises challenges in interpreting and applying the results to ensure that appropriate risk management and mitigation activities can be implemented.
- Best practices for RCSA have matured in the past few years and can be leveraged to ensure a successful program is implemented.

REVIEW QUESTION

1. Which of the following best describes how risk and control self-assessments (RCSA) can be used to manage fraud risk for Basel II?
   a. An RCSA can be used to gather business environment and internal control factors that relate to fraud risks.
   b. An RCSA should be used to collect fraud-related loss events.
   c. RCSAs are designed primarily to provide estimates of capital for fraud risk exposures.
   d. RCSAs are generally not designed to consider fraud risk.
   e. RCSAs only consider internal fraud risks and not external fraud risks.

NOTE

1. Bank for International Settlements, "International Convergence of Capital Measurement and Capital Standards: A Revised Framework," 2004, section 676.

CHAPTER 11

Scenario Analysis

Scenario analysis is a challenging element in the operational risk framework. Scenario analysis provides the operational risk framework with a tool to explore the rare but plausible losses that could arise as a result of operational risk. In this chapter, we discuss the various methods used for scenario analysis and explain the important elements of a robust scenario analysis program.

ROLE OF SCENARIO ANALYSIS

Scenario analysis has become an important element in operational risk management and measurement, and the methods used have evolved rapidly over the past few years. Firms use scenario analysis to evaluate their exposure to high-severity events. Unlike RCSA analysis, scenario analysis focuses on "fat-tail" events, or rare catastrophic events. These types of events can put the firm at serious risk. For this reason, scenario analysis was a required element in calculating operational risk capital requirements under Basel II for any firm undertaking the Advanced Measurement Approach (AMA).

Firms that do not have AMA requirements are also pursuing scenario analysis programs, as they provide a valuable insight into the major risks faced and provide the opportunity for an engaging dialogue with the business lines.

The role of scenario analysis in the operational risk framework is illustrated in Figure 11.1.

Scenario analysis is used to derive reasoned assessments of plausible severe losses. The assessments are then used to explore "what-if" cases that may be beyond the current experience of the firm. External data plays a key role in scenario analysis, as it provides insight into what has already

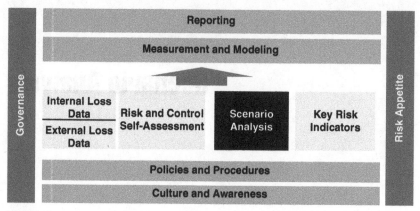

FIGURE 11.1 Scenario Analysis in the Operational Risk Framework

occurred in other firms. However, in addition to learning from experiences outside the firm, scenario analysis considers events that might not yet have occurred at any firm.

A somewhat helpful definition of scenario analysis and its uses can be found in Basel II. However, areas of ambiguity that have proven challenging to the industry are highlighted as follows:

> *A bank must use scenario analysis of expert opinion in conjunction with external data to evaluate its exposure to high-severity events. This approach draws on the knowledge of **experienced** business managers and risk management experts to derive **reasoned** assessments of **plausible** severe losses. For instance, these expert assessments could be expressed as parameters of an assumed statistical loss distribution. In addition, scenario analysis should be used to assess the impact of deviations from the correlation assumptions embedded in the bank's operational risk measurement framework, in particular, to evaluate potential losses arising from multiple simultaneous operational risk loss events. Over time, such assessments need to be validated and re-assessed through comparison to actual loss experience to ensure their reasonableness.[1] [emphasis added]*

Finding a process that taps experienced business managers and risk managers and that produces reasoned assessments of plausible losses is challenging indeed. Who is "experienced"? What constitutes a "reasoned" assessment? What do we mean by "plausible"?

In March 2021, the Bank of International Settlements (BIS) summarized the current state of scenario analysis in the financial services sector as follows:

> *Scenario analysis – Scenario analysis is a method to identify, analyse and measure a range of scenarios, including low probability and high severity events, some of which could result in severe operational risk losses. Scenario analysis typically involves workshop meetings of subject matter experts including senior management, business management and senior operational risk staff and other functional areas such as compliance, human resources and IT risk management, to develop and analyse the drivers and range of consequences of potential events. Inputs to the scenario analysis would typically include relevant internal and external loss data, information from self-assessments, the control monitoring and assurance framework, forward-looking metrics, root-cause analyses and the process framework, where used. The scenario analysis process could be used to develop a range of consequences of potential events, including impact assessments for risk management purposes, supplementing other tools based on historical data or current risk assessments. It could also be integrated with disaster recovery and business continuity plans, for use within testing of operational resilience. Given the subjectivity of the scenario process, a robust governance framework and independent review are important to ensure the integrity and consistency of the process.*[2]

SCENARIO ANALYSIS APPROACHES

There are several different methods that can be used to conduct scenario analysis. Some firms use a workshop approach; some conduct interviews or analyze data in small teams. Some firms conduct many scenario analysis workshops, covering each risk category in each business; some run only a few scenarios at the corporate level. Some firms have standard scenarios for every business line to consider; some prefer that each business line develop their own.

Whatever the approach is, the purpose of the scenario analysis program is to identify those rare, but plausible, large events that should be incorporated into the operational risk framework. In practice, this means that people will be asked extremely difficult questions such as, "How big could such an event be?" or "Could it happen in the next 20 years?"

If the output of scenario analysis is to be used directly in the capital calculation, then it will need to be a particularly robust, repeatable, and well-documented activity. Operational risk capital under an AMA framework is supposed to capture the risk at a 99.9 percent confidence level. In other words, it should be sufficient to cope with a 1-in-1,000-year event.

Conversations with business managers on whether something could happen in 1,000 years has proved unfruitful, and so most firms have developed ways to get close to the very rare by considering the rare. For example, a 1-in-10-year event might be easier to discuss, and several data points might be collected to allow for the data collected to be extrapolated out to the rarer event.

The Basel Committee recognized the challenges banks were facing with this element of the framework and provided some further guidance in their 2011 AMA Guidelines as follows:

> *Scenario data provides a forward-looking view of potential operational risk exposures. A robust governance framework surrounding the scenario process is essential to ensure the integrity and consistency of the estimates produced. Supervisors will generally observe the following elements in an established scenario framework:*
>
> *a. A clearly defined and repeatable process;*
> *b. Good quality background preparation of the participants in the scenario generation process;*
> *c. Qualified and experienced facilitators with consistency in the facilitation process;*
> *d. The appropriate representatives of the business, subject matter experts and the corporate operational risk management function as participants involved in the process;*
> *e. A structured process for the selection of data used in developing scenario estimates;*
> *f. High quality documentation which provides clear reasoning and evidence supporting the scenario output;*
> *g. A robust independent challenge process and oversight by the corporate operational risk management function to ensure the appropriateness of scenario estimates;*
> *h. A process that is responsive to changes in both the internal and external environment; and*
> *i. Mechanisms for mitigating biases inherent in scenario processes. Such biases include anchoring, availability and motivational biases.*[3]

We consider each of these aspects as we explore the variety of methods being used today to meet the challenges of scenario analysis.

The use of scenario analysis in capital calculation has proven so difficult that the latest capital calculation guidance from BIS has removed it as an element for the new approaches that are scheduled to be implemented in coming years. However, until those new approaches are implemented, scenario analysis remains a contributor to the AMA approach and continues to be an effective methodology for operational risk management beyond capital calculation.

(a) A Clearly Defined and Repeatable Process

Scenario analysis contents might vary considerably from one set to another, but the process needs to be consistent. To achieve this it is necessary to develop written procedures and standards that will be applied every time a scenario analysis activity is run.

Experience has shown many firms that their auditors and regulators will pore over these documents and will carefully compare them to the process that actually occurred. It is therefore important to ensure that the defined process is not aspirational but is achievable over and over again.

A robust scenario analysis process does not need to be, and should not be, overly complex. Rather, it should meet the criteria outlined earlier, while also providing the maximum benefit and least disruption to the businesses that are involved.

For this reason, much of the scenario analysis process is likely to reside in the corporate operational risk function, in the form of preparation, facilitation, and post-scenario documentation and validation.

(b) Background Preparation

Section b of the AMA Guidelines calls for "good quality background preparation of the participants in the scenario generation process."[4]

Interviews

Preparation for scenario analysis is very similar to preparation for RCSA workshops and questionnaires. The facilitator or preparation team interviews the key business managers and support managers for the area under consideration. Background documentation from audits, compliance reviews, and Sarbanes-Oxley assessments is reviewed. Internal and external loss events are analyzed.

Internal Loss Data

The internal loss data of a firm certainly provides a floor for losses, but it does not show what *could* go wrong; it only shows what *has* gone wrong. The facilitators of a scenario analysis discussion should be aware of the history of losses, but it should not be shared directly with those participating in the discussion as this introduces a hard-to-overcome anchoring bias, as discussed later.

External Loss Data

One of the most important inputs into the scenario analysis process is external loss data.

For example, if a scenario analysis workshop is being conducted on the risk category Internal Fraud, then the firm might have some internal data, but often very little. However, internal fraud as a category includes unauthorized trading, and the industry has several egregious examples of unauthorized trading that have resulted in losses in the many billions of dollars. Information on these external events can be helpful in developing a what-if scenario for the firm.

In scenario analysis, the questions should not be focused so much on why that event *could not* happen at this firm (as most businesses will contend), but rather on how such an event *could* happen at this firm. How many controls would have to fail at once? What sort of positions would the trader have to be able to hold? And so on.

External events provide an excellent opportunity to stimulate discussion on the rare, but plausible, risks in this category.

In addition to the storylines from the news, external data from a consortium such as ORX can provide a helpful benchmarking floor. For example, if your firm is a member of ORX and the ORX data show that in the industry firms of your size have experienced losses over $50 million on average once every five years in this risk category, then is there any reason why your firm is different?

RCSA Results

Another valuable source of background information is the RCSA program. RCSAs will have identified the high risks in each area and can be used to help populate a straw man of possible scenarios for consideration. However, something that is low risk in the RCSA might still qualify as a scenario, as it may be that frequency was the main driver that was keeping the risk low. If something could generate a very large loss, regardless of frequency, then that is an item for consideration in scenario analysis. Therefore, RCSA results need to be carefully reviewed as part of the background preparation.

Scenario analysis should also feed back into the RCSA program, further enriching the risks library that is constantly evolving in the operational risk framework.

Compliance and Audit Findings

Compliance and audit findings can be helpful in challenging claims that a control or a set of controls is working well. These should be carefully reviewed as part of the background preparation and should be on hand for the facilitator to refer to as needed.

Key Metrics and Analysis

Some risk categories may lend themselves to preparatory statistical analysis. For example, when discussing scenarios regarding the risk category Damage to Physical Assets, a scenario might be raised concerning a terrorist attack destroying a building. There are sources of data available on the frequency of attacks globally and in large cities and on the range in impact zone from a single attack. This data can be used alongside the firm's own data on its office locations to develop a model to assist with the estimation of severity and frequency.

The use of such metrics is referred to as factor analysis by some firms and is gaining momentum across the industry. This type of analysis alleviates the difficulties in estimation and seems to be well received by regulators so far. However, according to the AMA guidelines discussed previously, the role of the business expert must still exist and so even this type of analysis requires subjective confirmation from the business and risk managers.

Straw Man Scenario List

Based on research in all these elements, a list of possible scenarios can be brought to the participants for their consideration, or a list of scenarios can be determined for an interview based process.

Participants in scenario analysis activities are better equipped to consider scenarios if they are provided with appropriate background resources.

(c) Qualified and Experienced Facilitators with Consistency in the Facilitation Process

The AMA Guidelines call for "qualified and experienced facilitators with consistency in the facilitation process."[5]

If the scenarios are being discussed in a group environment, such as a workshop, then there needs to be a neutral facilitator who not only knows the process completely but is also proficient at managing the conversations to ensure that no one person, or small group, is dominating the discussion and that all ideas are heard.

The skills needed often mean that scenario analysis workshops can be run only one at a time as the facilitation resources are in short supply.

(d) The Appropriate Representatives

The AMA Guidelines call for the involvement of all of "the appropriate representatives of the business, subject matter experts and the corporate operational risk management function as participants involved in the process."[6]

The written procedures for scenario analysis should probably include a list of the required quorum. If the firm has a scenario analysis process that requires each business line to complete a scenario analysis workshop for each risk category, then each category may have a different quorum. For example, Employment Practice and Workplace Safety would require a representative from the human resources department.

Most scenarios benefit from attendance by representatives from the legal department, compliance, operations, and technology. Some may also benefit from representation from the finance department. The quorum requirements should be set appropriately.

If the quorum is not met, then it may be necessary to cancel and reschedule the workshop, or it might be possible to loop the missing participants into the review process afterward.

(e) A Structured Process for the Selection of Data

The AMA Guidelines call for "a structured process for the selection of data used in developing scenario estimates."[7]

At the heart of scenario analysis activity is the gathering of data to be used to develop the scenario analysis estimates. In a workshop environment, these data include all background preparation data and the estimates that are solicited from the participants during the workshop. While the workshop environment may be a free-flowing conversation, there need to be checkpoints incorporated into the process to ensure that all procedural requirements are being met. For example, a workshop might be designed to gather a worst-case dollar amount for each scenario. If so, there needs to be a defined process by which the worst-case estimates are gathered from the participants in the room and their final consensus reached.

In an interview-based approach, the same challenges exist in ensuring that the way responses are gathered is carefully structured so that the process can be clearly documented and is repeatable.

To meet this requirement, firms have adopted questionnaires and templates that assist the facilitators in keeping the process in line and ensuring that the data are clearly gathered and documented.

Once the data have been gathered, through background preparation and through expert discussion and debate, they can then be used to draw conclusions on the possible severity and frequency for each scenario.

Some firms collect data at the risk category level rather than at the scenario level. For example, there may be five scenarios that have been identified in the Clients, Products, and Business Practices risk category. Some firms gather severity and frequency information for all five, and some firms gather severity and frequency for the group of five (e.g., how many of these scenarios could happen in the next 10 years in total?).

Conclusions drawn and decisions made need to be clearly documented as discussed next.

(f) High-Quality Documentation Which Provides Clear Reasoning and Evidence Supporting the Scenario Output

The AMA Guidelines require "high-quality documentation which provides clear reasoning and evidence supporting the scenario output."[8]

In the early days of operational risk scenario analysis, there was a reluctance to document the discussions. Sensitive issues are often raised, and there may be disagreements during the discussions before consensus is reached. The idea of documenting all those details left most firms feeling uncomfortable and their legal departments feeling anxious.

However, in the past few years, the regulatory pressure to ensure that all conclusions are supported by documented reasoning and evidence has led to a more highly documented process despite these concerns.

While the whole conversation does not need to be recorded, there does need to be a well-documented summary at the end of the process that outlines the thought processes, the data and evidence that was weighed and considered, and the reason that consensus was reached on certain conclusions such as severity and frequency.

It is hard for a facilitator to both facilitate the process and document what happens. For this reason, in workshop scenario analysis activities there is often a second neutral participant, perhaps from the corporate operational risk function, whose sole role is to document the proceedings. This is not a court reporter–type activity, but requires a deep understanding of the process and procedures to ensure that all important aspects are captured in the documentation.

It is difficult to go back afterward to look for consensus on something that was missed, and a robust documentation template can assist with ensuring that all important data points and rationales have been captured.

(g) Independent Challenge and Oversight

The AMA Guidelines call for a "robust independent challenge process and oversight by the corporate operational risk management function to ensure the appropriateness of scenario estimates."[9]

In a workshop, if the facilitator is provided by the corporate operational risk function, then they can take on the dual role of challenge also. If a third-party facilitator is used, then the corporate operational risk function can be a participant in the workshop and challenge as a member of the quorum.

In all types of scenario analysis, the corporate operational risk function can meet this challenge and oversight requirement by being actively involved in all preparation work, in the scenario analysis activities, and in the review of the documentation.

It is also helpful to establish a formal challenge and review process after the activity. This can consist of a simple e-mail documentation review by all participants or by a follow-up meeting to walk through the final documented conclusions.

(h) A Process That Is Responsive to Changes

The AMA Guidelines require "a process that is responsive to changes in both the internal and external environment."[10]

A scenario analysis activity should capture the current state of the business and control environments and should be designed to ensure that any changes in those environments will trigger a new activity as appropriate.

Many firms revisited their Internal Fraud scenario analysis after the 2012 UBS unauthorized trading event, and external events are helpful triggers for such reassessments. It is also important to revisit scenario analysis when a major business change occurs, such as an acquisition or divestiture. Similarly, a major control change such as a technology infrastructure rollout may trigger a new scenario analysis in impacted business and risk categories.

Regardless of triggers, scenario analysis should be conducted on a timely basis to ensure that it remains up-to-date as regards the current internal and external environment. For this reason, many firms will require their scenario analysis to be updated once a year even if no trigger has arisen.

However, the resource challenge can prove overwhelming and less frequent updates might be practically necessary.

(i) Mechanisms for Mitigating Biases

The AMA Guidelines draw attention to the need for "mechanisms for mitigating biases inherent in scenario processes. Such biases include anchoring, availability and motivational biases."[11]

In all methods there are biases that enter the process and that require careful consideration. While an expert may be knowledgeable on the subject matter of the scenario under discussion, they might not have the statistical background to understand the implications of certain estimates and decisions regarding impact and frequency of events. They are also likely to be untrained in the biases that can arise in such exercises and how to compensate for them.

Therefore, it is important to ensure that scenario analysis workshops and interviews are facilitated by someone who does have that experience or, at the very least, has an appreciation for the dangers of statistical and behavioral bias in the process.

Where possible, the process should avoid the introduction of biases when providing background or supporting data.

The Australian Prudential Regulation Authority produced a working paper in 2007 that addressed the inherent biases that occur in scenario analysis for operational risk and identified two classes of bias: judgmental and motivational.[12] This paper has stood the test of time and still provides strong guidance on how to address bias in scenario analysis today.

Judgmental bias occurs during the estimation process as the experts are swayed by the background data and the form of the questions. An example of judgmental bias is *availability* bias, which occurs when estimates are influenced by the availability of data. For example, past operational risk event data may be supplied to scenario analysis participants in the form of internal and external loss event data.

This data can influence the perception of likely size and frequency of events, and indeed the type of events that can occur. If an expert has recently experienced a particular event, they are more likely to deduce that that event can occur with a higher frequency and with a similar impact. For example, someone who has recently been in a car accident is likely to estimate the frequency of car accidents as higher than someone who has not.

Similarly, if the firm or the industry has recently experienced a large event, the scenario analysis participants are more likely to estimate that that event could occur again soon, and at the same impact level.

Another example of judgmental bias is *anchoring*. Anchoring occurs where participants are offered an initial estimate from which to base their estimate. For example, internal and external data may anchor the estimates so that likely impacts beyond that size are considered unlikely, and frequencies that differ from the past are discounted as less plausible.

Scenario analysis should provide an opportunity to look forward and consider what could occur in the future, and not only what has already occurred in the past. Therefore, judgmental bias can seriously undermine the process if not carefully considered. For this reason, it may be best not to provide internal loss data and to only use it as a floor. The facilitator can have access to this data and refer to it if the scenario participants are estimating close to, or below, that floor.

The careful use of internal and external data, and facilitation by the operational risk department, can help to overcome these biases. By addressing these biases up front, the participants can be assisted in resisting them and keeping their estimation processes less constrained to the judgmental influences.

Motivational bias occurs where the estimates of the participants are influenced not by the data presented, but by the personal interest of the participants themselves. More crudely, this can be referred to as "gaming the system." Senior management may be particularly susceptible to this bias, as they may perceive an estimate that suggests a potentially high impact as reflecting poorly on their department's risk management practices.

In addition, if scenario analysis is used as an input into a capital calculation for operational risk capital, then participants will be aware that high estimates may result in high capital and so may resist estimating the fat-tail events effectively.

Overcoming motivational bias is more challenging than overcoming judgmental bias. One way to avoid gaming of the scenario analysis estimates is to ensure that allocation of capital is driven not only by scenario analysis but also by RCSA, KRI, and loss data results. Alternatively, scenario analysis can be done at the top of the house, rather than at the business unit level, and then allocated down to business lines using a combination of operational risk information.

The facilitator of the scenario analysis workshop might also set parameters for the estimates that preclude underestimating. For example, they might set minimum limits at past event levels if they are in fact larger or more frequent than the estimates.

SCENARIO ANALYSIS OUTPUT

Different methods produce different outputs, but the goal of scenario analysis is to produce reasoned assessments of plausible severe losses, and so outputs need to support that goal.

Some scenario analysis methods produce an average loss estimate, a worst-case loss estimate, and frequency estimates for each of these values. Some produce just the worst-case estimate and a single frequency estimate. Others produce a range of loss estimates, with frequency estimates for each loss. Still others produce the latter range plus a maximum loss estimate.

One example of possible scenario analysis output is illustrated in Table 11.1. In this table, the firm has taken the approach of collecting the number of events that might occur in a category rather than the number of times a single scenario might occur. They are collecting a range of frequencies for each risk category in a selection of severity ranges.

For example, in the Clients, Products, and Business Practices category they have decided upon all the scenarios that apply and are now estimating how many of those scenarios could occur in total.

In the $1 million to $5 million bucket (A), they have agreed that it is plausible that they could experience five events in this category. Hence, they have entered a frequency of five. However, in the greater than $100 million bucket (B), they have agreed that such a large event could occur only once every 10 years. Hence, they have entered a frequency of 0.1.

The total frequency (C) represents how many events could occur in this category in a single year and is simply the sum of the buckets.

The final column (D) contains a maximum loss amount that has been agreed in the scenario analysis workshops.

Some categories do not have any entries (E), as the group has determined that in fact no event could occur at that size. Of course, such an estimation process as represented in Table 11.1 would have to have be supported by robust procedures, supporting evidence, and a well-documented rationale.

The output drives how the scenario analysis information is then used for risk management or for capital calculation purposes, and the model that is applied to calculating capital for the firm. This capital model may have many other elements, and capital calculation methods are considered further in Chapter 12.

While designed to produce fat-tail estimates, scenario analysis is often also responsible for the identification of significant mitigation activities that should be undertaken in order to lessen the risks identified.

This can mean that some overlap occurs between the RCSA program and scenario analysis, particularly if the workshop RCSA method is being used. Indeed, some firms have combined the two elements of the operational risk framework, and at the end of an RCSA workshop they will ask the participants to consider the same risks in an environment where all controls fail. In this way participants can extrapolate from known and relatively well-controlled risks to extreme but plausible fat-tail events.

TABLE 11.1 Sample Scenario Analysis Output

Risk Category	Frequency/Severity Buckets						Total Annual Frequency	Max Single Loss
	$1 to $5m	$5 to $10m	$10 to $20m	$20 to $50m	$50 to $100m	> $100m		
Clients, Products, and Business Practices	5.0(A)	3.0	1.0	0.5	0.2	0.1(B)	9.8(C)	$600m(D)
Execution, Delivery, and Process Management	10.0	5.0	2.0	0.5	0.2	0.1	17.8	$150m
External Fraud	1.0	0.5	0.2	0.1	–	–	1.8	$45m
Internal Fraud	1.0	0.5	0.1	0.1	0.1	0.1	1.9	$1,000m
Damage to Physical Assets	3.0	1.0	1.0	0.5	0.2	0.1	5.8	$100m
Employee Practices and Workplace Safety	5.0	3.0	2.0	1.0	0.5	–	22.5	$75m
Business Disruption and Systems Failures	6.0	4.0	2.0	1.0	–(E)	–	13	$40M

Most operational risks that have a high impact occur as a result of multiple control failings, and the RCSA process can help with the thought processes behind imagining such events. The risk is identified in an RCSA. The controls are scored for effectiveness, and the residual risk assessed. Then the same risk is considered in a situation where all controls fail in order to envisage the fat-tail event.

KEY POINTS

- Firms use scenario analysis to evaluate their exposure to high-severity events by deriving reasoned assessments of plausible severe losses.
- There are several different methods for scenario analysis, including workshops and interviews. A robust scenario analysis process includes:
  - A clearly defined and repeatable process
  - Good-quality background preparation
  - Qualified and experienced facilitators
  - The appropriate quorum of participants
  - A structured process for the selection of data
  - High-quality documentation
  - A robust independent challenge process
  - A process that is responsive to change
  - Bias minimization
- The output from scenario analysis can be used as an input into capital calculations and to inform the firm of potentially catastrophic operational risk losses.

REVIEW QUESTIONS

1. The Basel II definition of scenario analysis requires which of the following elements as part of the process?
   I. Knowledge of experienced business managers
   II. Knowledge of experienced risk management experts
   III. Knowledge of external independent advisers
   IV. Reasoned assessments of plausible severe losses
   a. I, II, and III
   b. I and II only
   c. I, II, and IV only
   d. All of the above

2. During a scenario analysis workshop, a senior manager becomes concerned that an honest but high estimate of plausible losses will reflect badly on her management skills. How might this significantly impact the results? Select the best answer.
   a. The results may reflect a motivational bias.
   b. The results may reflect a judgmental bias.
   c. The results will be unaffected.
   d. The results will reflect the true opinion of the senior manager.

NOTES

1. Bank of International Settlements, Basel Committee on Banking Supervision, "International Convergence of Capital Measurement and Capital Standards: A Revised Framework," Comprehensive Version, 2006, section 675.
2. Bank of International Settlements, Basel Committee on Banking Supervision, "Revision to the Principles for Sound Management of Operational Risk," March 2021, section 35(f), https://www.bis.org/bcbs/publ/d515.htm.
3. Basel Committee on Banking Supervision, "Operational Risk—Supervisory Guidelines for the Advanced Measurement Approaches," June 2011, www.bis .org/publ/bcbs196.pdf, section 254.
4. Ibid., (b).
5. Ibid., (c).
6. Ibid., (d).
7. Ibid., (e).
8. Ibid., (f).
9. Ibid., (g).
10. Ibid., (h).
11. Ibid., (i).
12. Emily Watchorn, "Applying a Structured Approach to Operational Risk Scenario Analysis in Australia," APRA Working Paper, September 2007.

CHAPTER 12

Capital Modeling

In this chapter, we explore the various methods for the calculation of operational risk capital and the challenges faced in adopting the Advanced Measurement Approach. New replacement methods are also considered, as these are scheduled for adoption in coming years. Different capital modeling methods are discussed and compared, and the use and importance of correlation and insurance offsets are considered. Finally, the disclosure requirements are introduced.

While banks are required to hold capital if they are subject to Basel II requirements, fintechs do not have this requirement. Fintechs rely on sponsor banks for the provision of much of their banking services, and those sponsor banks are subject to capital requirements in accordance with their national regulators.

OPERATIONAL RISK CAPITAL

Firms that are required to, or that choose to, calculate operational risk capital can select from several methods.

Basel II originally provided three main approaches to calculating operational risk capital: the Basic Indicator Approach, the Standardized Approach, and the Advanced Measurement Approach (AMA) (see Figure 12.1). These three methods will be considered first as they are still in place at the time of writing and were affirmed in 2019.[1] However, future simplification of the calculation is scheduled for implementation soon and those new approaches are considered later in this chapter.

If an AMA is being used, then the calculation will draw on the underlying elements, as is illustrated in Figure 12.2. If a simpler approach is being used, then the underlying elements need not feed into the model.

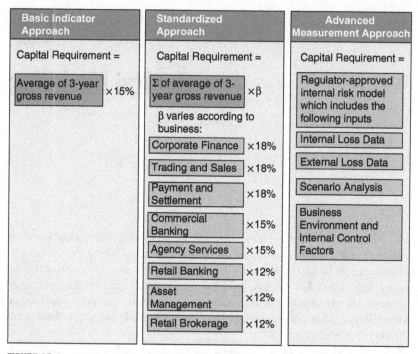

FIGURE 12.1 The Three Basel II Operational Risk Capital Methods

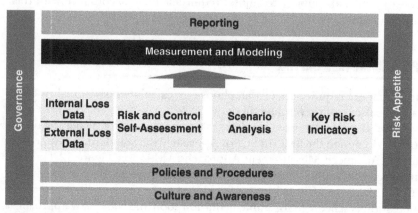

FIGURE 12.2 The Role of Capital Modeling in the Operational Risk Framework

Under the Basel II rules, banks are encouraged to move toward the more sophisticated approaches as they develop their operational risk management tools. Basel II expected international active banks to select either the Standardized or Advanced Measurement Approaches. Many national regulators also brought in mandatory requirements that forced large financial institutions to adopt the Advanced Measurement Approach for operational risk if they wished to be approved for Basel II overall.

Recent analysis of the effectiveness of the advanced methods has led to a change in direction, as is discussed later.

BASIC INDICATOR APPROACH

Under the Basic Indicator Approach (BIA), the capital calculation is arrived at through a simple calculation of the average gross revenue for the past three years, multiplied by 15 percent. The 2019 Bank of International Settlements (BIS) guidance outlines the approach as follows:

Banks using the Basic Indicator Approach must hold capital for operational risk equal to the average over the previous three years of a fixed percentage (denoted alpha) of positive annual gross income. Figures for any year in which annual gross income is negative or zero should be excluded from both the numerator and denominator when calculating the average. The charge may be expressed as follows:[2]

$$K_{BIA} = \left[\left(GI_{1..n} \times \alpha \right) \right] / n$$

where:

K_{BIA} = *the capital charge under the Basic Indicator Approach*

GI = *annual gross income, where positive, over the previous three years*

N = *the number of the previous three years for which gross income is positive*

α = *15 percent, which is set by the Committee, relating the industry-wide level of required capital to the industry-wide level of the indicator*

Gross income is defined as net interest income plus net noninterest income.[3]

Firms that used this approach were still encouraged to adopt all of the risk management elements that are outlined in the "Sound Practices"[4] document. Therefore, even though loss data, RCSA, scenario analysis, and business environment internal control factors (BEICF) are not needed for the capital calculation, they are needed as part of the operational risk framework to ensure that the firm can adequately identify, assess, monitor, and mitigate operational risk as required in the "Sound Practices" document.

If a bank has negative or zero income for any of the three years, then BIA instructs them to remove those years from both the numerator and denominator when calculation the average revenue.

EXAMPLE

Alpha Bank has the following revenue results from the past three years:

	Year One	Year Two	Year Three
Annual Gross Revenue (in $100m)	15	20	25

To calculate the BIA capital charge $K_{BIA} = \left[\left(GI_{1..n} \times \alpha \right) \right] / n$ we insert the values

$$GI = \left(15 + 20 + 25 \right)$$
$$N = 3$$
$$\alpha = 15\%$$

As follows:

$$K_{BIA} = \frac{\left[\left(60 \times 0.15 \right) \right]}{3}$$

To give a result:

$$K_{BIA} = 3$$

Therefore, Alpha Bank must hold $300 million operational risk capital under Basel II using the Basic Indicator Approach.

EXAMPLE

Alpha Bank has the following revenue results from the past three years:

	Year One	Year Two	Year Three
Annual Gross Revenue (in $100m)	15	–20	25

To calculate the BIA capital charge $K_{BIA} = \left[\left(GI_{1.n} \times \alpha \right) \right] / n$ we insert the values

$$GI = (15 + 25)[\text{year two is not counted}]$$
$$N = 2[\text{year two is not counted}]$$
$$\alpha = 15\%$$

As follows:

$$K_{BIA} = \frac{\left[(40 \times 0.15) \right]}{2}$$

To give a result:

$$K_{BIA} = 3$$

Therefore, Alpha Bank would still hold $300 million operational risk capital under Basel II using the basic indicator approach even though it experienced negative revenue in year two.

The Basic Indicator Approach to capital is certainly simple to adopt but does little to reflect the operational risk in a firm, as it uses only revenue as a driver. A firm that has very strong controls will have the same operational risk requirements as a firm with very poor controls if they have had the same average revenue over the past three years.

Furthermore, a firm will enjoy much lower operational risk capital requirements in years when it is producing lower revenue, even if its controls have not changed at all.

STANDARDIZED APPROACH

The Standardized Approach (TSA) originally provided under Basel II is similar to the Basic Indicator Approach, except that different business lines have different multipliers. The Standardized Approach attempts to capture operational risk factors that are missing in the Basic Indicator Approach by assuming that different types of business activities carry different levels of operational risk. Sales and trading is riskier than retail brokerage, for example. The 2019 BIS guidance puts it thus:

> *Within each business line, gross income is a broad indicator that serves as a proxy for the scale of business operations and thus the likely scale of operational risk exposure within each of these business lines.*[5]

As a result, although the calculation method is the same, the multiplier used varies according to the business line. This will result in several separate calculations that are then brought together for the total operational risk capital.

> *The total capital requirement is calculated as the three-year average of the simple summation of the regulatory capital requirements across each of the business lines in each year. In any given year, negative capital charges (resulting from negative gross income) in any business line may offset positive capital charges in other business lines without limit.*

> *However, where the aggregate capital charge across all business lines within a given year is negative, then the input to the numerator for that year will be zero. The total capital charge may be expressed as:*

$$K_{TSA} = \left\{ \sum_{\text{years } 1-3} \max\left[\Sigma(GI_{1-8} \times \beta_{1-8}), 0 \right] \right\} / 3$$

where:

K_{TSA} = *the capital charge under the standardized approach*

GI_{1-8} = *annual gross income in a given year, as defined above in the basic indicator approach, for each of the eight business lines*

β_{1-8} = *a fixed percentage, set by the Committee, relating the level of required capital to the level of the gross income for each of the eight business lines. The values of the betas are detailed below.*[6]

Business Lines	Beta Factors
Corporate finance (β_1)	18%
Trading and sales (β_2)	18%
Retail banking (β_3)	12%
Commercial banking (β_4)	15%
Payment and settlement (β_5)	18%
Agency services (β_6)	15%
Asset management (β_7)	12%
Retail brokerage (β_8)	12%

The TSA calculation of operational risk capital is no more difficult than the BIA, but it does have significantly more steps, as a calculation must be made for all business lines in order to produce the final capital result.

In the following example, Beta Bank has only three lines of business and is using the TSA calculation method for its operational risk capital.

EXAMPLE

Beta Bank has the following revenue in $100 million for the past three years for its three lines of business: trading and sales, commercial banking, and asset management.

	Year One	Year Two	Year Three
Trading and sales	15	20	25
Commercial banking	10	5	10
Asset management	5	5	5

To calculate the TSA capital charge

$$K_{TSA} = \frac{\left\{\sum_{\text{years }1-3} \max\left[\sum(GI_{1-8} \times \beta_{1-8}), 0\right]\right\}}{3}$$ we insert the appropriate β values:

	Year One	Year Two	Year Three
Trading and sales	$15 \times 18\% = 2.7$	$20 \times 18\% = 3.6$	$25 \times 18\% = 4.5$
Commercial banking	$10 \times 15\% = 1.5$	$5 \times 15\% = 0.75$	$10 \times 15\% = 1.5$
Asset management	$5 \times 12\% = 0.6$	$5 \times 12\% = 0.6$	$5 \times 12\% = 0.6$
Total	4.8	4.95	6.6

(continued)

(continued)

Entering these totals into the TSA calculation:

$$K_{TSA} = \frac{\{4.8 + 4.95 + 6.6\}}{3}$$

To give a result:

$$K_{TSA} = 5.45$$

Therefore, Beta Bank would hold $545 million operational risk capital under Basel II using the Standardized Approach.

If there is negative or zero income during one of the three prior years, TSA takes a different treatment approach than that used in the BIA. In the BIA, any years that have negative or zero income are removed from both the denominator and the numerator. However, under TSA:

> *In any given year, negative capital charges (resulting from negative gross income) in any business line may offset positive capital charges in other business lines without limit. However, where the aggregate capital charge across all business lines within a given year is negative, then the input to the numerator for that year will be zero.*[7]

Note that the denominator in TSA is set at 3.

EXAMPLE

If Beta Bank has negative revenue in any business line, then that can offset the capital charges for that year up to a maximum benefit of zero capital (no negative capital is permitted for a year).

Beta Bank has the following revenue in $100 million for the past three years for its two lines of business, corporate finance, and retail banking.

	Year One	Year Two	Year Three
Corporate finance	10	20	30
Retail banking	5	−25	−55

To calculate the TSA capital charge

$$K_{TSA} = \frac{\left\{\sum_{\text{years}1-3} \max\left[\Sigma(GI_{1-8} \times \beta_{1-8}), 0\right]\right\}}{3}$$ we insert the appropriate

β values:

	Year One	Year Two	Year Three
Corporate finance	$10 \times 18\% = 1.8$	$20 \times 18\% = 3.6$	$30 \times 18\% = 5.4$
Retail banking	$5 \times 12\% = 0.6$	$-25 \times 12\% = -0.3$	$-55 \times 12\% = -6.6$
Total	2.4	0.6	−1.2

Because a negative number must not be entered into the calculation, we replace −1.2 in year three with zero. Entering these totals into the TSA calculation:

$$K_{TSA} = \frac{\{2.4 + 0.6 + 0\}}{3}$$

To give a result:

$$K_{TSA} = 1$$

Therefore, Beta Bank would hold $100 million operational risk capital under Basel II using the Standardized Approach.

Alternative Standardized Approach

Basel II allowed a national regulator to permit a bank to use an Alternative Standardized Approach (ASA) provided "the bank is able to satisfy its supervisor that this alternative approach provides an improved basis by, for example, avoiding double counting of risks."[8]

Under the ASA, the operational risk capital charge/methodology is the same as for the Standardized Approach except for two business lines—retail banking and commercial banking. For these business lines, loans and advances—multiplied by a fixed factor "m"—replaces gross income as the exposure indicator . . .

The ASA operational risk capital requirement for retail bank-
ing (with the same basic formula for commercial banking) can be
expressed as:

$$K_{RB} = \beta_{RB} \times m \times LA_{RB}$$

where:

K_{RB} = *the capital charge for the retail banking business line*
β_{RB} = *the beta for the retail banking business line*
LA_{RB} = *total outstanding retail loans and advances (non-risk-*
weighted and gross of provisions), averaged over the past
three years
m = *0.035*

For the purposes of the ASA, total loans and advances in the retail
banking business line consist of the total drawn amounts in the follow-
ing credit portfolios: retail, SMEs treated as retail, and purchased retail
receivables. For commercial banking, total loans and advances consist
of the drawn amounts in the following credit portfolios: corporate,
sovereign, bank, specialized lending, SMEs treated as corporate and
purchased corporate receivables. The book value of securities held in
the banking book should also be included.

Under the ASA, banks may aggregate retail and commercial banking
(if they wish to) using a beta of 15 percent.
Similarly, those banks that are unable to disaggregate their gross
income into the other six business lines can aggregate the total gross
income for these six business lines using a beta of 18 percent, with
negative gross income treated as described in paragraphs OPE25.3
and OPE25.4.

As under the Standardized Approach, the total capital requirement
for the ASA is calculated as the simple summation of the regulatory
capital charges across each of the eight business lines.[9]

Future of the Basic and Standardized Approaches

The BIA and TSA methodologies can produce an unanticipated result as is
demonstrated in the following example.

EXAMPLE

In the prior example Beta Bank had the following revenue in $100 million:

	Year One	Year Two	Year Three
Corporate finance	10	20	30
Retail banking	5	–25	–55
Total	15	–5	–25

This resulted in a TSA capital charge of $100 million.

If Beta Bank was calculating its capital under the BIA approach to calculate the BIA capital charge $K_{BIA} = \left[\left(GI_{1.n} \times \alpha \right) \right] / n$ we insert the values

$$GI = 15$$
$$N = 1$$

[Years two and three are not counted in the nominator or denominator as they have negative total income.]

$$\alpha = 15\%$$

As follows:

$$K_{BIA} = \frac{[15 \times 0.15]}{1}$$

To give a result:

$$K_{BIA} = 2.25$$

Therefore, Beta Bank would hold $100 million operational risk capital under Basel II using the Standardized Approach, but $225 million under the Basic Indicator Approach.

This was likely not the intent of the Basel Committee, and they recognized that making allowances for negative income might produce an inappropriate result.

> *If negative gross income distorts a bank's Pillar 1 capital requirement . . . supervisors will consider appropriate supervisory action under Pillar 2.*[10]

Therefore, if the use of negative income offsets produces an unpalatable or inappropriate result, then a bank may see its regulators adding on capital under the Pillar 2 requirements of Basel II. As discussed in Chapter 2, Pillar 2 provides a mechanism for additional capital requirements to cover any material risks that have not been effectively captured in Pillar 1.

The revised Standardized Approach that is discussed later in this chapter also addresses this issue.

ADVANCED MEASUREMENT APPROACH

The Advanced Measurement Approach (AMA) allowed a bank to design its own model for calculating operational risk capital. The Basel Committee recognized that they were allowing significant flexibility for the design of the AMA capital model and established prerequisites for its use as follows:

General Standards for Using the AMA

> *In order to qualify for use of the AMA a bank must satisfy its supervisor that, at a minimum:*
>   *Its board of directors and senior management, as appropriate, are actively involved in the oversight of the operational risk management framework;*
>   *It has an operational risk management system that is conceptually sound and is implemented with integrity; and*
>   *It has sufficient resources in the use of the approach in the major business lines as well as the control and audit areas.*[11]

In addition, a bank's regulator must monitor the proposed AMA to ensure that it is appropriate before it can be relied upon for the calculation of capital:

> *A bank's AMA will be subject to a period of initial monitoring by its supervisor before it can be used for regulatory purposes. This period will allow the supervisor to determine whether the approach is credible and appropriate.*[12]

The four elements of the framework—internal loss data, external loss data, scenario analysis, and business environment internal control factors—must be included in the model.

> *As discussed below, a bank's internal measurement system must reasonably estimate unexpected losses based on the combined use of internal and relevant external loss data, scenario analysis and bank-specific business environment and internal control factors.*[13]

The final prerequisite is that there must be an appropriate method for allocating the capital to the businesses to incent good behavior.

> *The bank's measurement system must also be capable of supporting an allocation of economic capital for operational risk across business lines in a manner that creates incentives to improve business line operational risk management.*[14]

Quantitative Requirements of an AMA Model

Once the prerequisites have been met, there are several quantitative requirements that must be adhered to for an AMA model.

One Year and 99.9 Percent

The first requirement is that the model must hold capital for a one-year horizon at 99.9 percent confidence level. In other words, the capital held must be sufficient to cover all operational risk losses in one year with a certainty of 99.9 percent.

This is the equivalent of asking for a bank to hold operational risk capital that will protect it from a 1-in-1,000-year fat-tail event.

> *Given the continuing evolution of analytical approaches for operational risk, the Committee is not specifying the approach or distributional assumptions used to generate the operational risk measure for regulatory capital purposes. However, a bank must be able to demonstrate that its approach captures potentially severe "tail" loss events. Whatever approach is used, a bank must demonstrate that its operational risk measure meets a soundness standard comparable to that of the internal ratings-based approach for credit risk (i.e., comparable to a one year holding period and a 99.9th percentile confidence interval).*[15]

Model Governance

The second requirement is that the model must be subject to full model governance.

> *In the development of operational risk measurement and management systems, banks must have and maintain rigorous procedures for operational risk model development and independent model validation.*[16]

Model Design

The third requirement concerns the design of the AMA model and several stipulations that must be met.

The first stipulation is that the model must represent the operational risk framework as outlined in Basel II and supporting guidance.

> *Any internal operational risk measurement system must be consistent with the scope of operational risk defined in OPE10.1 and the loss event types defined in Table 1.*[17]

In effect, this means that calculations should be made for all seven risk categories. Some firms calculate capital at the top of the firm and then allocate operational risk capital down into the business lines. Others calculate capital at the business line. Table 12.1 shows a matrix for capital calculations using the Basel business lines. However, a firm might have different headings in the first column to better represent their own business line structure.

The second stipulation is that the model must capture all expected and unexpected losses and may only exclude expected losses under certain strict criteria.

> *Supervisors will require the bank to calculate its regulatory capital requirement as the sum of expected loss (EL) and unexpected loss (UL), unless the bank can demonstrate that it is adequately capturing EL in its internal business practices. That is, to base the minimum regulatory capital requirement on UL alone, the bank must be able to demonstrate to the satisfaction of its national supervisor that it has measured and accounted for its EL exposure.*[18]

The third stipulation is that the model must provide sufficient detail and granularity to ensure that fat-tail events are captured.

TABLE 12.1 Example Capital Calculation Matrix

	Internal Fraud	External Fraud	Clients, Products, and Business Practices	Execution, Delivery, and Process Management	Employment Practices and Workplace Safety	Damage to Physical Assets	Business Disruption and System Failures
Corporate Finance							
Trading and Sales							
Retail Banking							
Commercial Banking							
Payment and Settlement							
Agency and Custody							
Retail Brokerage							
Asset Management							

A bank's risk measurement system must be sufficiently "granular" to capture the major drivers of operational risk affecting the shape of the tail of the loss estimates.[19]

The fourth stipulation is that the bank must sum all calculated cells or defend any correlation assumptions that are made in its AMA model.

Risk measures for different operational risk estimates must be added for purposes of calculating the regulatory minimum capital requirement. However, the bank may be permitted to use internally determined correlations in operational risk losses across individual operational risk estimates, provided it can demonstrate to the satisfaction of the national supervisor that its systems for determining correlations are sound, implemented with integrity, and take into account the uncertainty surrounding any such correlation estimates (particularly in periods of stress). The bank must validate its correlation assumptions using appropriate quantitative and qualitative techniques.[20]

The fifth stipulation simply reinforces the requirement that all four elements must be in the model.

Any operational risk measurement system must have certain key features to meet the supervisory soundness standard set out in this section. These elements must include the use of internal data, relevant external data, scenario analysis and factors reflecting the business environment and internal control systems.[21]

Finally, the bank must weight these four elements appropriately.

A bank needs to have a credible, transparent, well-documented and verifiable approach for weighting these fundamental elements in its overall operational risk measurement system.[22]

The Basel rules also provide many qualitative requirements that must be met in order for a bank to qualify for an AMA model for Basel II. Many of these have been discussed in prior chapters, for example the rules regarding the collection and use of loss data, the challenges of scenario analysis, and the use of BEICF from RCSA and KRI elements in the operational risk framework.

While the four elements must be considered in the capital calculation methodology, many banks use some of these elements to allocate capital, to stress-test their models, or to adjust their models rather than using them to provide direct inputs into the capital calculation. Regulators have accepted many different models for AMA and the modeling of operational risk capital is developing rapidly as different approaches are tried and tested by the banking industry.

Many firms, however, spent many years wrestling with building and receiving approval for their AMA models, and the most recent guidance has removed the AMA option. At the time of this writing, this sunsetting of the AMA model was to occur in 2023, but that date has been moved out several times.

As a result, the AMA is still currently a viable approach to calculating operational risk capital under existing Basel II rules and so we will consider some of the modeling options that are available below.

Loss Distribution Approach to Modeling Operational Risk Capital

A loss distribution approach (LDA) model relies on internal losses as the mainstay of its design. A simple LDA model uses only internal losses as direct inputs into the model and uses the remaining three elements for stressing or allocation purposes.

A bank must have at least three years of loss data to put into its AMA model, regardless of design, as the data may be rich enough to form the basis of a capital model.

> *Internally generated operational risk measures used for regulatory capital purposes must be based on a minimum five-year observation period of internal loss data, whether the internal loss data is used directly to build the loss measure or to validate it. When the bank first moves to the AMA, a three-year historical data window is acceptable.*[23]

Despite this stipulation, regulators leaned toward requiring all available data to be included, even beyond the five-year requirement. In their 2011 AMA Guidelines, the Basel Committee noted:

> *The Basel II Framework requires banks to base their internally generated operational risk measures on a minimum historical observation period of five years (three years when an institution first moves to an AMA). For certain ORCs with low frequency of events, an observation period greater than five years may be necessary to collect sufficient data to generate reliable operational risk measures and ensure that all material losses are included in the calculation dataset.*[24]

The advantage of a loss distribution approach is that the model is based on real historical data that is relevant to the firm.

The disadvantage of a loss distribution approach is that the period of data collection is likely to be relatively short, and so may not have captured the fat-tail events that the capital calculation is supposed to protect the firm from. It certainly will not contain 1,000 years of data, and yet the model is supposed to provide a 99.9 percent confidence level. Some firms also find that they have insufficient loss data on which to build a model even if they have more than five years of data.

In addition, historical data does not necessarily reflect the future. The firm may have changed its products, processes, and controls.

Although there is a wide range of AMA modeling practices, even within the LDA approach, there are some standard methods that are worthy of discussion.

Step 1: Modeling Frequency

In order to develop a model of expected operational risk losses, the first step is to determine the likely number of events per year. This is the frequency of events.

The most popular distribution selection for modeling frequency is the Poisson distribution. This allows for a fairly simple approach to modeling frequency. In a Poisson distribution, there is only a single parameter (λ), which represents the average number of events in a given year. Both the mean and the variance are represented by this single parameter in a Poisson distribution. In more complex cases, a negative binomial distribution may be used, which allows for different values for the mean and variance.

The Poisson distribution works well for a situation where there is a whole number of events and where the probability in one time period is the same as in another time period. The Poisson distribution is built from the use of the average number of events using the following formula.

$$f(n) = \frac{\lambda^N e^{-\lambda}}{n!}$$

where:

$n = 0, 1, 2, \dots$
λ = average number of events in a year

In an LDA model, λ can be obtained simply by observing the number of events per year in the internal loss data history and calculating the average.

EXAMPLE

Lambda Bank has been gathering loss data for the past seven years and has observed the following number of events each year.

Year	1	2	3	4	5	6	7
# of loss events	746	810	765	940	780	695	850

$$\lambda = (746 + 810 + 765 + 940 + 780 + 695 + 850) / 7 = 798$$

The Poisson distribution that is derived from this approach represents the probability of a certain number of events occurring in a single year. As can be seen in Figure 12.3, lower lambdas produce more skewed and leptokurtic[25] annual loss distributions than higher lambdas.

Step 2: Modeling Severity

The next step in modeling expected operational risk losses is to determine the likely size of an event given the fact that an event has occurred. This is the severity of an event.

Unlike frequency, severity need not be an integer but can fall anywhere along a continuum. When a loss occurs, it might be $1.50, or it might be $133,892.25 or any other value. The severity distribution establishes the

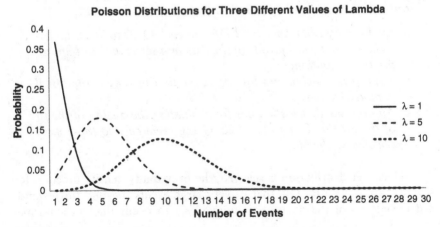

FIGURE 12.3 Comparing Three Different Poisson Distributions

probability of an event occurring over a wide range of values, from zero to very, very large losses.

The most common and least complex approach to modeling severity is to use a lognormal distribution, although low-frequency losses may fit better to other options such as Generalized Gamma, Transformed Beta, Generalized Pareto, or Weibull. Regulators take a keen interest in how well the selected distribution demonstrates "goodness of fit"—or in other words, how certain you are that the sample comes from the population with the claimed distribution. When selecting which approach to use, the AMA guidelines also provide the following guidance (emphasis added):

> *The selection of probability distributions should be consistent with all elements of the AMA model. In addition to statistical goodness of fit, Dutta and Perry (2007) have proposed the following criteria for assessing a model's suitability:*
>
> - *realistic (e.g., it generates a loss distribution with a realistic capital requirements estimate, without the need to implement "corrective adjustments" such as caps),*
> - *well specified (e.g., the characteristics of the fitted data are similar to the loss data and logically consistent),*
> - *flexible (e.g., the method is able to reasonably accommodate a wide variety of empirical data) and*
> - *simple (e.g., it is easy to implement and it is easy to generate random numbers for the purpose of loss simulation).*
>
> *The process of selecting the probability distribution should be well-documented, verifiable and lead to a clear and consistent choice. To this end, a bank should generally adhere to the following:*
>
> *a. Exploratory Data Analysis (EDA) for each ORC to better understand the statistical profile of the data and select the most appropriate distribution;*
> *b. Appropriate techniques for the estimation of the distributional parameters; and*
> *c. Appropriate diagnostic tools for evaluating the quality of the fit of the distributions to the data, giving preference to those most sensitive to the tail.*[26]

Whichever distribution is selected, the probability density function for severity will have a fat tail, that is, very large events (beyond three standard deviations of the mean) are more likely to occur than in a normal

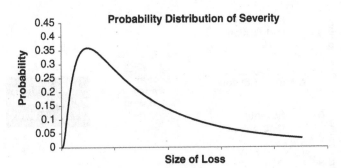

FIGURE 12.4 The Severity Probability Distribution

distribution. It will also be skewed to the right, as can be seen in the example in Figure 12.4.

Step 3: Monte Carlo Simulation

Once the frequency and severity distributions have been established, the next step is to use these distributions to generate many more data points in order to better estimate the capital needed to ensure with 99.9 percent certainty that likely losses for the next year are covered by appropriate capital.

Monte Carlo simulation provides a method by which frequency and severity distributions can be combined to produce many more data points that have the same characteristics as the observed data points. Excel can handle this process using built-in functionality, but often much more powerful statistical modeling tools are used.

First, a data point is selected from the frequency distribution. This gives us the number of events that are predicted to occur in year one. Values nearer the mean of the frequency distribution will be selected more often than values far from the mean. In this example, let us say that the number 50 is selected. Therefore, in year one the model assumes there were 50 events.

Next, the size of each of those 50 events is selected from the severity distribution. Again, values with a higher probability in the severity distribution will be selected more often than values with a lower probability. This will produce 50 losses for year one.

The value of all 50 losses is then added together to give the total value of losses for year one.

This process is repeated for year two, and then over and over again, a million times, thus giving the modeler many additional years of representative data. The data is then placed in size order, the largest total year loss, to the smallest total year loss.

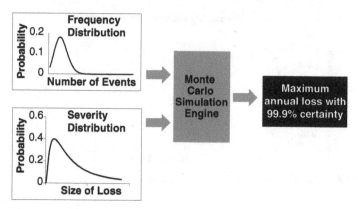

FIGURE 12.5   Using Monte Carlo Simulation

Finding the 99.9 percent confidence level is simply a case of selecting the one thousandth item in the ordered list. That value represents, with 99.9 percent certainty, the maximum loss that will be experienced in a single year.

This process is represented in Figure 12.5.

Correlation

Once all of the cells of the operational risk capital matrix have been populated, with a calculated capital amount for each risk category, and possibly also for every business line, then all of the cells must be simply added together to produce the total capital required. However, firms can take advantage of correlation assumptions between cells if these assumptions can be defended.

> *Risk measures for different operational risk estimates must be added for purposes of calculating the regulatory minimum capital requirement. However, the bank may be permitted to use internally determined correlations in operational risk losses across individual operational risk estimates, provided it can demonstrate to the satisfaction of the national supervisor that its systems for determining correlations are sound, implemented with integrity, and take into account the uncertainty surrounding any such correlation estimates (particularly in periods of stress). The bank must validate its correlation assumptions using appropriate quantitative and qualitative techniques.*[27]

Some firms have found the ORX data useful for this purpose. ORX data contains loss data for all risk categories for all firms that are consortium members. If a correlation matrix can be established for that large pool of data it might be possible to use those same assumptions for the internal AMA model of a member firm. With no correlation assumptions, the additive nature of the model can produce very high capital results. As a result there is an enormous amount of work (internally and with consulting firms) currently under way in the industry, as firms attempt to better support correlation assumptions for use in operational risk capital modeling.

Scenario Analysis Approach to Modeling Operational Risk Capital

A pure scenario analysis approach to modeling uses only scenario analysis data in the model. The other three required elements are used for stress testing, validation, or allocation.

Scenario analysis data is designed to identify fat-tail events, and therefore may provide rich data for the calculation of appropriate operational risk capital.

One of the advantages of a scenario analysis approach is that the data reflects the future as it is captured in a process that is designed to consider "what if" scenarios. In contrast, an LDA approach is only considering the past.

One of the major disadvantages of a scenario analysis approach is that the data is highly subjective, as it has probably been gathered in an interview or workshop estimation exercise. Also, scenario analysis produces only a few data points and so complex techniques have to be applied to model the data into a full distribution.

While the same methods for frequency and severity distributions and Monte Carlo simulations might be used as in the LDA approach described earlier, the lack of data in scenario analysis output can make the fitting of distributions particularly troublesome. A small change in assumptions can lead to very different results, and therefore the defense of all assumptions must be particularly robust in a scenario analysis approach.

The data for use in the model may look similar to the output example in Chapter 11 and shown again in Table 12.2, or it might be a simple series of maximum loss amounts per risk category, or per scenario.

There are many possible outputs from the many different scenario approaches in use. Whatever scenario analysis method is used, there will likely be a paucity of data points, and so a pure scenario analysis approach can be difficult to defend. Indeed, although some scenario-based models may have been approved in Europe, they are generally frowned upon by the regulators in the United States.

Certainly, the more reliance there is on scenario analysis, the more robust the scenario analysis program must be.

TABLE 12.2 Sample Scenario Analysis Output

Risk Category	Frequency/Severity Buckets						Total Annual Frequency	Max Single Loss
	$1 to $5m	$5 to $10m	$10 to $20m	$20 to $50m	$50 to $100m	> $100m		
Clients, Products, and Business Practices	5.0(A)	3.0	1.0	0.5	0.2	0.1(B)	9.8(C)	$600m(D)
Execution, Delivery, and Process Management	10.0	5.0	2.0	0.5	0.2	0.1	17.8	$150m
External Fraud	1.0	0.5	0.2	0.1	–	–	1.8	$45m
Internal Fraud	1.0	0.5	0.1	0.1	0.1	0.1	1.9	$1,000m
Damage to Physical Assets	3.0	1.0	1.0	0.5	0.2	0.1	5.8	$100m
Employee Practices and Workplace Safety	5.0	3.0	2.0	1.0	0.5	–	22.5	$75m
Business Disruption and Systems Failures	6.0	4.0	2.0	1.0	–(E)	–	13	$40m

There may well be cells in the model that rely on a pure scenario analysis model simply because there is little or no loss data available in that cell. It is acceptable to have different modeling techniques in different cells of the model as long as the differences are justified.

Hybrid Approach to Modeling Operational Risk Capital

Many firms have some version of a hybrid approach. In a hybrid approach, the loss data and scenario analysis output are both used to calculate appropriate operational risk capital.

Some firms combine the LDA and scenario analysis approaches by stitching together two distributions, for example, by using LDA for the left end of the distribution, or the expected losses, and scenario analysis for the right end of the distribution, or the fat-tail and unexpected losses. Some firms develop a LDA model and then use scenario analysis to stress the model to produce a more appropriate distribution. Some firms add their scenario analysis data points into their loss data and develop their frequency and severity distributions from the combined data pool.

In a hybrid approach, the advantages and disadvantages of both approaches are present.

INSURANCE

Businesses will often argue that they are not exposed to operational risk in certain risk categories or scenarios because they carry insurance against just such risks arising. However, insurance payments can be slow and contentious and therefore Basel II does not allow for insurance to be used to reduce the gross amount of the loss, except under very narrow circumstances.

Under the AMA, a bank will be allowed to recognize the risk-mitigating impact of insurance in the measures of operational risk used for regulatory minimum capital requirements, but only if specific, fairly onerous, criteria are met.

The recognition of insurance mitigation is limited to 20 percent of the total operational risk capital charge calculated under the AMA.

The qualifying criteria are as follows:

A bank's ability to take advantage of such risk mitigation will depend on compliance with the following criteria:

The insurance provider has a minimum claims paying ability rating of A (or equivalent).

- *The insurance policy must have an initial term of no less than one year. For policies with a residual term of less than one year, the bank must make appropriate haircuts reflecting the declining residual term of the policy, up to a full 100% haircut for policies with a residual term of 90 days or less.*
- *The insurance policy has a minimum notice period for cancellation of 90 days.*
- *The insurance policy has no exclusions or limitations triggered by supervisory actions or, in the case of a failed bank, that preclude the bank, receiver or liquidator from recovering for damages suffered or expenses incurred by the bank, except in respect of events occurring after the initiation of receivership or liquidation proceedings in respect of the bank, provided that the insurance policy may exclude any fine, penalty, or punitive damages resulting from supervisory actions.*
- *The risk mitigation calculations must reflect the bank's insurance coverage in a manner that is transparent in its relationship to, and consistent with, the actual likelihood and impact of loss used in the bank's overall determination of its operational risk capital.*
- *The insurance is provided by a third-party entity. In the case of insurance through captives and affiliates, the exposure has to be laid off to an independent third-party entity, for example through re-insurance, that meets the eligibility criteria.*
- *The framework for recognizing insurance is well reasoned and documented.*
- *The bank discloses a description of its use of insurance for the purpose of mitigating operational risk.*

A bank's methodology for recognizing insurance under the AMA also needs to capture the following elements through appropriate discounts or haircuts in the amount of insurance recognition:

- *The residual term of a policy, where less than one year, as noted above;*
- *A policy's cancellation terms, where less than one year; and*
- *The uncertainty of payment as well as mismatches in coverage of insurance policies.*[28]

Operational risk capital may run into many billions of dollars, so it is certainly worth pursuing a 20 percent reduction in that amount, and many firms have explored how best to take advantage of this opportunity. At the same time, many insurance companies are looking to produce insurance products that can meet the many criteria required. In the disclosure examples later in this chapter, firms have outlined their approach to the use of insurance to lower their operational risk capital requirements.

FUTURE OF CAPITAL REQUIREMENTS: BASEL III

Basel II regulators around the world have accepted all types of modeling approaches in AMA banks to date and the Basel Committee commented in their 2011 AMA Guidelines document on the wide range of practice that they had observed. In developing the Basel III capital requirements for operational risk, the Bank of International Settlements (BIS) noted that the AMA had not provided sufficient capital coverage for the economic crisis that occurred in 2008.

BIS's choice of values for alpha and beta in BIA and TSA were made with little supporting data, and the Basel Committee reviewed the assumptions that were made when those values were selected. This was always their intention and was clearly stated in Basel II.

> *The Committee intends to reconsider the calibration of the Basic Indicator and Standardized Approaches when more risk-sensitive data are available to carry out this recalibration. Any such recalibration would not be intended to affect significantly the overall calibration of the operational risk component of the Pillar 1 capital charge.*[29]

This reconsideration occurred in 2011–2012, and it was generally expected that the alpha and beta values had not stood up to testing now that data was available on business line operational risk losses.

In addition to questions being raised about the alpha and beta values of the BIA and TSA, there have been concerns raised about the range of practice found in the implementation of AMA calculations. In Basel II, the Basel Committee stated:

> *Supervisors will review the capital requirement produced by the operational risk approach used by a bank (whether Basic Indicator Approach, Standardized Approach or AMA) for general credibility, especially in relation to a firm's peers. In the event that credibility is lacking, appropriate supervisory action under Pillar 2 will be considered.*[29]

The review of the effectiveness of the operational risk capital approaches led eventually to the introduction of Basel III requirements for operational risk capital. This new approach was introduced in 2017 and required the sunsetting of the use of AMA, replacing it with a simplified Standardized Approach.

Therefore, while the industry continued to refine their AMA models, the rules have now changed and, at the time of this writing, the new approach must be adopted by January 2023.

Basel III Standardized Approach

In 2017, BCBS issued new guidance in "Finalizing Post-Crisis Reforms," as follows:

> *The standardised approach for measuring minimum operational risk capital requirements replaces all existing approaches in the Basel II framework. That is, this standard replaces paragraphs 644 to 683 of the Basel II framework.*
>
> *The standardised approach methodology is based on the following components:*
>
> i. *the Business Indicator (BI) which is a financial-statement-based proxy for operational risk;*
> ii. *the Business Indicator Component (BIC), which is calculated by multiplying the BI by a set of regulatory determined marginal coefficients (αi); and*
> iii. *the Internal Loss Multiplier (ILM), which is a scaling factor that is based on a bank's average historical losses and the BIC.*[30]

The new Standardized Approach disallows the use of an internal model that is derived from the four elements that make up the AMA approach and instead relies only on the internal loss experience of the firm and its business lines. The use of the other elements—external loss data, scenario analysis, and business environment internal control factors—as direct inputs to the model is no longer permissible once the new requirements go into effect (2023 at the time of this writing). However, the guidance regarding the sound principles of operational risk management still stand and so those elements are still required for the purposes of demonstrating effective operational risk management.

The calculation of the new Standardized Approach is as follows:

$$OTC = BIC \times ILM$$

where:

OTC = operational risk capital
BIC = business indicator component
ILM = internal loss multiplier

Banks that have a BI of €1 billion or less have a simplified requirement for capital and are required to hold capital that is equal to their business indicator component (BIC), with no adjustment for the internal loss multiplier (ILM). This allows smaller banks to avoid the strict requirements for internal loss data collection that are required for the inclusion of the ILM in the calculation.

The BIC is calculated from the business indicator.

The Business Indicator BI

The first building block of the new Standardized Approach is the business indicator (BI). As stated earlier, the BI is a financial-statement-based proxy for operational risk.

The BI comprises three components: the interest, leases, and dividend component (ILDC); the services component (SC); and the financial component (FC).

The BI is calculated as follows:

$$BI = ILDC + SC + FC\,^{31}$$

The three factors that make up the BI are derived as outlined below. First, the ILDC is derived as follows:

$$ILDC = Min\left[ABSII(II - IE); 2.25 * IEA\right] + DI$$

where:

II = Average interest income over the prior three years
IE = Average interest expense over the prior three years
IEA = Average interest-earning assets over the prior three years
DI = Average dividend interest over the prior three years

Secondly, the services component (SC) is derived as follows:

$$SC = Max[OOI; OOE] + Max[FI; FE]$$

where:

OOI = Average other operating Income over the prior three years
OOE = Average other operating expense over the prior three years
FI = Average fee income over the prior three years
FE = Average fee expense over the prior three years

Finally, the financial component (FC) is derived as follows:

$$FC = Abs\left(Net\ PLTB\right] + Abs\left(Net\ PLBB\right)$$

where:

$Net\ PLTB$ = Average net P&L trading book over the prior three years
$Net\ PLBB$ = Average net P&L banking book over the prior
                  three years

The definitions of what makes up each of these indicators is outlined in the annex of the latest Basel guidance, as shown in Table 12.3.

Business Indicator Component: BIC

The next step in the new Standardized Approach calculation is to derive the BIC from the BIs as follows:

To calculate the BIC, the BI is multiplied by the marginal coefficients (αi). The marginal coefficients increase with the size of the BI as shown in Table 1. For banks in the first bucket (i.e. with a BI less than or equal to €1bn) the BIC is equal to BI × 12%. The marginal increase in the BIC resulting from a one unit increase in the BI is 12% in bucket 1, 15% in bucket 2 and 18% in bucket 3. For example, given a BI = €35bn, the BIC = (1 × 12%) + (30 − 1) × 15% + (35 − 30) × 18% = €5.37bn.[32]

Table 1 BI Ranges and Marginal Coefficients

Bucket	BI Range (in €bn)	BI Marginal Coefficients (α_i)
1	≤1	12%
2	1 < BI ≤ 30	15%
3	> 30	18%

TABLE 12.3 Definitions of the Business Indicator Component

BI Component	P&L or Balance Sheet Items	Description	Typical Subitems
Interest, lease, and dividend	Interest income	Interest income from all financial assets and other interest income (includes interest income from financial and operating leases and profits from leased assets)	■ Interest income from loans and advances, assets available for sale, assets held to maturity, trading assets, financial leases, and operational leases ■ Interest income from hedge accounting derivatives ■ Other interest income ■ Profits from leased assets
	Interest expenses	Interest expenses from all financial liabilities and other interest expenses (includes interest expense from financial and operating leases, losses, depreciation, and impairment of operating leased assets)	■ Interest expenses from deposits, debt securities issued, financial leases, and operating leases ■ Interest expenses from hedge accounting derivatives ■ Other interest expenses ■ Losses from leased assets ■ Depreciation and impairment of operating leased assets
	Interest-earning assets (balance sheet item)	Total gross outstanding loans, advances, interest bearing securities (including government bonds), and lease assets measured at the end of each financial year	
	Dividend income	Dividend income from investments in stocks and funds not consolidated in the bank's financial statements, including dividend income from nonconsolidated subsidiaries, associates and joint ventures.	

(Continued)

TABLE 12.3 (*Continued*)

BI Component	P&L or Balance Sheet Items	Description	Typical Subitems
Services	Fee and commission income	Income received from providing advice and services. Includes income received by the bank as an outsourcer of financial services.	Fee and commission income from: ■ Securities (issuance, origination, reception, transmission, execution of orders on behalf of customers) ■ Clearing and settlement; asset management; custody; fiduciary transactions; payment services; structured finance; servicing of securitizations; loan commitments and guarantees given; and foreign transactions
	Fee and commission expenses	Services	Fee and commission expenses from: ■ Clearing and settlement; custody; servicing of securitizations; loan commitments and guarantees received; and foreign transactions
	Other operating income	Income from ordinary banking operations not included in other BI items but of similar nature (income from operating leases should be excluded)	■ Rental income from investment properties ■ Gains from noncurrent assets and disposal groups classified as held for sale not qualifying as discontinued operations (IFRS 5.37)
	Other operating expenses	Expenses and losses from ordinary banking operations not included in other BI items but of similar nature and from operational loss events (expenses from operating leases should be excluded)	■ Losses from noncurrent assets and disposal groups classified as held for sale not qualifying as discontinued operations (IFRS 5.37) ■ Losses incurred as a consequence of operational loss events (e.g. fines, penalties, settlements, replacement cost of damaged assets), which have not been provisioned/reserved for in previous years ■ Expenses related to establishing provisions/reserves for operational loss events

BI Component	P&L or Balance Sheet Items	Description	Typical Subitems
Financial	Net profit (loss) on the trading book		■ Net profit/loss on trading assets and trading liabilities (derivatives, debt securities, equity securities, loans and advances, short positions, other assets and liabilities) ■ Net profit/loss from hedge accounting ■ Net profit/loss from exchange differences
	Net profit (loss) on the banking book		■ Net profit/loss on financial assets and liabilities measured at fair value through profit and loss ■ Realized gains/losses on financial assets and liabilities not measured at fair value through profit and loss (loans and advances, assets available for sale, assets held to maturity, financial liabilities measured at amortized cost) ■ Net profit/loss from hedge accounting ■ Net profit/loss from exchange differences

Internal Loss Multiplier: ILM

The final step in calculating capital for operational risk using the new Standardized Approach is to derive the Internal Loss Multiplier (ILM). It is clear at this point that the only element of the operational risk framework that now has a direct input into the capital calculation is the operational loss experience of the bank itself.

In this way, the new approach removes the qualitative elements of scenario analysis and of business environment and internal control factors and simply asks: (1) What does your bank do (BIC)? and (2) How many losses have you experienced (ILM)?

The internal loss multiplier is derived as follows:

$$ILM = \ln\left\{ \exp(1) - 1\left\{ \frac{LC}{BIC} \right\}^{0.8} \right\}$$

Where the loss component (LC) = 15 times average annual operational risk losses incurred over the previous 10 years.

> *The calculation of average losses in the Loss Component must be based on **10 years** of high-quality annual loss data. The qualitative requirements for loss data collection are outlined in paragraphs 19 to 31. As part of the transition to the standardised approach, banks that do not have 10 years of **high-quality loss data** may use a minimum of five years of data to calculate the Loss Component. Banks that do not have five years of high-quality loss data must calculate the capital requirement based solely on the BI Component. Supervisors may however require a bank to calculate capital requirements using fewer than five years of losses if the ILM is greater than 1 and supervisors believe the losses are representative of the bank's operational risk exposure.[33] [emphasis added]*

This is a significant change from the original Basel requirements regarding the use of internal loss data in capital calculations, as the period of losses has been expanded from five years of experienced losses (three at the outset) to 10 years. The structure of the calculation ensures that a bank's loss experience directly influences its capital requirement.

> *The ILM is equal to one where the loss and business indicator components are equal. Where the LC is greater than the BIC, the ILM is greater than one. That is, a bank with losses that are high relative to its BIC is required to hold higher capital due to the incorporation of*

internal losses into the calculation methodology. Conversely, where the LC is lower than the BIC, the ILM is less than one. That is, a bank with losses that are low relative to its BIC is required to hold lower capital due to the incorporation of internal losses into the calculation methodology.[34]

This means that large events will have a long-term impact on the capital requirements of a bank, and in effect, they will be punished for their errors even long after they may have fixed the underlying control failures that led to those errors. Conversely, a bank that has a low level of losses will be able to benefit from lower capital regardless of whether its current control environment is flawed.

While this does not appear to directly incentivize banks to ensure that they have a strong control framework, the BCBS has determined that this is in fact a more consistent and measurable approach than the AMA has proven to be.

The new guidance also provides comprehensive requirements for the collection of internal loss data as discussed in Chapter 7. These are outlined fully in Sections 5 and 6 of the 2017 BCBS document "OPE 25 – Basel III: Finalizing post-crisis reforms."

As a large event might have a high impact on capital long after the control weaknesses have been remediated, it is possible for a bank to petition for the removal of certain operational risk events under the new framework as follows:

Exclusion of losses from the Loss Component

27. *Banking organisations may request supervisory approval to exclude certain operational loss events that are no longer relevant to the banking organisation's risk profile. The exclusion of internal loss events should be rare and supported by strong justification. In evaluating the relevance of operational loss events to the bank's risk profile, supervisors will consider whether the cause of the loss event could occur in other areas of the bank's operations. Taking settled legal exposures and divested businesses as examples, supervisors expect the organisation's analysis to demonstrate that there is no similar or residual legal exposure and that the excluded loss experience has no relevance to other continuing activities or products.*

28. *The total loss amount and number of exclusions must be disclosed under Pillar 3 with appropriate narratives, including total loss amount and number of exclusions.*

> 29. A request for loss exclusions is subject to a materiality threshold to be set by the supervisor (for example, the excluded loss event should be greater than 5% of the bank's average losses). In addition, losses can only be excluded after being included in a bank's operational risk loss database for a minimum period (for example, three years), to be specified by the supervisor. Losses related to divested activities will not be subject to a minimum operational risk loss database retention period.[35]

As can be seen, such exclusions will be rare and will only be allowed after a period of inclusion in the capital calculation (e.g., three years) and with strong evidence that it is appropriate to now exclude the loss. If granted, the exclusion must be noted in the disclosures of that bank.

Disclosure

Pillar 3 of Basel II requires disclosure of capital calculation results and explanations of methodologies used.

> Description of the AMA, if used by the bank, including a discussion of relevant internal and external factors considered in the bank's measurement approach.[23]

Under the new Standardized Approach, this disclosure requirement will be updated as follows:

> All banks with a BI greater than €1bn, or which use internal loss data in the calculation of operational risk capital, are required to disclose their annual loss data for each of the ten years in the ILM calculation window. This includes banks in jurisdictions that have opted to set ILM equal to one. Loss data is required to be reported on both a gross basis and after recoveries and loss exclusions. All banks are required to disclose each of the BI sub-items for each of the three years of the BI component calculation window.[36]

The following extracts are from banks' annual reports describing their AMA methods and their operational risk capital amount. In the earlier days of Basel II, banks were more open to describing the inner workings of their AMA methods. More recent disclosures have been at a higher level. Credit Suisse provided some insight into their scenario-based approach in their 2010 Annual Report Disclosure as follows:

The economic capital/AMA methodology is based upon the identification of a number of key risk scenarios that describe the major operational risks that we face. Groups of senior staff review each scenario and discuss the likelihood of occurrence and the potential severity of loss. Internal and external loss data, along with certain business environment and internal control factors, such as self-assessment results and key risk indicators, are considered as part of this process.

Based on the output from these meetings, we enter the scenario parameters into an operational risk model that generates a loss distribution from which the level of capital required to cover operational risk is determined. Insurance mitigation is included in the capital assessment where appropriate, by considering the level of insurance coverage for each scenario and incorporating haircuts as appropriate . . .

Operational risk increased following the update of scenario parameters to recognize higher litigation risks.[37]

In its most recent annual report, the bank takes a much-higher-level approach to describing its current AMA methodology:

Operational risk *RWA reflect the capital requirements for the risk of loss resulting from inadequate or failed internal processes, people and systems or from external events. For calculating the capital requirements related to operational risk, we received approval from FINMA to use the advanced measurement approach (AMA). Under the AMA for measuring operational risk, we have identified key scenarios that describe our major operational risks using an event model.*[38]

Credit Suisse's risk-weighted assets for operational risk in 2011 was disclosed as CHF36,088 million and in 2020 had risen to CHF58,655 million.

In contrast to Credit Suisse's scenario analysis methodology, Deutsche Bank currently uses a loss data AMA methodology that has remained consistent for the past 10 years. Deutsche Bank's 2020 annual report describes its methodology as follows:

We calculate and measure the regulatory and economic capital requirements for operational risk using the Advanced Measurement Approach (AMA) methodology.

Our AMA capital calculation is based upon the loss distribution approach. Gross losses from historical internal and external loss data (Operational Risk data eXchange Association consortium data) and external scenarios from a public database (IBM OpData) complemented by internal scenario data are used to estimate the risk profile (i.e., a loss frequency and a loss severity distribution). Our loss distribution approach model includes conservatism by recognizing losses on events that arise over multiple years as single events in our historical loss profile. Within the loss distribution approach model, the frequency and severity distributions are combined in a Monte Carlo simulation to generate potential losses over a one year time horizon. Finally, the risk mitigating benefits of insurance are applied to each loss generated in the Monte Carlo simulation.

Correlation and diversification benefits are applied to the net losses in a manner compatible with regulatory requirements to arrive at a net loss distribution at Group level, covering expected and unexpected losses.

Capital is then allocated to each of the business divisions after considering qualitative adjustments and expected loss.

The regulatory and economic capital requirements for operational risk are derived from the 99.9% percentile; see the section "Internal Capital Adequacy" for details. Both regulatory and economic capital requirements are calculated for a time horizon of one year.[39]

Deutsche Bank's RWA for operational risk in 2011 was €4.8 billion and in 2020 had risen to €69 billion.

In 2011, JPMorgan Chase was not AMA approved but chose to disclose its methodology and operational risk capital amount. It had adopted a hybrid AMA model that used loss data and added additional data from scenarios:

Operational risk capital

Capital is allocated to the lines of business for operational risk using a risk-based capital allocation methodology which estimates operational risk on a bottom-up basis. The operational risk capital model is based on actual losses and potential scenario-based stress losses, with adjustments to the capital calculation to reflect changes in the quality of the control environment or the use of risk-transfer products. The Firm believes its model is consistent with the Basel II Framework.[27]

Their economic capital for operational risk in 2011 was $8.5 billion. In 2020 JP Morgan calculated their RWA for operational risk as $385 billion and provided the following guidance on how they believed their methodology met the AMA requirement:

> *The primary component of the operational risk capital estimate is the Loss Distribution Approach ("LDA") statistical model, which simulates the frequency and severity of future operational risk loss projections based on historical data. The LDA model is used to estimate an aggregate operational risk loss over a one-year time horizon, at a 99.9% confidence level. The LDA model incorporates actual internal operational risk losses in the quarter following the period in which those losses were realized, and the calculation generally continues to reflect such losses even after the issues or business activities giving rise to the losses have been remediated or reduced. As required under the Basel III capital framework, the Firm's operational risk-based capital methodology, which uses the Advanced Measurement Approach ("AMA"), incorporates internal and external losses as well as management's view of tail risk captured through operational risk scenario analysis, and evaluation of key business environment and internal control metrics. The Firm does not reflect the impact of insurance in its AMA estimate of operational risk capital.*[40]

Whatever approach is taken to modeling capital for operational risk, the model must be stress-tested and back-tested for validity, and it is expected that models will continue to evolve as experience develops. The validity and verification requirements discussed in Chapter 8 must be applied to all modeling activities and a special model validation team is usually established in order to meet those needs.

KEY POINTS

- Basel II provides three main approaches to calculating operational risk capital: the Basic Indicator Approach (BIA), the Standardized Approach (TSA), and the Advanced Measurement Approach (AMA).
- Basel III will require the adoption of a new Standardized Approach that does not allow for the use of an AMA method.
- Firms that are currently required to, or choose to, calculate operational risk capital using AMA can select from several methods. They may base their calculations on loss distribution approach (LDA), on scenario analysis, or on a combination of the two.

- Under AMA
  - A model is generally built through the combination of a frequency distribution and a severity distribution using Monte Carlo simulation.
  - A calculation must be done for each risk category.
  - Capital must be allocated to the business lines appropriately.
  - Correlation assumptions must be strongly defended.
  - The model must be validated.
- The use of insurance to mitigate capital is limited.
- Capital amounts and the factors used must be disclosed under Pillar 3 of Basel II and Basel III.

REVIEW QUESTIONS

1. Basel II provided what three main approaches to calculating operational risk capital?
   I. The Basic Indicator Approach
   II. The Standardized Approach
   III. The Advanced Measurement Approach
   IV. The Loss Distribution Approach
   a. I, II, and III
   b. I, II, and IV
   c. II, III, and IV
   d. I, III, and IV
2. Basel III allows which of the following approaches to calculating operational risk capital?
   I. A basic indicator approach
   II. A standardized approach
   III. An advanced measurement approach
   a. I, II, and III
   b. I and II
   c. III only
   d. II only

NOTES

1. Basel Committee on Banking Supervision, OPE Calculation of RWA for operational risk, OPE10, "Definitions and Application," version effective as of December 15, 2019, https://www.bis.org/basel_framework/chapter/OPE/10.htm.

2. Basel Committee on Banking Supervision, OPE Calculation of RWA for operational risk, OPE20, "Basic Indicator Approach," version effective as of December 15, 2019, sections 20.1–20.3, https://www.bis.org/basel_framework/chapter/OPE/20.htm.

3. Ibid., section 20.3 clarifies that this definition is intended to (1) be gross of any provisions (e.g., for unpaid interest); (2) be gross of operating expenses, including fees paid to outsourcing service providers; (3) exclude realized profits/losses from the sale of securities in the banking book; and (4) exclude extraordinary or irregular items as well as income derived from insurance.

4. Basel Committee on Banking Supervision, Risk Management Group, "Sound Practices for the Management and Supervision of Operational Risk," 2011, https://www.bis.org/publ/bcbs195.pdf.

5. Basel Committee on Banking Supervision, OPE Calculation of RWA for operational risk, OPE25, "Standardised approach," version effective as of December 15, 2019, section 25.2, https://www.bis.org/basel_framework/chapter/OPE/25.htm.

6. Ibid., sections 25.3–25.4.

7. Ibid., section 25.3.

8. Ibid., section 25.9.

9. Ibid., sections 25.9–25.15.

10. Footnoted in OPE20 and OPE25—see notes 2 and 5 above.

11. Basel Committee on Banking Supervision, OPE Calculation of RWA for operational risk, OPE30, "Advanced Measurement Approach," version effective as of December 15, 2019, section 30.6, https://www.bis.org/basel_framework/chapter/OPE/30.htm.

12. Ibid., section 30.7.

13. Ibid.

14. Ibid.

15. Ibid., section 30.9.

16. Ibid., section 30.11.

17. Ibid., section 30.11 (1).

18. Ibid., section 30.11 (2).

19. Ibid., section 30.11 (3).

20. Ibid., section 30.11 (4).

21. Ibid., section 30.11 (5).

22. Ibid., section 30.11 (6).

23. Ibid., section 30.14.

24. "Operational Risk—Supervisory Guidelines for the Advanced Measurement Approaches," 2011, www.bis.org/publ/bcbs196.pdf, section 180.

25. A leptokurtic distribution is more concentrated around the mean than would be observed in a normal curve.

26. See note 24, sections 195–196.

27. See note 11, section 30.11 (4).

28. Ibid., sections 30.20 and 30.21.

29. Bank for International Settlements, "International Convergence of Capital Measurement and Capital Standards: A Revised Framework," 2004, sections 249–650, footnote 103.

30. Bank for International Settlements, Basel Committee on Banking Supervision, "Basel III—Finalizing Post Crisis Reforms," December 2017, 128, https://www .bis.org/bcbs/publ/d424.htm.

31. Ibid.

32. Ibid., 129.

33. Ibid.

34. Ibid.

35. Ibid., 133.

36. Ibid., 134.

37. Credit Suisse Annual Report 2011, 99.

38. Credit Suisse Annual Report 2020, 129.

39. Deutsche Bank Annual Report 2020, 103.

40. JP Morgan Annual Report 2020, 145.

CHAPTER 13

Reporting

In this chapter, we investigate reporting tools that empower the operational risk function with the opportunity to contribute to the business decision making at the firm. We consider loss data reporting in some depth and also discuss reporting on the other elements in the framework, including risk and control self-assessment, key risk indicators, and scenario analysis. Examples of fictional data are used to demonstrate how risk analysis can be applied to raw data in order to provide relevant reporting conclusions that can drive business decision making.

ROLE OF REPORTING

An operational risk framework is designed to identify, assess, monitor, control, and mitigate operational risk. All of the elements of the framework contribute to these goals, but without effective reporting even the best of programs will be ineffective in changing the risk culture of the firm. The place of reporting in the operational risk framework is illustrated in Figure 13.1.

The reporting of operational risk is key to the program's success. There are many ways to ensure that the reporting of each element drives action and to protect against the danger of producing reporting that receives a "so what?" response.

Generally, an operational risk department will be looking to report on several things, including:

- Operational risk event (loss) data for the previous period
- Remediation action being taken
- Key risk indicators (KRIs)

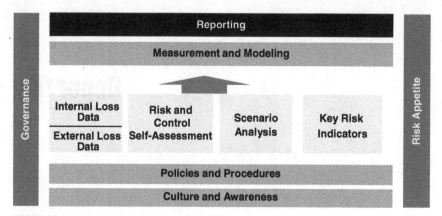

FIGURE 13.1 The Role of Reporting in the Operational Risk Framework

- Results of risk and control self-assessment (RCSA)
- Results of scenario analysis
- Capital calculation
- Whether the operational risk department is on track with its deliverables

However, the chief risk officer (CRO), risk committee, or other executive management may have different expectations, and they are more likely to be looking for reporting that addresses:

- Where is our risk?
- What action do we need to take?
- Who is under control?
- Who is not?
- Are we meeting our regulatory requirements?

Effective reporting is presented in a way that demonstrates the risk analyst role of the operational risk department. Just as market and credit risk specialists are focused on risk analysis, so too operational risk specialists should be risk analysts. Market risk and credit analysts:

- Analyze raw data
- Analyze trends and predictors
- Follow news articles
- Present opinions
- Present capital at risk (value at risk [VaR] and stressed VaR)
- Recommend action and hedging strategies

In the same way, operational risk managers should take on the same responsibilities for operational risk and should not just be data gatherers but should also:

- Analyze raw data
- Analyze trends and predictors (KRIs)
- Follow news articles
- Present opinions
- Present capital at risk
- Recommend action and mitigating strategies

OPERATIONAL RISK EVENT REPORTING

Operational risk event (loss) data reporting is often the central reporting activity in an operational risk function. Operational risk event data can be a mine of vital information that can contribute to effective operational risk management and measurement. However, it can also be redundant data if it is not properly presented in a way that can drive decision making.

Operational risk event data reporting typically looks something like the fictional example seen in Table 13.1.

While these data are somewhat self-explanatory, the method of collection and underlying assumptions might lead to a misinterpretation of the data. Therefore, it is important to ensure that the recipients of the event data reporting understand the background.

Impact of Gains on Internal Event Reporting

For example, in Table 13.1 the data may actually contain gains as well as losses. It may be an operational risk *event* report rather than a *losses* report. Table 13.1 shows that there were eight events in Investment Banking in December 2020 and that the net value of events was $10,000. However, there is no more detail provided on the nature of those eight events, and there may be significant information that is being masked from view.

An example of the underlying data for investment banking is seen in Table 13.2.

From the underlying data it is clear that one of the events was a gain of $12,500 and this gain is skewing the net events so that they total $10,000, when in fact operational risk losses totaled $22,500 if gains are excluded. The amount at risk might actually be $35,000—the absolute value of the events, as it was probably only luck that the seventh event was a gain instead of a loss.

TABLE 13.1 Example Operational Risk Event Data Table

Business Line	Absolute $ Value of Events	# Events	December 2020 Gross $ Value of Events	$ Recovery	Net $ Value of Events	Trend	12-Month Total # Events	Gross $ Value of Events	Net $ Value of Events
Fixed Income	150,000	10	(65,000)	5,000	(60,000)	⇕	185	(650,000)	(350,000)
Investment Banking	35,000	8	(10,000)		(10,000)	⇑	65	(435,000)	(400,000)
Equities	250,000	65	(208,000)	55,000	(153,000)	⇐	450	(8,500,000)	(2,500,000)
Asset Management	120,000	28	(120,000)	25,000	(95,000)	⇕	235	(11,350,000)	(5,500,000)
Private Wealth Management	70,000	35	(70,000)		(70,000)	⇒	625	(12,560,000)	(2,000,000)
Total	625,000	146	(473,000)	85,000	(388,000)		1560	(33,495,000)	(10,750,000)

TABLE 13.2 Example Investment Banking Operational Risk Event Detail

	Absolute	Gross	Recovery	Net	Total Net Loss
	Investment Banking Events in $, December 2020				
Event 1	2,000	(2,000)	0	(2,000)	(2,000)
Event 2	2,000	(2,000)	0	(2,000)	(2,000)
Event 3	4,000	(4,000)	0	(4,000)	(4,000)
Event 4	2,000	(2,000)	0	(2,000)	(2,000)
Event 5	5,000	(5,000)	0	(5,000)	(5,000)
Event 6	2,000	(2,000)	0	(2,000)	(2,000)
Event 7	12,500	12,500	0	12,500	0
Event 8	5,500	(5,500)	0	(5,500)	(5,500)
Total	35,000	(10,000)	0	(10,000)	(22,500)

Therefore, it is important to ensure that the recipients of a report such as Table 13.1 are aware of whether gains are being netted against losses. Perhaps this nuance would be lost on the audience. If so, the absolute dollar value of the events might be a better indicator of operational risk and the report might be changed to reflect that.

Trends in Internal Losses

The fictional operational risk data Table 13.1 includes a trend column. This trend needs more explanation in order to be informative. The presenter of the report will need to clarify whether the trend relates to month-on-month changes, changes relative to the average over the past year, or some other benchmark. The trend could also relate to any of the previous columns, and so clarification is needed as to whether it relates to the number of events or to the dollar amount of the absolute, gross, or net amount.

Trends can be helpful, as they can indicate a changing risk environment that may require action. Trends of loss size against number of events might provide insight into improving or worsening control environments. An example of using trends to compare events and net losses is provided in Figure 13.2.

It can also be helpful to compare trends in business lines and in risk categories to see where the risks are elevated. This information is particularly helpful when considering entering into a new business. Trends and history from similar business lines can be used to help with the assessment of the likely operational risk exposures that may arise in this new business line.

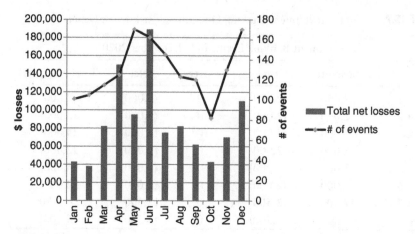

FIGURE 13.2 Trending Loss Amount vs. Number of Events

Risk Analysis of Table 13.1

There may be a story behind the raw numbers that is not apparent without explanation and analysis from the operational risk department. Looking again at the fictional operational risk event in Table 13.1, it is clear that there is a large difference between the total gross amount of losses ($33,495,000) and the total net amount ($10,750,000) of losses for the past 12 months.

This difference begs for analysis and explanation and suggests that this firm is very good at recovering amounts lost in operational risk events. Recoveries are usually achieved through expert employees who intervene and recover some, or all, of the initial loss amount. Recoveries are more often driven by people than by automated systems, suggesting that the excellent recovery rate reflected in this data is dependent on experienced personnel.

This analysis takes on significance if the firm is currently downsizing or has experienced a significant structural change in its staffing model, such as all of the employees working remotely due to a global pandemic. An operational risk manager could use this loss data to alert senior management that they might experience an increase in net losses due to weaker recovery rates as a result of the current downsizing or remote working strategy of the firm.

The recovery rate might also be used to drive a discussion about what efforts could be made to further improve the recovery rates and what the cost benefit might be of such initiatives.

This type of analysis, linking operational risk data to the business activities and strategies of the firm, demonstrates the relevance and importance of the operational risk function and properly provides increased transparency into operational risk exposures.

Internal Losses by Risk Category

The same operational risk event data can also be presented by risk category rather than by business line, as follows. The fictional data in Table 13.1 provides a view into how each business is doing compared to the other business lines. There may be opportunities for more analysis if the data are cut differently, by risk category, as in Table 13.3.

Risk Analysis of Table 13.3

Several stories can be told from this cut of the data. It is clear that most of the events occur in the Execution, Delivery, and Process Management category as it has experienced 1,100 events over the past 12 months—significantly higher than any other category.

However, the highest loss amounts occur in the Clients, Products, and Business Practices category, which has the lion's share of the dollar value of the losses at $18.5 million over the past year. This suggests that the latter are more prone to fat-tail events.

The firm will want to confirm whether this pattern of losses is to be expected, and it can be helpful to compare risk category data to external benchmarks. The data can be compared to benchmarks from sources such as the ORX consortium data discussed in Chapter 8.

Further analysis of these data shows that this firm has a good experience with recoveries from fraud events. They have experienced 32 internal events and two external events, but the net losses are small compared to the gross losses, indicating that there have been successful recoveries in these cases.

Timeliness

A report that tracks the timeliness of reporting of internal loss data events can be a powerful tool in driving culture change within a firm. Transparent reporting of loss reporting behavior can be very effective in inspiring better behavior and can drive reporting times down.

If loss data is reported late, it not only exposes the firm to unmitigated risks, but it may also impact the capital calculation if the firm has an AMA or Standardized Approach that uses loss data as a direct input into the model.

Timeliness can be tracked in several ways:

- Time from occurrence to identification
- Time from identification to entry in the loss database
- Time from entry to sign-off

It should be noted that legal losses often have a long time lag between occurrence and identification, and this needs to be handled thoughtfully

TABLE 13.3 Example Operational Risk Event Data Cut by Risk Category

Risk Category	Absolute $ Value of Events	December 2020					12-Month Total		
		# Events	Gross $ Value of Events	$ Recovery	Net $ Value of Events	Trend	# Events	Gross $ Value of Events	Net $ Value of Events
Business Disruption and System Failure	5,000	8	(5,000)	$5,000	0	⇕	45	(650,000)	(150,000)
Clients, Products, and Business Practices	265,000	28	(158,000)	0	(158,000)	⇕	88	(18,500,000)	(7,450,000)
Execution, Delivery, and Process Management	190,000	97	(145,000)	80,000	(65,000)	⬆	1,100	(6,540,000)	(2,400,000)
Damage to Physical Assets	20,000	10	(20,000)	0	(20,000)	⇕	235	(1,200,000)	(200,000)
Employment Practices and Workplace Safety	120,000	2	(120,000)	0	(120,000)	➡	56	(3,450,000)	(500,000)
Internal Fraud	25,000	1	(25,000)	0	(25,000)	⇕	32	(2,655,000)	(50,000)
External Fraud	0	0	0	0	0	⇕	4	(500,000)	0
Total	625,000	146	(473,000)	85,000	(388,000)		1560	(33,495,000)	(10,750,000)

when tracking timeliness of loss data. Any combination of the above criteria can be used to drive better reporting behavior. Timeliness can often be adversely impacted due the slow response of another department, and this can also be reflected in reporting statistics. For example, the front office areas might complain that the finance department is very slow to complete their portion of the data when accounting issues are involved. Tracking the timeliness of all events that impact the finance department can be made transparent and encourage more efficiencies in the finance area.

External Loss Data Reporting

Operational risk reporting often includes a summary and analysis of relevant external events over the past reporting period. These should be reviewed for relevance and lessons learned. It is always more popular to discuss bad things that have happened to competitors than it is to talk about bad things that have happened at the firm. Significant external events offer an opportunity to consider "could it happen here?"

Senior management are often very engaged in such discussions, and this can lead to proactive operational risk mitigation activities that can be led by the operational risk function or kicked off and tracked by that function.

Any emerging trends, such as an increase in regulatory fines in a particular area, should be compared to the firm's internal experience and current risk and control environment.

For example, if external data indicate that there has been an increase in the levying of regulatory fines for breaches in the Foreign Corrupt Practices Act (FCPA), then the operational risk manager might propose a review of the firm's current FCPA training and awareness to ensure that these controls are functioning at peak levels of effectiveness.

If the firm is a member of a consortium of loss data, then the internal loss results should be compared to the benchmarking results that the consortium makes available. Comparisons between external and internal data should always be treated with caution, as there may be significant differences in the business models, products, and control environments that could lead to incorrect conclusions.

However, as discussed earlier, external data can provide helpful awareness of risks that may not yet have occurred at the firm but that should be seriously addressed.

RISK AND CONTROL SELF-ASSESSMENT REPORTING

The output from RCSAs is generally reported in detail to the participating department and in summary or thematic form to senior management. While the full RCSA output demonstrates that analysis and recommendations are based on strong underlying data, the details themselves are rarely of interest to the risk committee or CRO.

Instead, the operational risk department can analyze the RCSA output and identify areas that require escalation and raise themes that are best addressed on a firm-wide basis.

For example, if multiple departments have identified through RCSAs that their employee training is weak, then a firm-wide training and development initiative might be a more appropriate response than many individual training programs.

The operational risk department might also have noticed underlying themes during their facilitation of the RCSA exercise, such as a lack of awareness of appropriate fraud controls. This might give rise to a firm-wide initiative to raise awareness of appropriate fraud risk mitigation activities.

RCSA thematic data might also be enhanced by regular monitoring of triggers that have been identified as requiring a reassessment of all or part of an RCSA. A large internal or external event might result in a recommendation by the operational risk department that the firm, or one division of the firm, revalidate the risk and control scores for that particular risk. For example, a sudden increase in fines for FCPA breaches might result in the next operational risk report to senior management including a request to reassess all corruption and bribery risks in the firm.

KEY RISK INDICATOR REPORTING

KRIs are particularly well suited to dashboard-type reporting. There are many tools available to present data to management in a way that highlights red flags and allows for drill-down capabilities to review the underlying sources of data.

However, complex and comprehensive KRI reports are often provided to senior management without sufficient analysis and explanation, leaving the audience with a "so what?" response. For this reason, an operational risk department might decide to review all KRI reports with the departments that own the data and only provide a summary to senior management. Exception reporting of red flags that require escalation might be more valuable than a comprehensive KRI report that shows all KRIs for the firm.

KRI reports are often designed to use color to indicate whether there is a concern, with different thresholds for red, yellow, or green.

The dangers with KRI reporting are that a sea of green might give a false sense of security and a sea of red might produce panic, when the underlying KRIs and thresholds have not yet been proven to be indicative of raised or lowered risk.

Careful explanation and analysis must therefore accompany any KRI dashboard reporting that is provided to senior management.

SCENARIO ANALYSIS REPORTING

The results of the scenario analysis program may drive changes to any Advanced Measurement Approach (AMA) to calculating operational risk capital. They may also produce important mitigating actions that require escalation to senior management.

While the details of the scenario analysis output are unlikely to be of interest to senior management, the implications of those results and their impact on capital will certainly be of interest. In the same way, any proposed mitigating actions may need to be presented to senior management for approval and funding. Scenario analysis results can also give an organization's senior management a good indication of the firm's "top risks" and help the firm manage against them.

The scenario detail will be of importance to any department that is impacted by the results and should be included in their department-level reporting. The form of scenario analysis reporting will depend on the type of program that is in place.

CAPITAL REPORTING

Operational risk capital will need to be reported to senior management and the board, who are likely to be very interested in the drivers of capital and, if an AMA model is in place, any reporting of capital will need to be accompanied by a simple, but complete, explanation of the model and its drivers. As operational risk capital is a direct and sometimes significant driver of risk-weighted assets (RWA), senior management would benefit from understanding how operational risk capital drives RWA. Also, firms can do informative peer analysis of operational risk capital by leveraging public information (e.g., Bloomberg) or data provided from a consortium like ORX to create useful peer comparison. Key metrics to compare across the industry can include:

- Op Risk RWA as a percentage of total RWA
- Op Risk RWA as a percentage of total revenue

Finally, but importantly, looking at operational risk RWA by business unit can help drive business decisions. If the BIA or TSA approach is being used for capital calculation, then it may be prudent to include a reminder of the method being used. Capital calculation methodologies will soon be simplified when the new Standardized Approach becomes mandatory. As firms prepare for this transition they should use the reporting forum to explain how the capital calculation will be impacted and to share a parallel run calculation to ensure that senior management is prepared for the change.

ACTION TRACKING REPORTING

There are usually many action items generated by an operational risk management framework. Actions arise from operational risk events that require actions to ensure a recovery of the lost amount, or to prevent a repeat of the same event. Actions arise during an RCSA as control improvements are identified and mitigating actions are agreed upon. Actions arise during scenario analysis as fat-tail events are discussed and firm-wide mitigating actions proposed.

In addition to all of the action items that arise in the operational risk framework, there are usually other action items that are operational risk–related but are owned by other areas of the firm. For example, the Sarbanes-Oxley team and the audit department will be tracking their own set of action items, most of which are in fact operational risk related.

Some firms integrate all action tracking into one tool and one business process; this is discussed further under "Governance, Risk, and Compliance" in Chapter 16. However, many firms still do not yet have an integrated action tracking process. This does not prevent the operational risk department from adding value to the organization by bringing the reporting of those action items into one report so that management can have a clearer view of the operational risk of the firm.

For example, an integrated report could look like something like the example in Table 13.4.

An integrated action table is helpful in assessing which business lines or support areas are managing their risks effectively. The example in Table 13.4 shows the output at a firm where there are different action tracking methods in operational risk, in audit, and in Sarbanes-Oxley (SOX). Operational risk is tracking all completed open and past due items, audit only tracks past due items once they are more than 90 days late, and SOX only tracks whether items are open.

Ideally, all groups will eventually align to one action tracking method, but even though there are different approaches, reporting can still occur and

TABLE 13.4 Example of Integrated Action Tracking Reporting

Business Unit	Operational Risk			Internal Audit		SOX	Total
	Completed	Open	Past Due	Open	> 90 Days Past Due	Open	Open Action Items
Finance	25	5	2	6	3	8	19
Human Resources	20	2	2	3	0	0	5
Legal	10	0	0	2	2	0	2
Operations	45	5	4	8	3	1	14
Technology	28	8	2	7	1	5	20
Fixed Income	10	2	0	5	1	2	9
Investment Banking	8	1	1	8	1	0	9
Equities	5	1	1	12	2	5	18
Asset Management	14	2	1	12	7	0	14
Private Wealth Management	13	5	5	2	2	1	8
Total	178	31	18	65	22	22	118

can still be helpful. All departments have action items to track, both support areas and front office business lines. This is unlike operational risk data reporting, where Table 13.1 showed only the front office business lines, as they own the loss. In loss data reporting, some firms do also track events by cause and so may have results for support areas also.

Risk Analysis of Table 13.4

As a raw table of data, this report does leave the observer wondering "so what?" Where is there an area of concern or a need for escalation? Further analysis is helpful to present the information in a way that supports business decision making.

Table 13.4 suggests that the finance, technology, and equities departments need to move more urgently to address the outstanding action items in their areas as they have the highest number of open action items.

If the operational risk department has been successful in partnering with the SOX and audit departments to such a degree that all three are categorizing their action items by the same risk categories, then it is also possible to produce a risk category cut of the same data.

Such a cut might produce data that could populate a pie chart such as the one shown in Figure 13.3.

From this view we can see that the majority of open action items in this fictional set are in the execution, delivery, and process management category. However, perhaps the late action items tell a different and more compelling story, as shown in Figure 13.4.

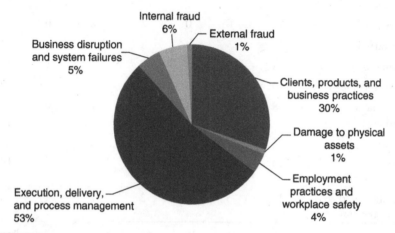

FIGURE 13.3 Fictional Action Open Items by Risk Category, Pie Chart

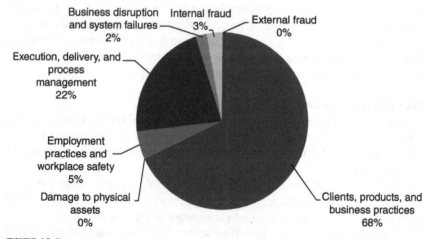

FIGURE 13.4 Fictional Late Action Items by Risk Category, Pie Chart

From this view it is clear that the real concern should be around the resolution of the many late Clients, Products, and Business Practices items, as these relate to a risk category that is prone to fat-tail events.

This demonstrates how analysis and explanation by the operational risk department can lead to decision points for senior management. This chart would best be presented along with a request to follow up on all late Clients, Products, and Business Practices action items in the firm, to ensure they are reprioritized as high priority and addressed as soon as possible.

A CONSOLIDATED VIEW

All of this operational risk data can be brought together into one view, to provide a snapshot of the current overall risk profile for each department. Just one example of how this might be done is shown in Table 13.5. If this report is for the CRO, risk committee, or board, then the overall risk rating should be the independent view of the corporate operational risk function, acting in its role as a second line of defense.

DASHBOARDS

Some firms bring together all of their reporting into one view so that the total risk exposure for each department can be clearly seen and compared. There are many sophisticated software solutions for this type of reporting. Some have drill-down capabilities so that an area of interest can be clicked on in order to see the underlying data.

KEY POINTS

- Strong, analytical reporting is fundamental to a successful operational risk framework and provides the opportunity to drive business decision making.
- Reporting will usually include analysis of internal loss data, external loss data, risk and control self-assessment results, scenario analysis results, and capital.
- Action tracking across the firm can be consolidated under the operational risk framework.
- A risk profile can be subjectively determined from the underlying data.
- Dashboards are readily available today and provide drill-down capabilities for interactive reporting.

TABLE 13.5 Consolidated View of Operational Risk Outputs to Produce a Risk Profile

December 2020 Risk Profile Business Unit	New Losses $m		RCSA Score							Highest Scenario $m	Late Action Items	Overall Risk Rating
	Owned	Caused	CPBP	EDPM	IF	EF	EPWS	DPA	BDSF			
Finance	2.1		H	M	M	M	L	L	L	—	20	M
Human Resources	0.4		L	M	L	L	H	L	L	—	5	M
Legal	1.2		L	L	L	L	L	L	L	—	0	L
Operations	2.1		H	H	M	M	L	L	L	—	16	H
Technology	5.0		L	M	L	H	L	L	L	—	55	H
Fixed Income	11.0	2.0	M	M	M	M	M	L	L	2,000	12	M
Investment Banking	2.5	1.0	L	L	L	L	L	L	L	500	4	L
Equities	2.5	1.0	H	M	L	L	L	L	L	2,500	6	M
Asset Management	0.6	2.0	L	M	L	L	L	L	L	650	18	L
Private Wealth Management	1.2	1.0	L	L	L	L	L	L	L	100	42	L

REVIEW QUESTION

1. Which of the following is most likely to generate informed business decisions based on operational risk considerations?
   a. A table showing raw operational risk loss data
   b. A table containing the total capital required using the Basic Indicator Approach
   c. A list of themes raised through the RCSA process with proposed mitigating actions
   d. A list of the latest scenario analysis maximum loss estimates

CHAPTER 14

Risk Appetite

In this chapter, we explore the most challenging element of the operational risk framework: risk appetite. The risk appetite element of the framework is the glue that holds the framework together, as it provides context for the risks that are identified and assessed and ensures appropriate escalation and governance of operational risk.

However, there was little guidance on operational risk appetite in the original Basel II documents, and firms have struggled with this element in the past few years. Regulators have now provided further guidance that makes it clear that the board of directors, senior management, and businesses all have roles to play in setting and managing operational risk appetite. This guidance has proven helpful, and firms are now making real progress in addressing this element of the framework, albeit with a wide range of practices.

THE ROLE OF RISK APPETITE

Operational risk management, measurement, and capital modeling produce data, scores, and capital numbers that are designed to be used by the firm to identify, assess, monitor, control, and mitigate operational risk. All of these activities rely on an underlying understanding of the risk appetite of the firm.

Assessment of risk assumes that there is a gauge against which that assessment is measured. However, finding and expressing an operational risk appetite can prove to be very challenging. Unlike other risk categories, operational risk is inherent in the very existence of the firm. As such, a risk appetite of zero operational risk is untenable. What then is the appropriate level of operational risk?

Risk appetite usually matures as the operational risk program develops. Once operational risk loss event data is gathered, then management is able to determine whether they consider this level of losses to be acceptable or not. As RCSA data is gathered, the participants express whether they feel the risks to be high and in need of mitigation or whether they are at acceptable levels.

As scenario analysis workshops are conducted, participants engage in discussion around the worst possible cases and determine whether there may be mitigating actions required. As KRIs are designed and gathered, thresholds are determined and refined to reflect the risk levels that are considered acceptable.

Therefore, the operational risk framework itself supports the evolution of the operational risk appetite of the firm. Thresholds and scores will be adjusted as that appetite is refined or changes.

For that reason, most firms did not attempt to articulate their operational risk appetite until the operational program had had a few years to evolve and mature. The risk appetite is a critical pillar that holds the whole operational risk framework together, as is illustrated in Figure 14.1.

Before examining the rules and approaches that apply to operational risk appetite, it is necessary to establish terminology. Many firms use different terms in this space, referring to risk capacity, risk appetite, risk tolerance, and risk thresholds—often interchangeably and confusingly.

It may help to consider this area of the framework in all four ways, and for the purposes of this chapter we take the following approach. Risk capacity is the ability of the firm to absorb risk and is often related to the capital that it holds. Risk appetite is the firm's view on what risks it is willing or unwilling to take. Risk tolerance reflects specific levels of risk that will be permitted without the need for mitigation. Risk limits are thresholds

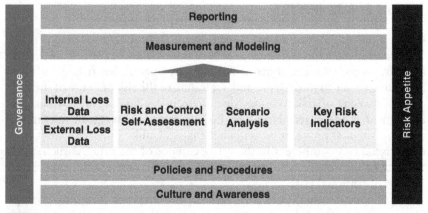

FIGURE 14.1 The Role of Risk Appetite in the Operational Risk Framework

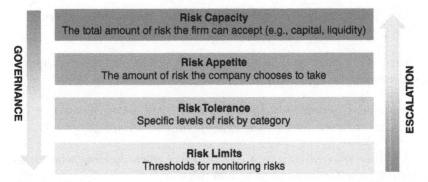

FIGURE 14.2 The Relationship between Risk Capacity, Appetite, Tolerance, and Limits

that are used to monitor measures of risk. The relationship between these is illustrated in Figure 14.2.

In Figure 14.2 it can be seen that the governance flows down from capacity, through appetite and tolerance to limits. It is also clear that the escalation of risk flows upward from limits to risk capacity. These flows impact the roles and responsibilities of the board, senior management, and the business lines and limit owners.

REGULATORY EXPECTATIONS

The regulators have evolved their thinking on risk appetite, not just in operational risk, but as an important element in corporate governance. Basel II only mentions the word *appetite* once, in the Pillar 2 section of the rules:

> *The [operational risk] framework should cover the bank's appetite and tolerance for operational risk, as specified through the policies for managing this risk.*[1]

In its 2003 "Sound Practices for the Management and Supervision of Operational Risk" document, the Basel Committee on Banking Supervision (BCBS) did not add much color. They referred to appetite in their principles:

> *Principle 6: Banks should have policies, processes and procedures to control and/or mitigate material operational risks. Banks should periodically review their risk limitation and control strategies and should adjust their operational risk profile accordingly using*

*appropriate strategies, in light of their overall risk **appetite** and pro-file.[2] [emphasis added]*

They talked about how the risk appetite should be used in remuneration considerations:

*Senior management should also ensure that the bank's remuneration policies are consistent with its **appetite** for risk.[3] [emphasis added]*

And they referred to it as a consideration when deciding whether to accept risk or self-insure against certain risks:

*In some instances, banks may decide to either retain a certain level of operational risk or self-insure against that risk. Where this is the case and the risk is material, the decision to retain or self-insure the risk should be transparent within the organization and should be consistent with the bank's overall business strategy and **appetite** for risk.[4] [emphasis added]*

But there was no Basel guidance provided as to how operational risk appetite could or should be articulated and initially little pressure from the regulators for banks to get any clear risk appetite statements in place.

However, there was a fundamental change in emphasis in this area when BCBS updated the 2003 "Sound Practices" guidance with the "Principles for the Sound Management of Operational Risk and the Role of Supervision" document in 2011. Instead of five mentions of *appetite*, there were now 19, and the bar had been significantly raised.

Perhaps most importantly, under the 2011 guidance the board of directors was now expected to approve and review the operational risk statement, and we have more clues as to what that statement should include:

Principle 4: The board of directors should approve and review a risk appetite and tolerance statement for operational risk that artic-ulates the nature, types, and levels of operational risk that the bank is willing to assume.[5]

The footnote provides additional guidance as to the meaning of *risk appetite* and *risk tolerance* were as follows:

"Risk appetite" is a high level determination of how much risk a firm is willing to accept taking into account the risk/return attrib-utes; it is often taken as a forward-looking view of risk acceptance.

> *"Risk tolerance" is a more specific determination of the level of variation a bank is willing to accept around business objectives that is often considered to be the amount of risk a bank is prepared to accept. In this document the terms are used synonymously.[6]*

In other words, BCBS did not clearly distinguish between *appetite* and *tolerance*, but they did start to define the concepts for us as *a forward-looking view of risk acceptance.*

The updated "Sound Practices" still required senior management to ensure that the operational risk framework was consistent with the risk appetite of the firm[7] and charged audit to "review the robustness of the process of how [risk appetite and tolerance] limits are set and why and how they are adjusted in response to changing circumstances."[8]

The "Sound Practices" document of 2011 also required a clear articulation of risk appetite, stating that the framework documents must:

> *. . . describe the bank's accepted operational risk appetite and tolerance, as well as thresholds or limits for inherent and residual risk, and approved risk mitigation strategies and instruments . . .[9]*

Documenting this description remained a challenge for banks, as they attempted to articulate a risk appetite for errors occurring due to inadequate or failed processes, people, systems, or external events. The simple answer is, of course, we don't want any mess-ups. But a bank or a fintech cannot have a risk appetite of zero, as this is not tenable.

Neither the U.S. regulators' AMA guidance nor the Committee of European Banking Supervisors guidelines on operational risk offered any further assistance with these challenges, making little or no mention of risk appetite. The only additional guidance that had been offered out of the Bank of International Settlements (BIS) is a footnote in their "2012 Core Principles for Effective Banking Supervision":

> *"Risk appetite" reflects the level of aggregate risk that the bank's Board is willing to assume and manage in the pursuit of the bank's business objectives. Risk appetite may include both quantitative and qualitative elements, as appropriate, and encompass a range of measures.[10]*

As a result, a fairly complex, and at times inconsistent, nomenclature had arisen in this element of the framework.

In 2007 the United Kingdom's Financial Services Authority (FSA) conducted a study[11] into the range of practices being used to define and use

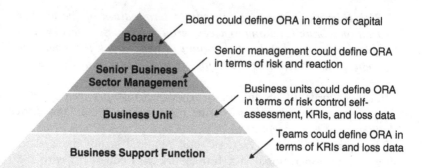

FIGURE 14.3 FSA Findings on How ORA Can Be Defined or Articulated at Several Levels Using Varying Metrics

operational risk appetite and tolerance within the operational risk frameworks of banks. They identified a very wide range of practices and simply summarized their findings to show the many ways that these terms were being used and thresholds being set.

Figure 14.3 is a reproduction of the diagram that the study used to demonstrate the many ways that risk appetite and tolerance could be managed. In their paper, the FSA refers to operational risk appetite as ORA and notes that qualitative and quantitative approaches were being developed across the industry.

This broad range of practices was noted, but not particularly criticized, and firms continued to take a slow-paced approach to the development of this element of their operational risk framework.

However, in 2009, the Senior Supervisors Group (SSG), which includes the major national banking regulators from Europe and the United States, issued a report, "Risk Management Lessons from the Global Banking Crisis of 2008"[12] (the "2009 SSG report"). This report, in the SSG's own words, "reviewed in depth the funding and liquidity issues central to the crisis and explored critical risk management practices warranting improvement across the financial services industry."[13] Two of the key findings of weakness were (1) the lack of robust risk appetite frameworks and (2) weaknesses in information technology (IT) infrastructure and data.

To further address these two items, in 2010 SSG issued "Observations on Development in Risk Appetite Frameworks and IT Infrastructure."[14] Therefore, while Basel was silent on more guidance on risk appetite, the national regulators offered their views on their expectations around risk appetite frameworks.

In 2015, BCBS updated their Corporate Governance Principles for Banks and provided additional guidance for banks that were looking to implement effective risk appetite frameworks. BCBS incorporated much of the language used by the SSG and provided the following definitions:

risk appetite	*The aggregate level and types of risk a bank is willing to assume, decided in advance and within its risk capacity, to achieve its strategic objectives and business plan.*
risk appetite framework (RAF)	*The overall approach, including policies, processes, controls and systems, through which risk appetite is established, communicated and monitored. It includes a risk appetite statement, risk limits and an outline of the roles and responsibilities of those overseeing the implementation and monitoring of the RAF. The RAF should consider material risks to the bank, as well as to its reputation vis-à-vis policyholders, depositors, investors and customers. The RAF aligns with the bank's strategy.*
risk appetite statement (RAS)	*The written articulation of the aggregate level and types of risk that a bank will accept, or avoid, in order to achieve its business objectives. It includes quantitative measures expressed relative to earnings, capital, risk measures, liquidity and other relevant measures as appropriate. It should also include qualitative statements to address reputation and conduct risks as well as money laundering and unethical practices.*[11]

The SSG's approach to risk appetite continues to be a helpful framework when considering how to implement an effective risk appetite framework. This approach applies to all aspects of the risk framework, not just the operational risk framework.

This brings us to the most recent guidance from BCBS, "Revisions to the Principles for the Sound Management of Operational Risk," which was published in March 2021. BCBS acknowledged that "several principles had not been adequately implemented, and further guidance would be needed to facilitate their implementation," and they included "articulation of operational risk appetite and tolerance statements" as one of those areas.[12] They finally dedicated a whole principle to providing guidance on how to determine and articulate a risk appetite for operational risk:

> **Principle 4:** *The board of directors should approve and periodically review a risk appetite and tolerance statement for operational risk that articulates the nature, types and levels of operational risk the bank is willing to assume.*

> 26. *The risk appetite and tolerance statement for operational risk should be developed under the authority of the board of directors and linked to the bank's short- and long-term strategic and financial*

plans. Taking into account the interests of the bank's customers and shareholders as well as regulatory requirements, an effective risk appetite and tolerance statement should:

a. be easy to communicate and therefore easy for all stakeholders to understand;

b. include key background information and assumptions that informed the bank's business plans at the time it was approved;

c. include statements that clearly articulate the motivations for taking on or avoiding certain types of risk, and establish boundaries or indicators (which may be quantitative or not) to enable monitoring of these risks;

d. ensure that the strategy and risk limits of business units and legal entities, as relevant, align with the bank-wide risk appetite statement;

e. and be forward-looking and, where applicable, subject to scenario and stress testing to ensure that the bank understands what events might push it outside its risk appetite and tolerance statement.

27. The board of directors should approve and regularly review the appropriateness of limits and the overall operational risk appetite and tolerance statement. This review should consider current and expected changes in the external environment (including the regulatory context across all jurisdictions where the institution provides services); ongoing or forthcoming material increases in business or activity volumes; the quality of the control environment; the effectiveness of risk management or mitigation strategies; loss experience; and the frequency, volume or nature of limit breaches. The board of directors should monitor management adherence to the risk appetite and tolerance statement and provide for timely detection and remediation of breaches.[13]

Banks and fintechs can now use this additional guidance to evaluate whether their risk appetite frameworks are appropriate and complete.

IMPLEMENTING A RISK APPETITE FRAMEWORK

SSG had three key findings regarding risk appetite in 2010 that continue to resonate today, more than 10 years later:

1. Many firms had made progress in conceptualizing, articulating, and implementing a risk appetite framework (RAF).

2. An effective RAF greatly improves a firm's strategic planning and tactical decision making.
3. Strong and active engagement by a firm's board of directors and senior management plays a central role in ensuring that a RAF has a meaningful impact on the organization.

SSG also observed three important characteristics that led to a more effective implementation of a risk appetite framework:

1. Strong internal **relationships** at the firm.
2. The board of directors ensures that senior management establishes strong **accountability** for the risk appetite, with clear incentives and constraints for business lines.
3. A common risk appetite **language** is in use across the firm, expressed through qualitative statements and appropriately selected risk metrics.

SSG provided further guidance on implementing a risk appetite framework under the following categories, and we consider each in turn.

- The Risk Appetite Framework as a Strategic Decision-Making Tool
- Risk Appetite Governance: The Board, "C-Suite," and Business Lines
- Promoting a Firmwide Risk Appetite Framework
- Monitoring the Firm's Risk Profile within the Risk Appetite Framework

The Risk Appetite Framework as a Strategic Decision-Making Tool

Having a risk appetite framework in place allows for business decisions to be considered in the context of risks being taken relative to the board or senior management's appetite for risk.

For example, a decision to expand a business line should include considerations of how the risk profile may change with that expansion. If that change is well understood and meets with the approval of the senior management, then the expansion will proceed. In contrast, if the risks in an existing business are either beyond the appetite of the firm or are not well understood, then the risk appetite framework can facilitate exiting that business for risk reasons.

Risk appetite discussions often lead to important related discussions on the strategic direction of the firm and its core competencies. Firms have often taken a step back and spent time rearticulating their strategy and business goals before moving forward with linking these to their risk appetites.

Putting a written risk appetite statement down on paper is challenging and usually results in a very-high-level statement that expresses the strategic priorities of the firm. The BCBS Corporate Governance definition of risk appetite provides additional guidance to banks on this:

> *The written articulation of the aggregate level and types of risk that a bank will accept, or avoid, in order to achieve its business objectives. It includes quantitative measures expressed relative to earnings, capital, risk measures, liquidity and other relevant measures as appropriate. It should also include qualitative statements to address reputation and conduct risks as well as money laundering and unethical practices.*[14]

A clear risk appetite should be resilient enough to prevent business lines from drifting away from the core strategy of the firm and to assist the firm in staying within its own strategic plans. However, it should also be able to evolve to reflect changing business environments and strategic decisions to move in a new direction.

Appetite Governance: The Board, "C-Suite," and Business Lines

SSG clearly outlined that in order for a RAF to be successfully implemented, the relative roles and responsibilities of the board, senior management, and the business lines should be as follows:

- The board of directors, with input from senior management, sets overarching expectations for the risk profile.
- The CEO, CRO, and CFO translate those expectations into incentives and constraints for business lines, and the board holds the businesses accountable for performance related to the expectations.
- Business lines, in turn, manage within the boundaries of these incentives and constraints, and their performance depends in part on the RAF's performance.[17]

This can be illustrated using an amended appetite triangle, as shown in Figure 14.4.

Successful risk appetite governance relies on a strong and well-informed board, a good partnership among the senior management team, and a business strategy and budgeting process that is integrated and transparent.

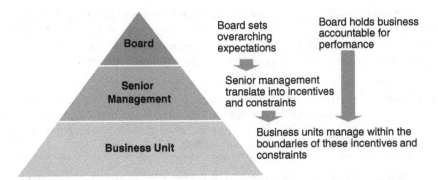

FIGURE 14.4   Risk Appetite Governance

Promoting a Firmwide Risk Appetite Framework

There is still a wide range of practice today in how widely a firm's risk appetite statements and approaches are disseminated across the firm. Some firms educate only those in senior roles and in business areas where risk is actively managed. Others will run a town hall campaign to ensure that every member of the firm understands the risk appetite of the firm and how to manage within it.

Operational risk is unique in this area, as every member of the firm does actively manage operational risk in some way. Whether they are a security guard, a bond trader, a controller, an IT programmer, or a client relationship manager, all staff will manage the risk of inadequate or failed people, process, systems, or external events.

For this reason, once an operational risk appetite is stated and an approach is established for the risk appetite framework, it will likely be important to include training and awareness on this subject in any firmwide operational risk training that is rolled out.

The most effective way to embed the framework is to hold people accountable for remaining within that appetite. In some firms, the consequences of nonadherence to risk principles or appetite statements can lead to loss of compensation, loss of promotion opportunity, or even dismissal from the firm.

Monitoring the Firm's Risk Profile within the Risk Appetite Framework

Setting limits for market and credit risk is a fairly clear-cut process. Limits can be set for traders, for trading desks, for business lines, and for the firm.

Value at risk (VaR) limits can be set and monitored and business decisions taken with reference to those limits and the current use of the limits. Credit can be denied to counterparties that have credit profiles that are outside the credit risk appetite of the firm. BCBS defines risk limits as follows:

risk limits   *Specific quantitative measures or limits based on, for example, forward-looking assumptions that allocate the bank's aggregate risk to business lines, legal entities as relevant, specific risk categories, concentrations and, as appropriate, other measures.*[15]

Setting "limits" for operational risk is very challenging. Unlike market and credit risk, in operational risk it is not possible to simply unwind a position to get back under a risk limit. When the operational risk loss is identified, the event has already occurred, and the loss is realized. Unwinding a position may not reduce the operational risk. It is also not feasible to set a "limit" on how many mistakes you can make.

However, there are mechanisms for monitoring operational risk, other than the use of limits.

MONITORING OPERATIONAL RISK APPETITE

In operational risk, it may be inappropriate to consider having an *appetite* for some risks. For example, should a firm have a set *appetite* for internal fraud? For this reason, it can be helpful to consider risk *tolerance* instead. What level of internal fraud will the firm tolerate, even though its appetite is zero?

Using the language adopted earlier in the chapter, let us consider possible risk capacity, appetite, tolerance, and limit statements for operational risk. See Figure 14.5.

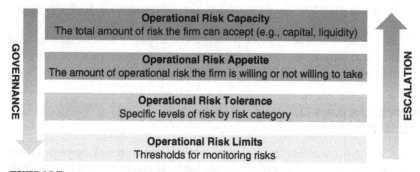

FIGURE 14.5   Operational Risk Appetite Framework

Risk Capacity

The risk capacity for operational risk is the same as for all risk for the firm, as it is the total risk that the firm can withstand, and generally would be expressed in terms of its capital ratios or liquidity.

Operational Risk Appetite

Corporate operational risk appetite statements are likely to be qualitative statements, stating the amount of risk the firm chooses to take, is willing to take, or is not willing to take. In operational risk, these statements are often purposefully broad (vague even) as accepting operational risks as being within the appetite of the board or senior management is generally not palatable. Examples of such statements could be:

- The firm will comply with laws and regulations.
- The firm will avoid business activities that may have adverse reputational impact.
- The business is an equal opportunities employer.
- The firm will invest in a robust infrastructure to support its business.

Operational Risk Tolerance

Many of the regulatory rules interchange the terms *appetite* and *tolerance*, but a semantic difference between them is particularly useful in operational risk management. While operational risk appetite statements will need to be necessarily broad, operational risk tolerances can be much more specific, as they can outline specific levels of the risk that the firm is willing to take, in the context of the broader risk appetite statements. For example, some might be black-and-white qualitative statements:

- The firm has zero risk tolerance for internal fraud.

  Others might be more quantitative:

- Total annual operational risk losses will not exceed 1 percent of revenue.
- Total annual operational risk losses will not exceed $500 million.
- Employee turnover should not exceed 15 percent.
- High-risk audit items will be resolved within 90 days.
- High residual risks identified in an RCSA will be mitigated or accepted within three months.

Operational Risk Limits/Indicators

While operational risk does not lend itself to limits in the same way that market and credit risk do, it does have many ways in which risk levels can be monitored. The choice of operational risk tolerance statements will drive the tools that are used to monitor risk levels. Each of the four main building blocks of an operational risk framework offers opportunities for articulating and monitoring operational risk appetite.

Losses

Tracking operational risk events against tolerance statements can provide a view into the current level of operational risk. While losses are not forward-looking, there may be a tolerance statement regarding the number or size of losses, and these can be tracked by business line, by risk category, and by cause.

If losses are approaching thresholds that may exceed the tolerance statement, then the risk would be escalated to senior management for a decision on any necessary mitigating actions.

For example, a new business might be expected to keep its operational risk loss events below a certain percentage of revenue in order to have approval to continue.

Capital

If an AMA approach is being taken to operational risk capital, then the capital levels will move as losses are incurred, scenarios change, and business environment internal control factors change. If a firm has adopted the new Standardized Approach, then capital requirements will move with changing losses. Some firms set risk limit statements for their operational risk capital, requiring escalation to senior management if those levels are breached.

RCSA

When we explored the use of scoring in RCSAs in Chapter 10, we were in effect building risk tolerance. For example, if a scoring matrix is used for risk impact, then this assumes that the risk tolerance is set at the low, medium, and high levels that are expressed in that matrix. The example scoring matrix can be seen again in Table 14.1.

These qualitative risk impact tolerance statements allow for RCSA reporting that expresses the level of risk as against the risk tolerance of the firm. In Chapter 10, we saw that scoring methods for controls and risk impacts can be developed and combined to produce an overall risk severity score, as in Figure 14.6.

TABLE 14.1 Impact Scoring Example

Impact Type	Low	Medium	High
Financial	Less than $100,000	Between $100,000 and $1 million	Over $1 million
Reputational	Negative reputational impact is local.	Negative reputational impact is regional.	Negative reputational impact is global.
Legal or Regulatory	Breach of contractual or regulatory obligations, with no costs.	Breach of contractual or regulatory obligations with some costs or censure.	Breach of contractual or regulatory obligations leading to major litigation, fines, or severe censure.
Clients	Minor service failure to noncritical clients.	Minor service failure to critical client(s) or moderate service failure to noncritical clients.	Moderate service failure to critical clients or major service failure to noncritical clients.
Life Safety	An employee is slightly injured or ill.	More than one employee is injured or ill.	Serious injury or loss of life.

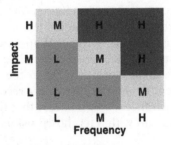

FIGURE 14.6 RCSA Risk Severity Scoring Matrix

Therefore, RCSA outputs can be used as a tool to monitor risk levels against the tolerance of the firm. In this example, if the tolerance statement states that all high risks must be remediated or accepted with a certain time period, then the RCSA is the tool by which that situation can be identified and tracked. When a risk reaches a level that breaches the threshold for "high," then necessary action can be taken.

Metrics

There are many metrics that can be used to monitor risk levels against risk tolerance statements. Any metrics that are identified as part of the operational risk KRI program should have thresholds set and should be used to produce reporting that allows for escalation of risks that are moving beyond the operational risk tolerance of the firm. As discussed in Chapter 9, the monitoring of business environment and internal control factors is an important element in the operational risk framework.

While RCSA provides monitoring at a fairly high level, metrics allow for monitoring at an individual control level, and sometimes, when a true KRI is identified, at the individual risk level. The risk appetite and tolerance of the firm are therefore very important when setting appropriate thresholds for metrics, as these metrics can then be used as "limits" for monitoring. The correct threshold will allow for appropriate escalation of rising risks so that business decisions can be made to keep the firm within its operational risk and appetite and its tolerance in the risk category.

RISK APPETITE TODAY

Risk appetite is a key area of concern for the board of a bank or fintech and needs to be effectively articulated and monitored. The regulatory expectation is now established that risk appetite must be articulated, and operational risk needs to be part of that articulation. Annual reports now include extensive sections addressing how risk appetite is established and governed, although the detailed risk appetite statements are rarely shared publicly and operational risk appetite is often expressed in only qualitative terms.

While it remains a challenging element in the framework, more and more senior management teams and boards are recognizing the benefits of setting appetites and tolerances to help ensure that the firm remains within its chosen strategic path and within its chosen risk boundaries.

KEY POINTS

- Operational risk appetite is a regulatory requirement under Basel.
- There is still a wide range of practice in risk appetite approaches today.
- The board and senior management have responsibilities to set, approve, and monitor risk appetite.
- Risk capacity is the ability of a firm to withstand risk.
- Risk appetite is the firm's willingness to take on risk.
- Risk tolerance expresses specific risk levels that will be acceptable.

- Risk limits/levels set thresholds for indicators above which escalation is required.
- Losses, RCSA, and KRIs all provide ways to monitor risk levels.

REVIEW QUESTION

1. Under Basel II, the board of directors has which of the following responsibilities for the firm's operational risk appetite statement?
   a. Review and approve
   b. Review only
   c. Approve only
   d. Develop, review, and approve

NOTES

1. Bank for International Settlements, "International Convergence of Capital Measurement and Capital Standards: A Revised Framework," 2004, section 737.
2. www.bis.org/publ/bcbs96.pdf, 4.
3. Ibid., section 21.
4. Ibid., section 41.
5. www.bis.org/publ/bcbs195.pdf, 5.
6. Ibid., p. 6, footnote 12.
7. Ibid.
8. Ibid., section 19, 5.
9. Ibid., section 27(c).
10. www.bis.org/publ/bcbs230.pdf, footnote 51.
11. Bank of International Settlements, Banking Basel Committee on Banking Supervision, "Guidelines – Corporate Governance Principles for Banks," July 2015, https://www.bis.org/bcbs/publ/d328.htm.
12. Bank of International Settlements, Banking Basel Committee on Banking Supervision, "Revisions to the Principles of the Sounds Management of Operational Risk," March 2021, https://www.bis.org/bcbs/publ/d515.htm.
13. Ibid., 8–9.
14. See note 11.
15. See note 11.

CHAPTER 15

Reputational Risk and Operational Risk

In this chapter we look more closely at reputational risk and the ways that an operational risk framework can be leveraged to help identify, assess, control, and mitigate reputational risk. Examples from recent headlines are used to highlight the significant reputational impact of most operational risk events, which often cause severe damage over and above the direct costs of the event. We explore the causes of reputational risk and the long-term effects that it can have on a firm.

Reputational risk is a critical concern for both fintechs and banks. Losing the trust of your customers can be a fatal blow to a firm's strategic plan, its growth trajectory, and investor confidence.

WHAT IS REPUTATIONAL RISK?

Regulatory guidance on the definition of reputational risk was fairly slim until the impact of the 2007 financial crisis made it clear that banks needed to do more to ensure that this risk type was well managed. The Bank of International Settlements (BIS) published comprehensive guidance on this area that became effective in December 2019. In this guidance they provided a definition for reputation risk:

> *Reputational risk can be defined as the risk arising from negative perception on the part of customers, counterparties, shareholders, investors, debt-holders, market analysts, other relevant parties or regulators that can adversely affect a bank's ability to maintain existing, or establish new, business relationships and continued access to sources of funding (e.g. through the interbank or securitisation markets).*

> *Reputational risk is multidimensional and reflects the perception of other market participants. Furthermore, it exists throughout the organisation and exposure to reputational risk is essentially a function of the adequacy of the bank's internal risk management processes, as well as the manner and efficiency with which management responds to external influences on bank-related transactions.*[1]

Reputational *risk* may be a misnomer, as it may be more practical to consider reputational *impact*. Any risk event—market, credit, operational, or strategic—can have a reputational impact. For this reason, some firms consider reputational impact in the other aspects of their risk management programs rather than managing a separate reputational risk activity. Others do consider reputational risk as its own category and manage it using the same tools that are available for operational and strategic risk.

Fintechs are particularly exposed to reputational risk, as many of them are still in the early growth stages of their strategic plan and a loss of reputation can deal a severe blow to their growth strategies.

First, let us consider whether there really is such a thing as reputational, or reputation, risk. Is this really a risk category, or is it simply a type of impact? In Chapter 10, we looked at the different potential impacts that might occur when an operational risk is identified and assessed in RCSA. There are direct and indirect financial costs, but there also may be client, regulatory, life safety, or reputation impacts.

As discussed in Chapter 1, and shown again in Figure 15.1, reputation risk sits at the heart of the risk wheel. If a risk event occurs in any

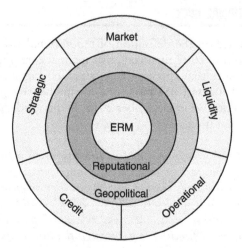

FIGURE 15.1   The Enterprise Risk Management Wheel

risk category on the outside spokes of the wheel, it can give rise to reputational risk.

A market risk event, a credit risk event, a strategic risk event, a liquidity risk event, and, of course, an operational risk event can have severe reputational consequences.

It might be better, then, to think of reputational impact rather than reputational risk. Whatever terminology we adopt, there is no doubt that damage to reputation can have serious consequences.

REPUTATIONAL IMPACT

We can easily identify reputational impacts by looking at two operational risk events that have occurred in recent years: the global COVID-19 pandemic and the London Interbank Offered Rate (LIBOR) scandal.

Global COVID-19 Pandemic

Late in 2019 the global pandemic emerged and quickly spread across the globe. This was (and at the time of this writing, still is) a catastrophic operational risk event that has led to tragic loss of life. This continuing operational risk event has cost many billions of dollars in economic impacts to businesses, governments, and individuals and is also fraught with reputational impacts for many companies, including fintechs and banks.

Companies quickly faced public and local government criticism for not moving quickly enough to protect their employees. Similarly, providers of basic supplies were vulnerable to reputational damage if they were perceived to be reacting too slowly to the event, leading to massive shortages at the outset and continuing supply chain issues over a year later. The quality of customer service in all organizations and the efficiency of their services during this crisis quickly became a hot topic. Those companies that treated their employees well and succeeded in continuing to supply good service fared better reputationally than those that did not.

Politicians faced the ire of their constituents as they struggled to maintain their base while also ensuring that the pandemic could be tackled effectively, and political careers were made and broken during the pandemic.

This is an operational risk event that was caused by natural disaster, and yet the reputational fallout was severe for all who were impacted.

Banking and Fintech Scandals

An operational risk event, where the cause is attributed to the internal actions of a bank, often gives rise to high levels of reputational damage. The LIBOR scandals of 2012 and 2013 tarnished the reputations of many banks.

It was alleged that several major banks had manipulated the LIBOR rate over an extended period, in order to benefit financially from the altered rate. The brush was quickly used to also tarnish other benchmark rates globally and regulators from many nations became engaged in uncovering the breadth and depth of the bad behavior.

Headlines from this period show the reputational wounds that were inflicted on those involved, above and beyond the direct operational risk losses that they suffered in direct fines.

Rigged Rates, Rigged Markets

Marcus Agius, the chairman of Barclays, resigned on Monday, saying "the buck stops with me." His was the first departure since the British bank agreed last week to pay $450 million to settle findings that, from 2005 to 2009, it had tried to rig benchmark interest rates to benefit its own bottom line.

New York Times, July 2, 2012[2]

RBS Managers Condoned Libor Manipulation

Royal Bank of Scotland Group Plc managers condoned and participated in the manipulation of global interest rates.

Bloomberg Business Week, September 25, 2012[3]

UBS and LIBOR

Horribly rotten, comically stupid.

The Economist, December 19, 2012[4]

As a result of its role in the alleged LIBOR manipulation, Barclays paid out $450 million in a settlement with British and U.S. regulators and lost its chief executive officer, Robert E. Diamond Jr.; its chairman, Marcus Agius; and its chief operating officer, Jerry del Missier, along with many other key senior managers.

Barclays then suffered a ratings hit as both Standard & Poor's (S&P) and Moody's rating agencies placed the firm on negative watch:

> *The abrupt changes alarmed the ratings agencies. Standard & Poor's said in its statement that "the negative outlook reflects our view of the current management flux and near-term strategic uncertainty."*
>
> *In a separate statement, Moody's said: "The senior resignations at the bank and the consequent uncertainty surrounding the firm's direction are negative for bondholders."[5]*

In addition, Barclays, along with many other alleged participants, faced multiple lawsuits from firms and individuals who alleged that the LIBOR manipulation impacted them adversely.

Charles Schwab Sues Banks Over Rate Manipulation

Charles Schwab is seeking unspecified compensatory and punitive damages from the banks. Other defendants include foreign banks like Barclays, Credit Suisse, Deutsche Bank, HSBC Holdings, Royal Bank of Scotland, Lloyds, WestLB and UBS.

New York Times, August 25, 2012[6]

Banks Rigged Libor to Inflate Adjustable-Rate Mortgages: Lawsuit

Homeowners in the U.S. are suing some of the world's biggest banks for fraud—not over any foreclosure issues but over the alleged Libor manipulation scam that they say sparked increases on their adjustable rate mortgages, and resulted in unlawful profits for the banks.

Forbes, October 15, 2012[7]

Finally, the threat of fines and lawsuits across the industry pushed stock prices down.

Barclays Libor Fine Sends Stocks Lower as Probes Widen

Barclays Plc (BARC)'s record $451 million fines for interest rate manipulation sent bank shares plunging as U.S. and U.K. authorities pursue sanctions in a global investigation of more than a dozen lenders.

Bloomberg.com, June 28, 2012[8]

The scandal eventually spread to other banks involved in LIBOR, and the New York and Connecticut attorneys general had 16 banks under investigation on this issue: Bank of America, Bank of Tokyo Mitsubishi UFJ, Barclays, Citigroup, Credit Suisse, Deutsche Bank, HSBC, JPMorgan Chase, Lloyds Banking Group, Norinchukin Bank, Rabobank, Royal Bank of Canada, Royal Bank of Scotland, Société Générale, UBS, and West LB. In December 2012, UBS agreed to settle with regulators for a huge $1.5 billion in total fines.

All of these banks faced the same reputational damage above and beyond the regulatory dollar fines that they were likely to pay. They faced the loss of key personnel (who might also face jail time), credit downgrading, litigation, and stock price devaluation.

While this might suggest that banks would become more attuned to the potential impact of reputational risk events that span the whole industry, unfortunately a similar scandal occurred more recently in Australia. The Royal Commission into Misconduct in the Banking, Superannuation and Financial Services Industry was established on December 14, 2017, to investigate multiple scandals that had rocked the Australian banking industry over prior years. The final report was published in 2019 and included a scathing executive summary that spoke to the tarnished reputation of Australian banks and suggested that their multiple failings had being motivated by greed:

> *Why did it happen? Too often, the answer seems to be greed— the pursuit of short term profit at the expense of basic standards of honesty.*[9]

The headlines picked up on this theme, and it was widely reported that every Australian bank (except Westpac) had been censured in the report. Several CEOs left their jobs, and the Australian regulators were ordered to pursue action against the banks.

The negative headlines have lingered, and there is still reporting at the time of writing in 2021 that reminds banking customers of the reputational damage that was inflicted on the Australian banks:

> *"Worse than ever": Australian bank culture has not improved since royal commission, staff say*
>
> *Workers insist pay is still linked to hitting sales benchmarks and leaderboards to track sales are rife.*
>
> *The Guardian,* April 6, 2021[10]

Fintechs have had their share of reputational risk in recent years, as their practices have come under scrutiny. Chime suffered from negative headlines in 2021 when they closed accounts as a result of their efforts to reduce fraud.

Backlash Over Chime Account Closings Highlights Risks in Fraud Detection

The neobank Chime is coping with growing pains, including a surge in customer complaints about suddenly closed accounts.

American Banker, July 7, 2021[11]

Robinhood bore the brunt of negative headlines when it was fined by FINRA in 2021.

Robinhood to pay $70 million fine after causing "widespread and significant harm" to customers

Popular investing platform Robinhood has agreed to pay nearly $70 million to the financial industry regulatory authority (FINRA) to settle allegations that the brokerage caused customers "widespread and significant" harm on multiple different fronts over the past few years.

CNBC, June 30, 2021[12]

A reputational risk event often results in multiple impacts, some of which are captured in the operational risk framework—but some might not be. Fines and litigation are captured in an operational risk framework, as they meet the definition of legal risk within the definition of operational risk:

> *Operational risk is defined as the risk of loss resulting from inadequate or failed processes, people and systems or from external events.*
> *This definition* ***includes legal risk***, *but excludes strategic and reputational risk.*[13]

However, other impacts such as stock price losses, credit downgrades, and loss of key personnel are not generally considered financial losses within this definition, and reputational risk is expressly excluded.

While the preceding examples arose out of operational risk events, reputational damage can arise from other events such as market risk and credit risk. Significant losses in either area can lead to serious questions about the ability of the firm to operate effectively in the markets, and this can lead to the loss of both clients and share value.

In addition to reputational impact arising from other risk types, it can also arise out of activities that are not risky in any other sense. For example, banks are increasingly avoiding investments and funding for environmentally unpopular or social unacceptable practices. It is common today for banks to issue glowing corporate social responsibility reports that outline their fair, environmentally sound, and socially responsible values and practices. UK banks are now required to share their climate change activities with their regulators, and there is pressure globally for all companies to be transparent about their efforts.

> *UK Banks to Reveal Exposure to Climate Crisis for First Time*
>   *Bank of England to examine risks rising temperatures and sea levels could pose for financial system*
>
> *The Bank of England will examine the risk of the climate crisis to financial institutions. UK banks will for the first time be forced to reveal their exposure to the climate crisis, highlighting the risks that rising temperatures and sea levels could pose for the financial system, as part of the Bank of England's climate stress tests this year.*
>
>

The Guardian, June 8, 2021[14]

These types of efforts can directly contribute to the reputation of a fintech or bank.

Stock Price Impacts

Financial losses as a result of a reputational event are generally captured in the operational risk framework, as they often stem from failed or inadequate people, systems, processes, or external events.

There are other impacts that are not captured in the operational risk framework, and these are drivers for strong reputational risk management.

One of these major drivers is the negative impact on share value that can result from a reputational event. As we saw earlier, the banking sector as a whole took a major stock hit as a result of the widespread LIBOR scandal. Barclays themselves saw an 18 percent slide during the early stages of the news breaking.

In 2005, Perry and de Fontnouvelle completed a study on the market reaction to operational risk announcements.[15] They examined the difference between internal fraud events and other events, on the assumption that internal fraud events carry a much higher reputational impact than, for example, execution errors.

Their research found that losses from internal fraud events resulted in larger impacts to share value than those that were not internal fraud, suggesting that reputational impact had real cost.

A similar study was conducted in 2010 by Gillet, Hubner, and Plunus. The authors examined stock market reactions to the announcement of operational losses by financial companies and attempted to disentangle operational losses from reputational damage. Their results showed:

> *... significant, negative abnormal returns at the announcement date of the loss, along with an increase in the volumes of trade. In cases of internal fraud, the loss in market value is greater that the operational loss amount announced, which is interpreted as a sign of reputational damage.*[16]

Robinhood recently experienced the negative impact of operational risk on its newly listed stock price. A concern around the compliance of its practices led to market concerns and shares tumbled quickly.

Robinhood Shares Tumble after Paypal News, SEC Scrutiny of Key Revenue Stream

New York, Aug 30 (Reuters) – Shares of Robinhood Markets Inc (HOOD.O), a popular gateway for trading meme stocks, tumbled nearly 7% on Monday on news that PayPal Holdings Inc (PYPL.O) may start an online brokerage and a report saying regulators were looking at a possible ban on a practice that accounts for the bulk of the company's revenue.[17]

Reuters, August 30, 2021

The apparent reputational impact on stock price can also be seen in the JPMorgan "Whale" case study in Chapter 18.

REGULATORY OVERSIGHT OF REPUTATIONAL RISKS

In December 2019, updated "Core Principles for Effective Banking Supervision" from the Basel Committee on Banking Supervision (BCBS) came into effect and listed the following essential criteria as guidance to banking regulators:

> *The supervisor understands and assesses how group-wide risks are managed and takes action when risks arising from the banking group and other entities in the wider group, in particular contagion and **reputation** risks, may jeopardize the safety and soundness of the bank and the banking system.*[18] *[emphasis added]*

The 2015 BCBS "Corporate Governance Principles for Banks" reinforced that the roles of the board, senior management, and the risk committee should include activities concerning reputational risk and that the risk management framework must include effective identification and measurement or reputation risk:

> *Risk identification and measurement should include both quantitative and qualitative elements. Risk measurements should also include qualitative, bank-wide views of risk relative to the bank's external operating environment. Banks should also consider and evaluate harder-to-quantify risks, such as reputation risk.*[19]

So the BCBS rules expect a firm to have strategies around its reputational risk and to identify, measure, and manage reputational risks impacts to the firm. This sounds very like the requirements for operational risk.

In Basel II itself, although reputational risk is expressly excluded from the Pillar 1 requirements for operational risk, it reemerges in Pillar 2. In the 2019 Pillar 2 summary, BCBS outlines this requirement:

> *Some areas are particularly important for supervisory review under Pillar 2. One such area is an assessment of corporate governance, including misconduct risk and firm-wide risk management, as well as those risks that are considered under Pillar 1 but not fully captured by Pillar 1 capital requirements. Examples of these risks are interest rate risk in the banking book; non-financial risks such as strategic risk, business model risk and **reputational** risk; and aspects of credit concentration risk.*[20] *[emphasis added]*

National regulators implemented their local rules for the supervision of Pillar 2 under regulations known as the ICAAP (Internal Capital Adequacy Assessment Process). In these documents they have included reputational risks as one of the material other risks that need to be captured as part of the bank's exercise to demonstrate that it holds adequate capital overall under Basel II.

Therefore, banks that are under the Basel II rules need to be able to identify, assess, and mitigate reputational risk. Banks that are not under Basel II frequently find that their regulators nevertheless expect Basel II–type standards to be in place for risk management.

Apart from the regulatory pressures, it is good business sense to actively manage risks that can seriously harm the firm.

REPUTATIONAL RISK MANAGEMENT FRAMEWORK

Although the Basel II definition of operational risk explicitly excludes reputational risk, some firms adopt an internal definition that expressly includes operational risk. As we saw in Chapter 1, Citi includes reputational risk in their definition of operational risk:

> *Operational risk is the risk of loss resulting from inadequate or failed internal processes, people or systems, or from external events. It includes the reputation and franchise risk associated with business practices or market conduct that the Company undertakes.*[21]

The operational risk framework is designed to identify, assess, control, and mitigate a risk that is difficult to quantify and that has a subjective and qualitative nature. The elements of the framework can also be effective in meeting the similar challenge of managing and measuring reputational risk. Indeed, several of the operational risk elements routinely consider the reputational impact of operational risks (although not of other risk types such as market, credit, or liquidity risks).

We can adapt the operational risk framework to meet reputational risk needs, and we can leverage existing operational risk activities to include the management and measurement of reputational risks. See Figure 15.2.

Drivers

The drivers for reputational risk management are very similar to the drivers of operational risk management:

- Managing all risks is sound business management.
- Excellence in reputation risk management provides transparency, foresight, and protection.

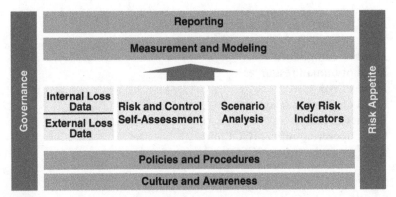

FIGURE 15.2 The Operational Risk Framework Structure Can Simply Be Renamed and Reused as a Reputational Risk Framework

- Strong reputational risk management can:
  - Lead to potentially fewer (bad) surprises
  - Allow for quicker recovery from events
  - Ensure that adequate capital is held to protect the firm from reputation risk events
  - Allow for full assessment of reputation risks prior to business decision making
  - Lead to increased investor/shareholder confidence

Governance

The same governance questions apply as for operational risk management: who owns the function, and what should the function own?

Some firms have an individual who is responsible for reputational risk across the firm. That person often resides in the legal department, but it could be argued that they should sit in the risk function in order to ensure that they have the appropriate independence.

There is often a franchise risk or reputation risk committee to which reputational risk issues are escalated. These issues might be raised from the operational risk area, or from other areas where no operational risks are anticipated and yet reputational risk remains.

For example, if a deal is being considered with a counterparty who has a less than stellar reputation or in an industry where there is strong public protest, such as some mining techniques, then there may be associated reputational risk.

In such cases, the deal can be brought to the franchise committee for consideration. There may be a single global committee, several independent regional committees, or a hierarchy of local and global committees.

The membership of such a committee should probably include:

- Head of corporate social responsibility
- Head of legal
- Head of compliance
- Head of human resources
- Head of risk
- Head of investor relations
- Business heads
- Chief operating officer (COO)
- Chief financial officer (CFO)

Event Data Collection

In the same way that operational risk losses are captured in a database for management and mitigation of the risks, reputational risk events could be captured in a database for the same purpose.

It may be more efficient to leverage the existing operational risk event database for this purpose. It is certainly fairly simple to add a reputational impact field to an operational risk event database to ensure that for all operational risk events, the reputational impact is being captured.

RCSA

As we saw in Chapter 10, it is possible to capture the reputational impact of an operational risk during the RCSA process. The sample reputational risk scale is shown again in Table 15.1.

The RCSA could also be leveraged to capture *all* reputational risks, including those not arising from operational risk, simply by expanding the scope of the RCSA. For example, once all operational risks have been identified, further questions could be asked concerning what reputational risks could also arise in other ways. The reputational impact scoring method could be used to assess the relative priority of those risks.

The use of the RCSA for this purpose would allow for reputational risks that have not yet occurred to be identified, assessed, and controlled and decisions made on whether they need to be mitigated.

An example of such a risk could be, "We invest in a company that has environmentally damaging practices."

Key Risk Indicators

In the same way that metrics can be used to help monitor whether operational risks are becoming more or less elevated, metrics can be used to monitor reputational impacts of operational risks. Metrics could also be

TABLE 15.1   Possible Reputational Impact Scoring Method for RCSA

Impact Type	Low	Medium	High
Reputational	Negative reputational impact is local.	Negative reputational impact is regional.	Negative reputational impact is global.

established to monitor reputational risk indicators that are unique to reputational risk.

For example, how many NGO protest letters has the firm received? How many of the firm's clients are currently under investigation for employing sweatshop labor? What percentage of U.S. mountaintop removal mining is funded by the firm?

The corporate social responsibility department could design and develop these types of metrics for review by the franchise or risk committee on a periodic basis.

Scenario Analysis

The scenario analysis program can be leveraged to ensure that reputational risk has been adequately captured for Pillar 2 capital purposes. There is a regulatory expectation that reputational considerations are included in stress testing when assessing capital adequacy for the firm.

The operational risk function will already have a scenario analysis program that handles the collection of data in the difficult and subjective area of very large operational risk exposures. This program will be well suited to provide the same structured output for reputational risk scenarios.

A scenario analysis program could be run separately for reputational risk, or reputational risk scenarios could be added to the existing operational risk scenario analysis program to improve efficiency.

Reporting

As with operational risk reporting, senior management are likely to be seeking reporting on reputational risk that addresses the following concerns:

- Where is our risk?
- What action do we need to take?
- Who is under control?
- Who is not?
- Are we meeting our regulatory requirements?

Reporting might be designed to go to the risk committee, to the franchise committee, or to both. It is important that the risk committee and the chief risk officer are aware of all risks in the firm and so some summary and escalation reporting process should be put in place to facilitate that.

As reputational risk issues often arise in the operational risk reporting process, it may be most efficient to combine overall reputational risk reporting with operational risk reporting.

Whatever approach is taken, the owner of reputational risk management at the firm should consider taking a risk analysis approach, and not just a data gathering approach. In other words, they should undertake to provide the following for reputational risk:

- Analyze raw data.
- Analyze trends and predictors (KRIs).
- Follow news articles.
- Present opinions.
- Present capital at risk and stress-testing impacts.
- Recommend action and mitigating strategies.

KEY POINTS

- Reputational risk is excluded from the Basel definition of operational risk. However, many firms include it in their internal definition of operational risk.
- The impact of reputational risk on capital occurs through its inclusion as a "material risk" under Pillar 2 of Basel II.
- Events that have a reputational impact often result in many knock-on negative impacts, including:
  - Litigation
  - Regulatory fines
  - Loss of key personnel
  - Stock price devaluation
- Studies have shown that operational risk events that have a higher reputational impact result in a more pronounced loss in share value.
- The operational risk framework can be leveraged for the effective management of reputational risk.

REVIEW QUESTION

1. Which of the following statements is true?
   a. The Basel II definition of operational risk includes reputational risk.
   b. Reputational risk is captured under Pillar 1 of Basel II.
   c. There is no reputational impact in operational risk.
   d. The impact of reputational risk is captured under Pillar 2 of Basel II.

NOTES

1. Bank for International Settlements, Basel Committee for Banking Supervision, "Supervisory Review Program, Risk Management," SRP 30, section 30.29, https://www.bis.org/basel_framework/chapter/SRP/30.htm.
2. www.nytimes.com/2012/07/03/opinion/rigged-rates-rigged-markets.html.
3. www.businessweek.com/news/2012-09-24/rbs-managers-said-to-condone-manipulation-of-libor-rates.
4. www.economist.com/blogs/schumpeter/2012/12/ubs-and-libor.
5. dealbook.nytimes.com/2012/07/05/attention-turns-to-barclays-future/.
6. dealbook.nytimes.com/2011/08/25/charles-schwab-sues-banks-over-rate-manipulation/.
7. www.forbes.com/sites/halahtouryalai/2012/10/15/banks-rigged-libor-to-inflate-adjustable-rate-mortgages-lawsuit/.
8. www.bloomberg.com/news/2012-06-28/barclays-451-million-libor-fine-paves-the-way-for-competitors.html.
9. Royal Commission into Misconduct in the Banking, Superannuation and Financial Services Industry, Executive Summary, 2019.
10. https://www.theguardian.com/australia-news/2021/apr/07/worse-than-ever-australian-bank-culture-has-not-improved-since-royal-commission-staff-say.
11. https://www.americanbanker.com/payments/news/backlash-over-chime-account-closings-highlights-risks-in-fraud-detection.
12. https://www.cnbc.com/2021/06/30/robinhood-to-pay-70-million-dollars-after-causing-users-significant-harm.html.
13. Bank for International Settlements, "International Convergence of Capital Measurement and Capital Standards: A Revised Framework," 2004, section 644.
14. https://www.theguardian.com/business/2021/jun/08/uk-banks-climate-crisis-bank-of-england.
15. Jason Perry and Patrick de Fontnouvelle, "Measuring Reputational Risk: The Market Reaction to Operational Loss Announcements," Federal Reserve Bank of Boston, 2005.
16. R. Gillet, G. Hubner, and S. Plunus, "Operational Risk and Reputation in the Financial Industry," *Journal of Banking & Finance* 34, no. 1 (2010), http://dx.doi.org/10.1016/j.jbankfin.2009.07.020.
17. https://www.reuters.com/business/finance/robinhood-shares-tumble-after-paypal-news-sec-scrutiny-key-revenue-stream-2021-08-30/.
18. Bank for International Settlements, Basel Committee on Banking Supervision, "BCP Core Principles for Effective Banking Supervision," effective December 2019, https://www.bis.org/basel_framework/standard/BCP.htm.
19. Bank for International Settlements, Basel Committee on Banking Supervision, "Guidelines: Corporate Governance Principles for Banks," July 2015, https://www.bis.org/bcbs/publ/d328.htm.
20. Bank for International Settlements, Basel Committee on Banking Supervision, "Pillar 2 Framework: Executive Summary," October 2019, https://www.bis.org/fsi/fsisummaries/pillar2.htm.
21. Citi Annual Report 2020, 64.

CHAPTER 16

Operational Risk and Convergence

In this chapter, we explore the continued enthusiasm for convergence, or governance, risk, and compliance (GRC). Both terms refer to the adoption of an integrated approach to managing the various elements of operational risk so that related activities can be leveraged, efficiencies attained, and more powerful risk management results achieved. We consider how a converged approach can be effective in assessment and in metrics and discuss the powerful reporting possibilities that can result from an integrated approach.

OPERATIONAL RISK AS A CATALYST FOR CONVERGENCE

Operational risk management aims to provide transparency into the operational risk exposures of the firm, by identifying, assessing, monitoring, controlling, and mitigating those risks. The depth and breadth of operational risk in every firm means that the operational risk department needs to take on a unique role. Not only must it build partnerships with all of the underlying operational risk activities, but it must also attain a governance structure that allows it to influence decision making at every level of the firm. In addition, it often has to facilitate a culture change across the firm so that operational risk management becomes a day-to-day embedded activity in the firm.

The rise of operational risk management has led to the emergence of integration and convergence initiatives and has energized enterprise risk management (ERM) discussions. The qualitative tools of the operational risk framework are being investigated by market, credit, strategic, reputational, and geopolitical risk specialists, as the purely quantitative models of the past have revealed weaknesses.

Operational risk management is an art as well as a science, requiring excellent influencing skills, communication skills, facilitation skills, and analytical skills for success.

The future of operational risk is still evolving, but it is certain that it will remain as an important and relevant risk management function in the financial services industry, and the discipline is being adopted across many other industries as the benefits of proactive operational risk management are realized.

In addition to its influence on other risk disciplines, the formal operational risk frameworks that have evolved in the past few years have led to improvements and integrations in many related activities. Audit, compliance, Sarbanes-Oxley, information security, business continuity, and many others have similar assessment, metrics, and reporting needs. As the operational risk framework has matured, the overlaps, duplications, and opportunities for leveraging have become more and more clear.

GOVERNANCE, RISK, AND COMPLIANCE (GRC)

There is strong movement toward integrating all operational risk–related activities, and this is often referred to as governance, risk, and compliance (GRC) or convergence. This integration refers to both the activities that are part of the operational risk framework and the other activities that exist outside that framework but are concerned with operational risk. These other activities include business continuity planning, information security, compliance desk reviews, legal event tracking, audit reports, and Sarbanes-Oxley assessments.

In Chapter 4, we examined the various governance structures that can be used to support an operational risk function. Some of these were more conducive to a GRC strategy at the firm, but it is possible to implement a GRC strategy in any governance structure. A GRC strategy requires senior management support and positive participation from all parties.

Without a GRC approach, there may be a waste of resources, contradictory reporting, incomplete analysis of risks, duplication of effort, and a misperception of risk exposures.

For example, when all operational risk–related functions work independently, they also interact separately with the business and support areas and report separately to management. The separate views of the risks and the separate representation of these views can be confusing and even misleading.

Let us take risk assessment as an example of where convergence can be beneficial.

Assessment Convergence

Without an integrated approach, the risk assessment activities in a firm can produce severe assessment fatigue, as business units and support areas are asked to complete a myriad of different assessments that often rely on the same key individuals in their area.

The first step in integrating risk assessment activities is to understand what the catalog of activities is. Firms are often surprised to discover that they have more than 20 assessments going on each year, all of which touch on subsets of operational risk categories. It can be helpful to map those activities to see where the overlaps and gaps are. Figure 16.1 illustrates an example mapping of assessment activities in a firm. In this diagram, two businesses units (BU 1 and BU 2) and three support areas (IT, Ops, and Finance) have listed the assessment activities that they are currently engaged in and where these activities touch on aspects of a Basel II operational risk category. For example, the SOX 404/302 assessment is undertaken by all business units and support areas and includes areas that are part of the Internal Fraud, Business Disruption and Systems Failures, and the Execution, Delivery, and Process Management risk categories.

In contrast, the anti–money laundering (AML) assessment is only undertaken by the business units and by operations. The AML assessment covers areas that would be under the Clients, Products, and Business Practices risk category.

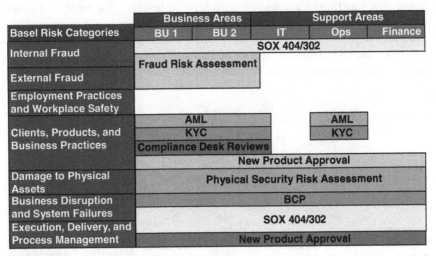

FIGURE 16.1 Map of Existing Assessment Activities against Operational Risk Categories

Figure 16.1 is a highly simplified version of the mapping that will occur when most firms attempt this exercise. The complexity of assessment activities, the amount of duplication, and the size of some of the gaps are often eye-opening.

However, each of the assessments is likely driven by regulatory requirements or strong business drivers, and so any simplification needs to ensure that the quality and completeness of assessments are not compromised.

The operational risk function will often discover that there are so many gaps in this patchwork that RCSA is necessary to ensure the completeness of risk assessment across all areas of the firm and across all risks that lie within each risk category.

For example, an existing fraud risk assessment might not capture all underlying internal and external fraud risks at Level 2 (Level 2 risks were discussed in Chapter 7), and it might not capture all departments.

The resulting multitude of necessary activities is often duplicative and burdensome on the firm. Figure 16.2 illustrates a nonconverged model, where all owners of risk assessments interact separately with their stakeholders in the firm. In this illustration only a handful of firm-wide assessments have been included, but it is easily apparent that there will be inefficiencies and resulting frustrations in this unconverged approach.

This is the model that was in place in many firms in the early stages of the implementation of the operational risk framework. RCSA became an additional assessment burden on the firm, and each assessment was run as a separate activity. To alleviate some of this stress on the firm, some operational risk functions have looked into how to leverage the results of other assessments in the RCSA so that at least that assessment is not unnecessarily duplicative.

For example, why ask questions about risks and controls that have already been assessed by the Sarbanes-Oxley (SOX) program? In fact, it is

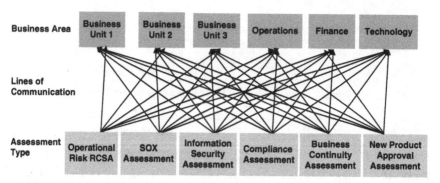

FIGURE 16.2 A Nonconverged Approach to Risk Assessment

dangerous to reassess any SOX risks and controls, as it is very important that the SOX certifications are not compromised by any new scoring that does not match the SOX conclusions.

Figure 16.3 illustrates how the RCSA program can leverage deep-dive underlying assessments while ensuring comprehensive cover of all risks in the Basel II operational risk categories.

Figure 16.3 illustrates how the SOX assessment can be leveraged in any fraud risk assessments and how the fraud risk assessment can then be leveraged in RCSA. By using the results from underlying assessments, the risk and control self-assessment (RCSA) process can avoid duplication and can ensure consistency of reporting among the different assessment teams.

Alternatively, this process could be designed so that the RCSA process now gathers all of the assessment information that is needed by the underlying assessments. For example, the RCSA program could ask for information above and beyond its own requirements so that the underlying assessment needs are met in that one assessment activity. If this approach is taken, then it allows for a highly simplified communication model for assessment at the firm, as is illustrated in Figure 16.4. This leveraging and sharing of assessment data can happen only if the data can be shared among the assessment teams.

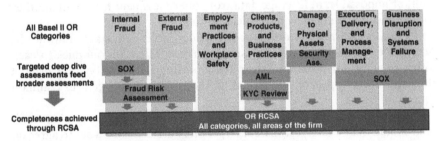

FIGURE 16.3 Leveraging Underlying Assessments in RCSA

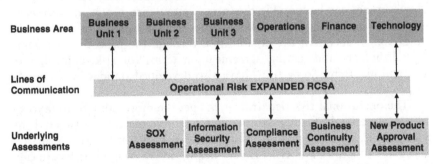

FIGURE 16.4 Simplified Communication Model with Expanded RCSA

Converged Assessment Data

The key to an effective GRC program is to provide a central repository for data that can be used by all parties. This is often a challenging undertaking, as each assessment is likely to have different systems, from sophisticated workflow tools to simple spreadsheets.

However, it is possible to share data without sharing tools. To achieve this, a central "golden source" of data needs to be established and an owner anointed for those data. The operational risk function is uniquely placed to drive such an initiative, as it needs to access all assessments data that relate to operational risk.

For this reason, GRC initiatives are often kicked off by the corporate operational risk function. At the very least, they will be a key stakeholder in such projects, including the data storage.

Assessment Taxonomies

Common data requires a convergence of language to ensure that all parties are using categorizations and definitions in the same way. All risk assessment owners will need to use the same terms when referring to risks and controls. They will likely also need to develop the same language for processes and for organizational hierarchies. Without these common taxonomies it is difficult, or impossible, to leverage data from one assessment for use in another, or to consolidate assessment results meaningfully.

Final converged taxonomies are a desirable end state, but in the meantime it is often possible to simply map different taxonomies to each other to allow for powerful integrated reporting. This can be done using a Rosetta Stone approach—where all libraries map into a central common library of terms.

Developing a taxonomy for each of the common elements is a huge task and should not be underestimated. To get every assessment owner to agree on the language that will be used for process, risk, control, and organizational hierarchy is a complex, political, and practically challenging undertaking.

Assistance can be found in the form of straw man taxonomies for each area. Many consulting firms today offer to provide these straw man taxonomies and to shepherd the organization through the process of engaging all stakeholders and getting agreement on terms for risk, control, process, and hierarchy. Some firms have also developed standard taxonomies for products.

The operational risk department can get the most value from taxonomies if they take the further step of mapping the connections between them. For example, for every process, what are the risks that may exist? A matrix that maps processes and risks is very helpful in ensuring all risks are captured whenever the same process is assessed in a different area of the firm.

For each risk, what are the expected types of controls? A matrix mapping risks to controls is very helpful in developing more standardized scoring methods for the effectiveness of controls. Therefore, using taxonomies and mapping matrices between them, the operational risk department can identify the following for an RCSA:

1. Which part of the organization hierarchy is being assessed?
2. Which processes exist in this area?
3. Which risks are associated with those processes?
4. What are the expected controls for those risks?
5. Have any underlying assessments already assessed those risks and controls?

Converged Assessment Tools

Figure 16.4 assumes that many fundamental elements are the same for all assessments represented in that model. For example, it assumes that the timing of the RCSA would be appropriate for the compliance assessments and that the sign-off requirements would be appropriate for the SOX assessments. However, in practice, this is often not the case. There may be critical deadlines for assessments and different required periods for assessments. To meet all of these requirements, an enhanced RCSA might then need to occur at too broad a scale and too often, with overburdensome sign-off requirements. A solution to this problem is to move all of the assessments onto a single assessment tool and allow each assessing team to conduct their assessments with the business units as needed. The fact that there are multiple assessments being conducted can be invisible to the business unit, if the business only interacts with a single assessment tool. That tool could send out assessment questions each month as needed, and the results parsed to the assessment areas that need them. By using sophisticated workflow tools, sign-off and scoring can all be built into the tool. In this way, assessment will have a standardized look and feel to the business unit, and duplication will be removed as the tool would provide recent results to the assessment teams and exclude them from this month's list of assessment questions for the business.

There are many such tools on the market today, but many firms are also selecting to build them in-house. They rely on robust taxonomies, excellent workflow capabilities, and centralized data.

A possible ideal end-state for such an approach is illustrated in Figure 16.5.

At its most robust, a converged, or GRC assessment strategy results in an integrated reporting platform that allows management to review assessment data from all sources across the firm.

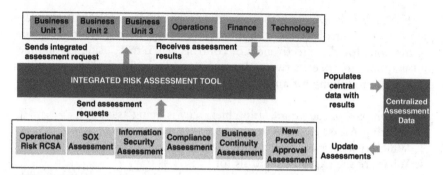

FIGURE 16.5   Communication Flows Using an Integrated Risk Assessment Tool

Convergence of Metrics

The need for metrics has grown exponentially in recent years. Metrics are gathered by risk assessment areas, control functions, and business departments. Some are used to measure efficiencies, some are used to monitor risk, and some are used to measure performance against strategic goals. As a result, many firms have found themselves entangled in multiple metrics initiatives that use communication and data gathering models similar to the confused communications illustrated in Figure 16.2. The technological complexities of having multiple metrics databases accessing the same metrics data can cause serious headaches in the information technology (IT) department and frustrations for the data owners.

Figure 16.6 illustrates the complexity of a nonconverged approach to metrics. In this illustration, the requests for metrics data are made by all areas of the firm. A business unit might request data from operations, operations may request data from technology, and technology may request data from finance. Each area of the firm has unique metrics needs and uses, and this often results in every area receiving multiple similar, but slightly different, requests for metrics data.

If standardized taxonomies have been developed for the firm, then a converged approach can also be taken to metrics gathering and usage. This approach generally looks very similar to a converged approach to assessment as a centralized data repository for metrics data is accessed by all metrics users and providers. Figure 16.7 illustrates how such an approach limits the data requests received by each area of the firm and allows users of metrics to access one location for all of their data needs.

There are many advantages to such a centralized metrics data approach:

- Consistent data quality standards can be applied.
- Consistent metrics reporting is ensured.
- "Golden sources" of data can be identified.

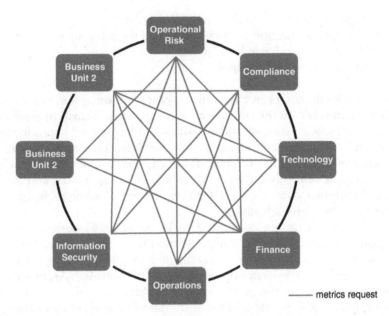

FIGURE 16.6 A Nonconverged Approach to Metrics Results in Multiple Data Requests

FIGURE 16.7 A Converged Approach to Metrics Data Warehousing

- Duplicate sources of data can be eliminated.
- Only one connection or "pipe" is needed to each source of data.
- Efficiency savings can be achieved.
- Best practices are leveraged.

Metrics initiatives in banks in the past were often doomed to failure. They often relied on the enthusiasm and support of a small number (sometimes one) senior manager and the cost and effort involved in producing useful results was often considered prohibitive. When cost-cutting cycles came along, the metrics initiative often was one of the first initiatives to be axed.

Fintechs generally have the advantage of having newer, and therefore possibly cleaner, data sets and structures and often look to their data strategies for competitive advantage.

Today, metrics are considered to be an essential element in a well-managed financial services company, whether it is a chartered bank or a start-up fintech. Regulators, boards, and executive management teams demand metrics to evidence the current state of controls, risks, performance, and efficiencies. As the permanence of metrics has now become evident, more and more firms are looking at the current complexities of their many metrics programs and are exploring initiatives to converge those programs, using a robust central data strategy.

This improved data management and warehousing approach also fits within the second major recommendation made by the Senior Supervisors Group (SSG) in its "2010 Observations on Development in Risk Appetite Frameworks and IT Infrastructure."[1] The risk appetite elements of this report were discussed in Chapter 14, but the second major recommendation was that banks make fundamental improvements in the quality of their data and the processes that surround that data.

Further guidance on data was provided by the Basel Committee on Banking Supervision (BCBS) in their 2013 paper, "Principles for Effective Risk Data Aggregation and Risk Reporting."[2] This paper addressed all aspects of risk reporting and highlighted the weaknesses in banks' abilities to effectively aggregate their risks, as was evidenced during 2007 financial crisis. The guidance applied to the Advanced Measurement Approaches to operational risk as well as to market and credit risk. In April 2020, a review of progress against the guidance concluded that:

None of the banks are fully compliant with the Principles in terms of building up the necessary data architecture and, for many, IT infrastructure remains difficult. But banks' efforts to implement the

> *Principles have resulted in tangible progress in several key areas, including governance, risk data aggregation capabilities and reporting practices.*[3]

CONVERGED OR GRC REPORTING

In addition to having assessment and metrics data mapped to standard taxonomies, and held in centralized data repositories, many firms are now looking at taking the same approach to their event data and their action tracking processes.

For example, all operational risk loss events, all audit items, and all regulatory exam results could be housed in one database. By housing all of these items in one location, mapped against standard taxonomies, it is now possible to also house all related action tracking in one location. This fully integrated approach is referred to as a GRC approach.

GRC Tools

The level of interest in a GRC approach has led software firms to develop off-the-shelf and configurable tools that promise to do some or all of the following:

- Provide workflow for many different assessments.
- Manage the capture and storage of loss event data.
- Manage the capture and storage of audit items.
- Manage the capture and storage of compliance items.
- Manage SOX processes and sign-off.
- Warehouse metrics for all operational risk-related functions.
- Provide taxonomy warehouses for process, risk, control, organizational hierarchies, and products.
- Support matrixed relationships between taxonomies.
- Provide all underlying data in dashboard and hard copy reporting.

Many banks have also decided to develop their own GRC tools and are linking them to other management information systems that they have in place. If firms achieve this integrated end state of convergence, they are then able to mine the data for insights. They are able to ask profound and powerful operational risk questions. For example, if the operational risk department has recently learned of a major external event in the area of unauthorized trading, they would be able to gather the following information with ease:

- What residual scores do all assessments show against unauthorized trading risks?
- What unauthorized trading loss events have occurred in the past five years?
- What outstanding audit items are there that relate to unauthorized trading processes and controls?
- What do our KRIs show us regarding controls that are related to unauthorized trading?

Similarly, the head of a business area could use a GRC tool to ask the following questions about his own department:

- What action items are currently outstanding and which are late? (All audit, all compliance, all SOX, and all operational risk actions items would be displayed in one dashboard.)
- What process has the weakest-scoring KRIs?
- What process has produced the most loss events and audit items in the past three years?

This type of proactive operational risk management is facilitated by a converged approach to operational risk and its related activities.

KEY POINTS

- Convergence or governance, risk, and compliance (GRC) are terms used to describe an integrated approach to managing operational risk activities and related activities across the firm.
- Assessment integration can lessen the assessment burden on a firm.
- Metrics convergence can result in higher-quality data practices and lessen the data request burdens on the firm.
- GRC reporting allows for powerful operational risk management reporting, including dashboard and management information systems that facilitate proactive operational risk management questions.
- Successful convergence requires the development and implementation of standard taxonomies for process, risk, control, and organizational hierarchy. Product taxonomies are also important in many cases.

REVIEW QUESTION

1. GRC is the common term used for
   a. governance, reliance, and content.
   b. global risk convergence.
   c. governance, risk, and compliance.
   d. global regulatory controls.

NOTES

1. www.fsa.gov.uk/pubs/other/ssg_2010.pdf.
2. BCBS 239, January 2013, https://www.bis.org/publ/bcbs239.pdf.
3. BCBS Progress in adopting the Principles for effective risk data aggregation and risk reporting, April 2020, https://www.bis.org/bcbs/publ/d501.htm.

CHAPTER 17

Best Practices in Related Risk Management Activities

There are many activities within a fintech or bank that manage a specific operational risk or subset of operational risks. Each of these may have existed well before the operational risk corporate function was formed and may be owned by specialists in that field. In addition to meeting all operational risk regulatory and business requirements, these risk areas often have their own unique regulations and business drivers.

As discussed in Chapter 16, the operational risk department must forge strong relationships with these areas in order to ensure the success of the framework and to ensure consistency in reporting and escalation of operational risks throughout the firm.

In this chapter, we will learn some more about each of these unique areas and their best practices.

NEW-PRODUCT APPROVAL

One of the most effective weapons against Clients, Products, and Business Practices events is a robust new-product approval process. This control should be designed to ensure that all risks are considered when a new product is being proposed. The market and credit risks may be well understood by those involved in proposing the new product, but they may be unaware of the resulting operational risks that may arise. Therefore, a new-product proposal should be reviewed by the legal, compliance, tax, information technology (IT), information security, business continuity, model governance, third-party risk management, operations, and finance departments before it is approved. Each of these departments should carefully consider the possible operational risks that may arise in the development, implementation, and maintenance of the new product.

Conditions may be raised and documented during the process so that the product owner is aware of the constraints that need to be built into the product to ensure that the firm's risk appetite is not breached.

If the operational risks are beyond the appetite of the firm, then they must be mitigated before the product is launched or, if this is not possible, the product proposal must be shelved.

If a product is approved, it is important to ensure that there is also a mechanism to ensure that it is monitored. Many products that were at the heart of the recent economic crisis did pass through a new-product approval process. However, they then grew at a rate beyond the expectations of all involved, and the risks were not reassessed at any point.

In today's highly competitive digital banking environment, a bank or fintech may be under significant pressure to continue to rapidly roll out innovative new products to attract and retain customers. The importance of the new-product approval process is heightened in this environment and needs to act as an opportunity for the risk department, the business leaders, and the support functions to pause and consider whether the product that is proposed meets the operational, compliance, reputational, and strategic risk appetite of the firm.

Effective new-product approval processes can be embedded in agile development methodologies by ensuring transparency into product requirements and builds at each step of the agile development process. Effective testing of the final product to ensure that it has met any conditions that were set is essential.

Risk and control self-assessments (RCSAs) can be useful in monitoring operational risks that arise as a product evolves. Key risk indicators (KRIs) can be attached to products to trigger a reassessment when they reach a particular volume.

SUPPLIER AND THIRD-PARTY RISK MANAGEMENT

The use of vendors or suppliers and third parties raises unique challenges for operational risk management. While activities and controls may be outsourced, operational risks are not. The firm still owns the risk. Therefore, it is necessary to ensure that there is a robust due diligence process to monitor operational risk management in any third parties that are providing key services or processes.

This can be achieved by requiring vendors to complete RCSAs, to deliver KRI data, and to inform the firm of operational risk events that occur. However, it may be difficult to ensure that such data is being collected to the same standards as the firm is applying internally.

Most firms now require third parties to complete in-depth risk assessments prior to engaging their services and may require quarterly reviews for the most critical vendors.

Some firms have amended their service-level agreements (SLAs) with vendors and third parties to require them to provide minimum data to assist with monitoring operational risks. Other firms have determined that these risks cannot be accurately monitored and have focused instead on developing robust contingency plans that can be implemented if the vendor fails. Other firms have spread their operational risk exposure by moving away from a single supplier and engaging several vendors where possible.

For banks, the regulatory expectations are high in the area of supplier risk management today. The failures of mortgage servicing companies came as a painful reminder to firms that were using those services that they had not reduced their risks; in fact, by handing over the controls they may have increased their risks.

Some firms are electing to move activities back in-house when they feel that they cannot get sufficient assurances through an SLA that controls are being well-managed and that risk is not rising.

LEGAL RISK MANAGEMENT

There is often tension between the operational risk department and the legal department, as the operational risk department is promoting transparency, whereas the legal department is focused on protecting the firm from legal risk exposures.

Legal Considerations in the Operational Risk Framework

This tension can lead to challenges around reporting loss data, RCSA scores, scenario analysis outcomes, and KRIs. Each of these elements of the operational risk framework can be responsible for alerting the firm to risks, and the legal department may be wary of the mitigation burden that this might then place on the firm. If a risk is known and is not mitigated, this could present problems in the future if related litigation were to arise.

It is important for the operational risk department to ensure that the policies and procedures surrounding operational risk identification, assessment, monitoring, control, and mitigation clearly state that there is no expectation that all risks can, or will, be mitigated. The legal department will often be eager to review these policies and procedures to ensure that they are clearly worded so as to prevent an inadvertent increase in legal risk.

Capturing Legal Risks Using the Operational Risk Framework

There are legal risks that will be captured in the operational risk program. Legal risk is a subset of operational risk, and therefore any losses related to litigation or legal disputes need to be captured in the operational risk event database and need to be considered in the RCSA and scenario analysis activities.

This raises additional concerns, as the contents of the loss database will be subject to the usual rules of discovery, and so might be requested by an adversary during litigation proceedings. For this reason, many firms provide very little information on legal events, restricting them to a simple description such as "pending litigation" and not completing the loss amount until the case has been settled or all appeals have been exhausted.

Recent developments have led to requirements to include reserve amounts in the loss database, and special care needs to be taken with those entries to ensure that privilege is not compromised.

REGULATORY RISK MANAGEMENT

The compliance department is sometimes surprised to find that the operational risk department is interested in its processes, procedures, reporting, and assessments. However, the regular monitoring and management of regulatory risks is an important element in operational risk management and a partnership between the two functions is mutually beneficial.

The operational risk function is often able to find strong KRIs that have been monitored regularly by the compliance department for many years, such as training and registration requirements. The compliance department is able to raise any concerns it has regarding regulatory compliance in a central operational risk forum, where they may be appreciated as risks that are beyond the risk appetite of the firm.

The governance structures around regulatory risk may need to evolve in order to ensure that the operational risk reporting and escalation processes and the compliance risk escalation processes are aligned.

PEOPLE RISK MANAGEMENT

People risk arises in all areas of operational risk management. Many controls are dependent on manual processes, and there can be some confusion as to how to capture the underlying people risks such as loss of key personnel, inadequate training, or inadequate cross-training.

These risks will often be raised by participants in an RCSA. However, the risk is not that people will leave or be untrained, but rather that this causes other risks to arise. Therefore, there may be a place in the operational risk framework for activities to protect the firm from people risks generally.

As a result, operational risk departments often engage with the human resources or training and development departments to develop programs that will help address firm-wide people risk themes. These themes may include:

- A need for training in nondiscriminatory behavior.
- A need for skills training in functional areas.
- A need for cross-training for critical activities.
- A staff survey to monitor KRIs regarding morale.
- Compensation surveys to ensure competitiveness.

The human resources department is understandably reluctant to share people-related data, as the data can be highly confidential and sensitive. It may take some time before the operational risk department can develop a relationship with human resources that will support the production of appropriate KRIs and activities that will mitigate people risks.

FRAUD RISK MANAGEMENT

There may be several activities in the firm that are designed to address fraud risks. The Sarbanes-Oxley Act (SOX) requires a firm-wide fraud risk assessment, compliance departments are tasked with monitoring trading to prevent unauthorized trading, and the operational risk department monitors Internal and External Fraud risk categories.

These activities can be combined to meet all needs. The compliance monitoring activities can be used as inputs into the operational risk RCSA program, and the SOX requirements can be met by that same RCSA program.

Many lessons were learned and controls improved as a result of the Société Générale event that was discussed at length earlier in Chapter 8. Since that event, however, there have been many other fraud scandals that were exposed during the economic crisis, and the UBS unauthorized trading scandal is discussed in Chapter 18. Hedge fund frauds, Ponzi schemes, insider trading scandals, and simple theft of funds have all occurred in the past few years. As a result, clients and regulators are raising their expectations regarding fraud risk controls, and firms are working to ensure that they have addressed internal and external fraud risks.

In addition, the level of external fraud in the banking and fintech sector has risen significantly in recent years. This may have been exacerbated by the online nature of banking that dominates the financial services industry today, by the economic pressures that many consumers have experienced, by the temptingly large volumes of stimulus and unemployment payments during the COVID-19 pandemic, and by the rise of organized fraud gangs that can globally access digital banking platforms.

There are best practices regarding fraud risk mitigation, including robust IT security, effective managerial supervision, and careful monitoring of activities. However, in addition to these controls, it is important to ensure that the culture of the firm is such that employees are aware of fraud risk and are comfortable with responding appropriately when faced with suspicious activity.

Whistle-blower hotlines, anonymous intranet sites, and annual training programs help to ensure that the firm's culture is strongly aligned to protect it against fraudulent activity. The operational risk department should work closely with the human resources department and legal and compliance departments to develop a framework for training, monitoring, and reporting that provides transparency and that supports a culture that resists fraudulent activities from within and from outside the firm.

TECHNOLOGY RISK MANAGEMENT

The current reliance of fintechs and banks on technology also exposes them to significant technology risks. The failure of a critical system, the loss of a network, or a programming error in a vital model can result in catastrophic losses to the firm. The case of Knight Capital, which suffered a technology glitch that wiped out the value of the firm, is discussed in Chapter 18.

The IT department will engage in technology risk management at a detailed level. They often collect metrics that monitor systems capacity, network outages, bug fixes, and security breaches. These metrics can be KRIs in the operational risk management framework, and the operational risk department will have a strong interest in understanding the underlying risks in the technology of the firm, as these represent the causes of events in many risk categories.

Technology solutions are often raised as mitigating actions where high residual risks have been identified in an RCSA or where an IT failure or inadequacy has resulted in a risk event. These mitigating actions can range from simple fixes to extensive firm-wide projects. The operational risk department can partner with the IT department to assist them in prioritizing these activities and assessing the cost benefit of large projects. The potential losses that are identified in the operational risk management program can be very helpful in understanding whether a major strategic IT project should be pursued by the firm.

CLIMATE RISK

A weather catastrophe can result in significant operational risk losses. The impact of global climate change has been felt in every region, with fires, floods, hurricanes, and tsunamis bringing disruption and danger to firms everywhere.

While weather cannot be controlled, it can be monitored, and the operational risk department should consider weather risks when working on RCSA and scenario analysis activities. The location of a branch or main office of a firm might significantly elevate the risk of a weather-related incident, and the assessment of those risks might lead to a residual risk level that requires mitigation or contingency plans.

Weather risks can impact employees as well as office locations, and some firms have travel tracking programs to ensure that they know the location of their employees, or at least their critical employees, at all times. In these programs, employees are required to log their business and personal travel plans in a central database.

For example, these systems resulted in some firms being able to quickly arrange for the retrieval of their personnel from Thailand following the tsunami in 2005 and are now often used to establish whether employees are accounted for after major hurricane events. Tracking systems can also be used to track whether there are any employees in areas that are subject to civil unrest and that may need to be extracted in an emergency.

The Basel Committee recently provided some guidance on the appropriate supervision of management of climate risk in its 2019 "Overview of Pillar 2 Supervisory Practices and Approaches."

Case Study: Integrating Climate-Related Risks in the Supervisory Review Process

In recent years, an increasing number of supervisors have increased their focus on how climate change can translate into financial risks for the financial sector. Financial institutions are exposed to the physical risks of climate change, as they may incur severe losses caused by weather events. Furthermore, the financial industry faces risks in relation to the transition to a carbon-neutral economy, due to considerable exposures to high-emission sectors. These exposures make them vulnerable to new climate policies, rapidly advancing carbon-neutral technology, and changing market conditions.

(continued)

(continued)

It is important that banks be aware of climate-related risks. A growing number of supervisors therefore expect banks to address the prudential risks from climate change through their existing risk management frameworks.

Some supervisors are taking steps to embed climate-related risks in the supervisory approach. For the supervisory review submission in 2019 in one jurisdiction, nonsignificant national banks and asset managers were asked to submit their own risk assessment on how climate-related risks affect their exposures and how they monitor and manage these risks.

In this submission, banks were asked to self-report on four thematic areas that represent core elements of how banks operate: governance, strategy, risk management and measurement, and disclosure:

1. Banks' governance on climate-related risks and opportunities: banks are asked to report on how climate-related prudential risks are embedded in their sound business and governance arrangements.
2. The actual and potential impact of climate-related risks on banks' strategy and financial planning: banks are asked to report on their strategic approach in managing the prudential risks and opportunities from climate change and their long-term view in setting their strategy.
3. Risk management and measurement: banks are asked to report on how the prudential risks from climate change are addressed through their existing risk management frameworks.
4. Climate-related financial disclosures that could promote more informed investment, lending, and insurance underwriting decisions: banks are asked to report on their approach for disclosure of prudential risks from climate change.

For all four areas, the supervisor developed a scorecard as a first attempt to map and benchmark the current level of climate risk management at institutions. It is important to note, however, that the outcome of the scorecard had no consequences for capital requirements or add-ons. At this stage, the main goal was to initiate a dialogue with banks on their exposures to climate-related risks, their governance and strategy in managing those risks, and what methodologies and metrics they had in place to limit their exposures to those risks. In addition, some supervisors from different jurisdictions were involved in efforts to size climate-related risks and explore how those risks can be incorporated in a supervisory framework.[1]

PANDEMIC PLANNING

Business continuity planning (BCP) functions were originally designed to provide controls and procedures that would protect the firm from downtime in the event of a loss of power, telecommunications, or access to buildings.

To respond to these risks, BCP plans were designed to provide robust data backup facilities, alternate work sites, and communications protocols to handle events such as a major power outage, terrorist attack, or weather catastrophe.

Over the past few years, concerns had arisen around the potential impact on the financial services industry of a pandemic, initially due to concerns over avian flu and swine flu and now the global spread of the COVID-19 coronavirus.

Traditional BCP contingency plans were often inadequate in a pandemic, as they relied heavily on the use of alternate sites. In a pandemic situation, there is a requirement for social distancing, where employees are unable to work together in close proximity. Also, there may be a high level of absenteeism in all industries and disruptions to the infrastructure and social norms as a result.

This called for a different approach to continuity planning, and operational risk departments have been involved in pandemic planning over the past few years. Pandemic flu exercises were held in the United Kingdom and in the U.S. financial services sectors in recent years, and the lessons learned from those exercises were implemented by operational risk teams and BCP teams across the industry.

In the first edition of this book, I noted that a pandemic flu would result in a truly global operational risk event, and the operational risk department in each region would need to address global as well as local considerations in its pandemic preparedness planning.

I noted that the following pandemic planning considerations were recommended by the U.S. government in the www.pandemicflu.gov website at that time:

1. Plan for the impact of a pandemic on your business.
2. Plan for the impact of a pandemic on your employees and customers.
3. Establish policies to be implemented during a pandemic.
4. Allocate resources to protect your employees and customers during a pandemic.
5. Communicate to and educate your employees.
6. Coordinate with external organizations and help your community.

In response to these guidelines, many firms developed sick leave, absenteeism, and travel policies that could be implemented should a serious pandemic occur. They also acquired medical and cleaning supplies that could be used as needed, including face masks, hand sanitizers, and, in some instances, antiviral medications.

The remote computing capabilities of many firms were upgraded to support remote log-on by all critical personnel, and calling trees and succession plans were updated. Critical vendors' pandemic plans were reviewed for completeness, and if they were found to be lacking, alternate vendors identified.

The arrival of the COVID-19 global pandemic tested all of these preparations, and it became clear that these plans had underestimated the length of the pandemic and some of the long-term supply chain impacts. Most firms assumed that a pandemic would be virulent and would burn out within a few months.

We have learned that it is possible for most fintechs and banks to operate completely remotely, and at the time of this writing, some firms have decided to remain fully or partially remote working permanently.

This global operational risk event has had a shocking death toll, and many more people are dealing with the long-term after-effects of having contracted the virus. Firms have now stress-tested their pandemic plans and have found ways to manage the complexities of occasional regional, national, or local shutdowns and rolling absenteeism across their own staff.

The personal mental, emotional, and physical toll on the workforce has required many operational risk, BCP, and human resource teams to develop programs to ensure that their employees have access to support to reduce the burnout that has pervaded the industry.

ORX reported that losses directly associated with COVID-19 in 2020 accounted for €2.1 billion (12.5 percent) of all operational risk losses among its members.[2]

The COVID-19 pandemic is the largest operational risk event in recent history and has underscored the need for effective preparation in the face of disaster, monitoring of risk during and after an event, and the importance of clear and effective communication across the firm.

STRATEGIC RISK

Strategic risk is specifically excluded from the Basel II definition of operational risk, but that does not mean that it is excluded from Basel II consideration nor from operational risk management programs. Managing strategic risk is critical in all fintechs and banks, and the operational risk framework offers support for that management.

Basel II has three pillars. Pillar 1 concerns the appropriate calculation of capital for market, credit, and operational risk and outlines some qualitative minimum standards for these risk management categories. Pillar 2 concerns the regulatory oversight that should be put in place to ensure compliance with Pillar 1, and also adds additional requirements to ensure that the firm is protected from risks that may not have been captured in Pillar 1. Pillar 3 refers to the disclosure requirements that firms need to adopt; for example, it outlines how to report on risk management practices and capital in the annual report.

Strategic risk is specifically mentioned in Pillar 2:

There are three main areas that might be particularly suited to treatment under Pillar 2: risks considered under Pillar 1 that are not fully captured by the Pillar 1 process (e.g. credit concentration risk); those factors not taken into account by the Pillar 1 process (e.g. interest rate risk in the banking book, business and **strategic risk***); and factors external to the bank (e.g., business cycle effects).[3]*

Other risks: Although the Committee recognizes that "other" risks, such as reputational and **strategic risk***, are not easily measurable, it expects industry to further develop techniques for managing all aspects of these risks.[4] [emphasis added]*

In December 2019, the Bank of International Settlements (BIS) provided further clarification of its view of the importance of effective strategic risk management:

Senior management should establish a risk management process that is not limited to credit, market, liquidity and operational risks, but incorporates all material risks. This includes reputational, legal and **strategic risks***, as well as risks that do not appear to be significant in isolation, but when combined with other risks could lead to material losses.[5] [emphasis added]*

Therefore, a firm that wishes to meet Basel II standards is required to consider business and strategic risk in its Pillar 2 framework. A weakness in the Pillar 2 framework can lead to capital penalties (or capital charges) from the firm's regulator. For this reason, some operational risk managers also consider business and strategic risks in their framework, so as to be able to demonstrate to regulators that these risks have been included in the risk management framework. For example, scenario analysis may be used to address both operational and strategic risks.

They may also use tools from the operational risk framework to help quantify appropriate capital additions for strategic risk, so preempting any regulatory suggestions for additions.

It is difficult to find an agreed upon definition of strategic or business risk, although the Committee of European Banking Supervisors (CEBS) has provided the following:

> *Strategic risk: the current or prospective risk to earnings and capital arising from changes in the business environment and from adverse business decisions, improper implementation of decisions or lack of responsiveness to changes in the business environment.*[6]

The U.S. Office of the Comptroller of the Currency's most recent definition is:

> *Strategic risk is the risk to current or projected financial condition and resilience arising from adverse business decisions, poor implementation of business decisions, or lack of responsiveness to changes in the banking industry and operating environment. The board and senior management, collectively, are the key decision makers that drive the strategic direction of the bank and establish governance principles. The absence of appropriate governance in the bank's decision-making process and implementation of decisions can have wide-ranging consequences. The consequences may include missed business opportunities, losses, failure to comply with laws and regulations resulting in civil money penalties (CMP), and unsafe or unsound bank operations that could lead to enforcement actions or inadequate capital.*[7]

Managing such risks is challenging and requires a qualitative approach. Because the operational risk program contains tools that are designed for managing and measuring qualitative as well as quantitative risk exposures, these tools can be very effective for managing and measuring strategic risk as well.

KEY POINTS

- Operational risk management often requires partnership with many related areas in the firm including those that own:
  - New product approval
  - Vendor, supplier, or third-party management
  - Legal risk
  - Regulatory risk
  - People risk

- Fraud risk
- Technology risk
- Weather risk
- Pandemic risk
- Strategic risk

REVIEW QUESTION

1. Which of the following is the best description of the Basel II requirements regarding strategic risk?
   a. There is no regulatory requirement to manage or measure strategic risk.
   b. Pillar 2 requires firms to manage and measure strategic risk.
   c. Pillar 1 includes strategic risk in the definition of operational risk.
   d. The only regulations regarding strategic risk are outside of Basel II rules.

NOTES

1. Bank for International Settlements, Basel Committee on Banking Supervision, "Overview of Pillar 2 Supervisory Review Practices and Approaches," June 2019, https://www.bis.org/bcbs/publ/d465.htm.
2. ORX Annual Member Banking Loss Report, 2021.
3. Bank for International Settlements, "International Convergence of Capital Measurement and Capital Standards: A Revised Framework," 2004, section 724.
4. Ibid.
5. Bank for International Settlements, Supervisory Review Process 30 (SRP 30), December 2019, https://www.bis.org/basel_framework/chapter/SRP/30.htm.
6. "Application of the Supervisory Review Process under Pillar 2," CEBS Consultation Paper (CP03 revised), 2005.
7. Office of the Comptroller of the Currency, "Comptroller's Handbook, Safety and Soundness, Corporate and Risk Governance," version 2.0, July 2019, 4.

CHAPTER 18

Case Studies

In this chapter, we dig deeper into five case studies: JPMorgan Whale, the Archegos Credit Suisse scandal, DNB Bank ASA anti–money laundering failings, UBS unauthorized trading, and the Knight Capital technology glitch.

JPMORGAN WHALE: RISKY OR FRISKY?

Are large losses at banks always a sign of poor governance, or are they sometimes merely the realization of losses that were expected, and even planned for, in the well-governed risk management of the firm? In May 2012, JPMorgan announced that it had lost $2 billion (possibly much more) on a hedging strategy that was being driven by Bruno Michel Iksil, aka "The London Whale," in its chief investment office. Was this poor governance, or were these losses predictable under JPMorgan's risk management practices? Was this acceptable risky behavior, or was it frisky misbehavior?

You can't win the game all of the time, and for every winner, there is a loser somewhere in the financial system. For each loss event that happens, we should ask the same question: Were these losses within the boundaries of the bank's known risk, or were they out of control?

We have all heard the worn-out caveat "investments may go down as well as up," and we all know that the banking industry sometimes makes money on its risk-taking activities and sometimes loses it on those same activities. So why all the noise in the press about these JPMorgan losses?

- "London Whale Harpooned"[1]
- "JPMorgan's 'Whale' Causes a Splash"[2]
- "Beached London Whale"[3]

Anything over a billion dollars still gets our attention, that's true. But even at that size, the steam would have gone out of the story very quickly if the loss had just been the result of an unfortunate market movement. That would have been a short-lived and dull story about market risk.[4]

So the question is: Was it well-managed risk taking that led to these unfortunate losses, or was there "frisky" behavior in a poorly governed trading desk?

This story had frisky written all over it. Both the *Wall Street Journal*[5] and Bloomberg[6] raised concerns about the size of Iksil's trades earlier in April, and hedge funds quickly responded and set about taking the other side of his trades, betting that the Whale's position was outsized and unmanageable. Jamie Dimon, CEO and chairman of JPMorgan, made comments that he certainly now regrets, calling the concerns raised "a complete tempest in a teapot."[7] How was it that outsiders were appropriately concerned about the trading strategy, but the firm itself was not?

Jamie Dimon later admitted,

In hindsight, the new strategy was flawed, complex, poorly reviewed, poorly executed, and poorly monitored. The portfolio has proven to be riskier, more volatile, and less effective as an economic hedge than we thought.[8]

Even JPMorgan's own risk management tools were not working effectively, as Dimon added:

We are also amending a disclosure in the first quarter press release about CIO's VaR, value at risk. We'd shown average VaR at 67. It will now be 129.[9]

Value at risk (VaR) is the strongest tool in the market risk manager's arsenal, providing an indication of the actual current risk taking of the firm measured against its expected levels of risk taking. If it is flawed, then they are flying blind.

These statements made by the senior management team suggested that they might have first learned of the Whale's positions from press reports, a possibility strengthened by the apparent decision to shut down the trading strategy just four days after it hit the press in April—and shutting it down may well have increased the losses, as this caused a sudden change in the market profile of those instruments.

The SEC swiftly opened a review[10] into the accounting practices used by JPMorgan, and the Justice Department opened a criminal inquiry[11] into the whole affair. Lawsuits[12] sprang up among disgruntled JPMorgan shareholders. Jamie Dimon, earlier dubbed "The King of Wall Street," battled sustained negative sentiment and watched his stock price take a beating every time more information hit the press. In 11 painful days JPM stock went

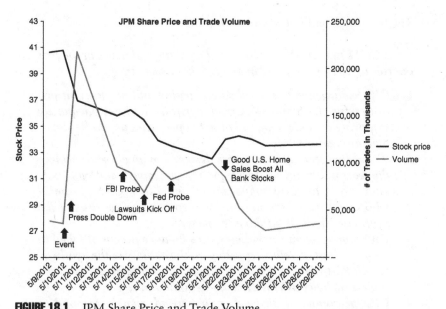

FIGURE 18.1 JPM Share Price and Trade Volume

from 40.64 to 32.51 and only recovered a little when all banks stocks got a boost on news of good U.S. home sales, as shown in Figure 18.1.

Dimon's rhetoric against regulation on Wall Street was now falling on deaf ears as everyone wondered[13] how he let such behavior go unchecked in his own backyard.

Risky or frisky? The positions being taken by the chief information office (CIO) desk were not being accurately captured by the firm's risk management tools, the trading was going on with little or no understanding at the senior management level, and the regulators suspected foul play. All this despite the fact that the whole purpose of the CIO desk is to hedge the firm's risk at the highest level and to protect it against large unexpected losses.

This author's verdict: frisky.

JPMorgan released two reports of the event in January 2102,[14] one by an internal task force, and the other conducted independently by the board. In the task force report, they were transparent about their own failings, as summarized by Bloomberg:

> *In a 129-page report issued yesterday, the bank described an "error prone" risk-modeling system that required employees to cut and paste electronic data to a spreadsheet. Workers inadvertently used the sum of two numbers instead of the average in calculating volatility. The firm also reiterated an assertion that London traders initially tried to hide losses that ballooned beyond $6.2 billion in last year's first nine months.*[15]

The task force had five key observations:

First, *CIO's judgment, execution and escalation of issues in the first quarter of 2012 were poor, in at least six critical areas:*

1. *CIO management established competing and inconsistent priorities for the Synthetic Credit Portfolio without adequately exploring or understanding how the priorities would be simultaneously addressed;*
2. *the trading strategies that were designed in an effort to achieve the various priorities were poorly conceived and not fully understood by CIO management and other CIO personnel who might have been in a position to manage the risks of the Synthetic Credit Portfolio effectively;*
3. *CIO management (including CIO's Finance function) failed to obtain robust, detailed reporting on the activity in the Synthetic Credit Portfolio, and/or to otherwise appropriately monitor the traders' activity as closely as they should have;*
4. *CIO personnel at all levels failed to adequately respond to and escalate (including to senior Firm management and the Board) concerns that were raised at various points during the trading;*
5. *certain of the traders did not show the full extent of the Synthetic Credit Portfolio's losses; and*
6. *CIO provided to senior Firm management excessively optimistic and inadequately analyzed estimates of the Synthetic Credit Portfolio's future performance in the days leading up to the April 13 earnings call. . . .*

Second, *the Firm did not ensure that the controls and oversight of CIO evolved commensurately with the increased complexity and risks of CIO's activities. . . .*

Third, *CIO Risk Management lacked the personnel and structure necessary to manage the risks of the Synthetic Credit Portfolio.*

Fourth, *the risk limits applicable to CIO were not sufficiently granular.*

Fifth, *approval and implementation of the new CIO VaR model for the Synthetic Credit Portfolio in late January 2012 were flawed, and the model as implemented understated the risks presented by the trades in the first quarter of 2012.*[16]

Jamie Dimon faced a 50 percent pay cut as a result, and many executive team members also saw their compensation significantly impacted.

FIGURE 18.2 ORX Classification of JPMorgan Whale Event
Source: Operational Riskdata eXchange Association (ORX).

Keywords	
Entity Type	FINANCIAL SERVICES\BANKING\COMMERCIAL\FULL SERVICE BANK
Business Unit Type	TRADING & SALES (BIS)\TRADING
Service/Product Offering Type	DERIVATIVES, STRUCTURED PRODUCTS AND COMMODITIES\DERIVATIVE PRODUCTS\CREDIT DERIVATIVES
Contributory/Control Factors	CORPORATE GOVERNANCE\BOARD OVERSIGHT,CORPORATE\MARKET CONDITIONS\CORPORATE & MARKET CONDITIONS,EMPLOYEE ACTION\INACTION\HUMAN ERRORS,LACK OF CONTROL\FAILURE TO TEST FOR DATA ACCURACY,MANAGEMENT ACTION\INACTION\UNDERTOOK EXCESSIVE RISKS,OMISSIONS\INADEQUATE STRESS TESTING,ORGANIZATIONAL STRUCTURE\ORGANIZATIONAL GAP(S),STAFF SELECTION\COMPENSATION\UNTRAINED/ INEXPERIENCED STAFF,STRATEGY FLAW\STRATEGIC FLAW
Loss Type:	Estimated
Loss Impact	DIRECT LOSS\WRITE-DOWN (BIS)\WRITE-OFFS
Loss Detection Sources	OTHER LOSS DETECTION SOURCES\PRESS DETECTED
Market Focus	INSTITUTIONAL SERVICES
Event Trigger	PROCESS RISK CLASS\TRANSACTIONAL AND BUSINESS PROCESS RISK\INADEQUATE/PROBLEMATIC TRANSACTION EXECUTION
Basel Levels I & II	Execution Delivery and Process Management\Transaction Capture, Execution & Maintenance\Other task misperformance
Basel Business Line	Trading & Sales\Proprietary Positions
Industry Event	
Rules and Regulations	

FIGURE 18.3 FIRST Classification of JPMorgan Whale Event

This internal report focuses heavily on what went wrong in the CIO office, but it does not clearly state the operational risk categories and causes.

Let us look at the two external data providers that we discussed earlier for their view on this event: ORX News Service[17] (ORX) and IBM FIRST Risk Case Studies[18] (FIRST). Both provide details on events that have happened in the industry and offer classifications of the event.

ORX classified the event as shown in Figure 18.2. They selected unauthorized trading as the risk category and inadequate policy/procedure, unauthorized activity, and management/control of staff as the three main causes.

FIRST classified the event as shown in Figure 18.3.

FIRST selected execution, delivery, and process management as the risk category and lists many contributing control factors, also including management, inaction, corporate governance, human errors, and excessive risk taking.

It is important to acknowledge that different interpretations of the Basel II risk categories are common, and external data sources need to be carefully used for this reason.

In the following case studies, you will have an opportunity to read the short descriptions of the event from the perspective of either ORX or FIRST and will determine the appropriate classifications of the risk type and major causes.

REVIEW QUESTIONS

Case 1   Case Credit Suisse Archegos Scandal 2021

Read the following IBM FIRST record of the event and respond to the questions that follow.

Event Summary

Rounds of margin calls that hit an obscure New York City-based hedge fund between March 24 and 26, 2021, led to the firm's collapse. They also appear to have inflicted significant losses on several banks that acted as prime brokers to Archegos Capital Management, the family office of investor Bill Hwang. Banks that had entered into large swaps positions with Archegos as their counterparty found themselves trying to liquidate blocks of shares in certain US media and Chinese tech stocks that Mr. Hwang favored. Early press estimates Credit Suisse's exposure to losses at Archegos in the range of $3 billion to $4 billion, while the bank itself said they would likely be "material to our first quarter results." On April 6 2021, after selling blocks of 60 million shares linked to Archegos, Credit Suisse announced in a trading update that it estimated its Archego-linked loss at CHF 4.4 billion (USD $4.7 billion). It also said that several executives and senior managers, including the head of investment banking and the chief risk officer, would leave the firm. On July 29, 2021, Credit Suisse released a summary of an independent report into its recent Archegos losses, saying that "conspicuous" risks posed by Archegos' positions were ignored by managers. By that date, the size of the losses had reached USD $5.5 billion. One key failure was not using dynamic *hedging, which caused the bank to pay $2.4 billion in "variable" margin collateral to Archegos between March 11 and March 19, augmenting its losses. The bank said 23 employees had been "disciplined" and nine dismissed, and $70 million in bonuses clawed back. The bank recently hired a new chief risk officer to strengthen a risk department that had previously been understaffed.*

Event Details

The dramatic collapse of Archegos Capital Management, a family office owned by Sung Kook "Bill" Hwang, between March 24 and March 26 is described in Event # 19063. Mr. Hwang had set up the firm, which did not have any external clients, to manage his assets in 2013 after the SEC had brought a complaint for insider trading against him (and his firm Tiger Asia Management) in 2012. The SEC's complaint against Mr. Hwang and Tiger Asia was eventually settled for payments totaling $44 million (#9260).

Mr. Hwang's Archegos made very large bullish bets on a small number of equities, including ViacomCBS, Discovery, and Chinese tech stocks such as IQIYI, Baidu, Tencent and GSK Techedu. These were set up by entering into derivatives contracts—including total return swaps—with various investment banks' primer broker units. The strategy involved leverage and depended on the value of the target stocks continuing to rise—or at least not losing value. Mr. Hwang reportedly ploughed almost all gains back into the same positions for several years, building up his leverage as he did so.

Archegos' downfall was triggered by Viacom CBS' issue of 30 million new shares on March 22, 2021 in an equity market that was hitting new highs. The new stock issue, offered at $85 a share and underwritten by Morgan Stanley, had the effect of diluting the pool of available stock. The offer was under-subscribed and Mr. Hwang was unable to buy any of the new offering, as some of his prime brokers had expected him to do. This caused Viacom-CBS' share price to fall sharply to around $55 and led to a margin call being issued to the heavily leveraged Archegos by one or more of Mr. Hwang's prime brokers. Archegos' forced sales in turn triggered further margin calls.

At least six banks were acting as prime brokers to Archegos or engaged in derivatives contracts with his firm. Until the first margin call was made, the banks were apparently unaware that they all had swaps contracts with him. As of early 2021, family office firms like Archegos were not subject to stringent SEC disclosure requirements imposed on other types of asset management firms.

(continued)

(continued)

On Thursday March 24, according to The Wall Street Journal, some of the firms involved, which included Goldman Sachs, Morgan Stanley, Credit Suisse, and Nomura, reportedly discussed by phone a proposal for handling a slower orderly sale of Archegos' assets over a period of several weeks—but no formal agreement was reached.

It has been reported that the Securities and Exchange Commission (SEC) and other regulators may be looking into whether such inter-broker discussions took place and whether any coordinated market activity was discussed. The Journal called such discussion among prime brokers "extremely unusual" and something that "has happened only a handful of times in recent memory," notably during the rescue of Long Term Capital Management, a fund that blew up in 1998 (#1062).

On Friday March 26, 2021 and into the weekend, Goldman Sachs and Morgan Stanley went ahead and started liquidating large blocks of shares that they held in collateral, even as Viacom CBS stock tanked. It is unclear at what level the decision was made, but it appears to have caught some of its rivals off-guard.

Goldman, which reportedly was late-coming in lending to Archegos, said any losses would be "immaterial." Wells Fargo said it had not experienced any losses after it closed out its exposures. Nomura and Credit Suisse were not major sellers in the falling market "fire sale" on March 26. Both banks were expected to announce significant losses due to the fall in value of securities formerly held by Archegos, or held by the banks on its behalf.

Control Failings and Contributory Factors

Inadequate Due Diligence Efforts; Failure to Disclose: *To some extent, all banks that lent to Archegos or entered into swaps contracts with him were unaware of the extent of his liabilities or the extent of leverage Mr. Hwang had taken on. This led to a "rush for the exits" as Archegos' holdings came under pressure to sell.*

Undertook Excessive Risks; Poor Judgment: *The decision to keep extending loans to Archegos raised questions about risk-management practices by prime brokers towards "family offices" and other wealthy investors.*

Lack of Internal Controls: *Internal reviews by banks (and possible future action by regulators) may lead to a reassessment of how large banks manage counterparty risk and collateral, and may lead to more disclosures related to swaps contracts.*

Inadequate Organizational Structures: *It appears that a July 2020 merger of risk-management and compliance functions into a single unit to save money may have backfired and even contributed to even larger losses.*

Corporate and Market Conditions: *A low-interest rate environment has pushed investors and lenders to take more risk in search of returns, and may have weakened risk-management. Margin calls were triggered by a share offering that disfavored Archegos' positions. Some of the banks appear to have had inadequate hedges in place.*

Corrective Actions and Management Response

The exposure of various banks' combined exposures to Archegos was estimated by JPMorgan Chase to be "in the range of $5 billion to $10 billion" on March 29, 2021.

Nomura Holdings told investors the same day that "an event occurred that could subject one of its US subsidiaries to a significant loss arising from transactions with a US client." Nomura estimated its claim against the client at "approximately $2 billion, subject to change depending on unwinding of the transactions and fluctuations in market prices."

Credit Suisse was reported to face an even larger exposure when "a significant US hedge fund [. . .] defaulted on margin calls made last week by Credit Suisse and certain other banks." It said that losses could be "significant and "material to our first quarter results." It followed earlier losses Credit Suisse suffered in loans to Luckin Coffee (#18521) in May 2020 and in buying asset-linked notes issued by Greensill Capital (#19055), a UK firm that engaged in supply-chain financing and went bust in early March 2021. Credit Suisse has said it expects to recover "most" of its Greensill-linked assets.

On April 1, 2021, Fitch ratings revised Credit Suisse's outlook to "negative" and affirmed its Issuer Default Rating at A–.

In a Trading Update[19] dated April 6, 2021, Credit Suisse said it would take a charge of CHF 4.4 billion (USD $4.7 billion) linked to its contracts with Archegos. The Financial Times reported April 6 that the bank had sold off blocks of 60 million shares, about 37 million of them in ViacomCBS. As a result of these and other charges, the bank expected to record a 1Q21 loss of about CHF 900 million ($960 million). Credit Suisse also said that several senior executives would leave: Lara Warner, chief risk and compliance officer, and Brian Chin, head of investment banking. At least five other senior managers would also depart. Bonuses would be cut, a share buyback cancelled, and dividends reduced.

(continued)

(continued)

Credit Suisse's chief executive Thomas Gottstein was referring to Archegos and Greensill on April 6, 2021 when he said: "The significant loss in our Prime Services business relating to the failure of a US-based hedge fund is unacceptable. In combination with the recent issues around the supply chain finance funds, I recognise that these cases have caused significant concern amongst all our stakeholders. Together with the Board of Directors, we are fully committed to addressing these situations. Serious lessons will be learned."

The Forensic Report (July 29, 2021)

On July 29, 2021, the investigative report written by the law firm Paul Weiss Rifkind was published by Credit Suisse. The 172-page report (available here[20]) suggests that Credit Suisse risk management in the Archegos case had been "lackadaisical" despite "persistent" defaults by Archegos, and that some standard risk-management checks had been waived, in order to retain Mr. Hwang as a valued customer.

Key areas of failure were mentioned: first, there was a failure to act on "known information" about Archegos, partially as a result of differences of views between the heads of the equities department and the prime brokerage services unit. This failure notably included a failure to obtain dynamic margin payments—i.e. increases in collateral as the risk increased—and failure to stop $2.4 billion in "variation margin" payments that Credit Suisse itself made to Archegos from March 11 to 19, 2021.

Second, senior managers in investment banking failed to push back and escalate concerns about the growing exposure. Third, there was a lack of investment in risk management personnel and technology. As experienced risk-management staff left, there was a "juniorization" of risk staff and a lack of investment in risk technology.

Key staff were overwhelmed by having multiple tasks and said they were overwhelmed by the volume of information available.

The report also cited a failure of "risk culture" in that potential exposures were not assessed, both in the light of Archegos' previous breaches of risk limits and past experience of defaults by another former client, Malachite. The report noted that since the collapse of Archegos 23 employees had been "disciplined" and forfeited bonuses, while nine were dismissed. Some $70 million in bonuses had been recovered.

Press reports noted that Credit Suisse also said it had hired a Goldman Sachs veteran, David Wildermuth, to be its new chief risk officer and who will also be a member of Credit Suisse's executive board.[21]

1. What Basel risk category does this event fall under?
2. What weaknesses in risk management did this event expose?

Case 2   DNB Bank ASA Anti–Money Laundering Scandal 2019

Read the following ORX record of the DNB Bank ASA AML event and respond to the questions that follow.

DNB ASA fined NOK 400 million for inadequate AML/CTF compliance and customer due diligence

On 3 May 2021, the Financial Supervisory Authority of Norway, Finanstilsynet, announced that it had fined DNB Bank ASA (DNB) NOK 400 million (USD 48 million, EUR 40 million) for due diligence failures and serious breaches of the updated Anti-Money Laundering and Counter-Terrorist Financing (AML/CTF) Act which came into force on 15 October 2018.

Finanstilsynet carried out AML/CTF inspections of DNB in 2016 and December 2018. In 2019, Wikileaks published a series of documents about Icelandic fishing group Samherji, implying that representatives of the Namibian authorities were paid bribes via DNB accounts and that the profits from wrongfully acquired fishing quotas allocated based on the bribes were transferred to Samherji through DNB. Finanstilsynet launched an investigation into the case in November 2019 and carried out a third audit in February 2020. These investigations uncovered many similar serious breaches in the bank's compliance with the AML/CTF Act, namely DNB's inadequate risk classification of customers, implementation of enhanced and ongoing customer measures, and monitoring and reporting failures.

Firstly, regarding the inadequate risk classification of customers, the AML/CTF Act states that the bank must obtain information about the customer so that the money laundering risk associated with the customer could be adequately assessed to ensure that higher-risk customers were followed up more frequently and control measures were implemented in the transaction monitoring system. In 2018, Finanstilsynet found varying quality in the risk classification and underlying documentation in DNB's Corporate Banking and Ocean Division. Finanstilsynet's 2020 audit revealed that DNB's procedures for completing risk classification in Corporate Banking and Markets were insufficient and its electronic system was inadequate as it did not capture obvious risk factors such as unidentifiable licensees. The audit also revealed major deficiencies in the database on which the risk classification was based.

(continued)

(continued)

Both the 2020 audit and the Samherji survey showed that DNB had a large backlog in collecting customer data necessary for correctly classifying customers. Regarding Samherji, DNB was repeatedly alerted about the breaches between 2015 and 2019, however, the bank failed to adequately remediate its deficiencies. The due diligence failures highlighted in the inspections were established before the Act came into force, but the violation was relevant for reclassifications that should have been carried out after this.

Additionally, there was limited or no analysis of how customers used the customer portfolio since the last due diligence measures were implemented following the initial inspections. For example, analysis of whether the transaction patterns matched the previously stated information, and whether this was in line with who the customer was. There was also little evidence of reinforced measures in the ongoing follow-up. The regulator found that DNB failed to follow up approximately 400 high-risk customers identified between 2015 and 2017. As of August 2020, 140 of these customers had still not been reviewed. One of the salient findings of the Samherji survey was the lack of implemented initial and ongoing enhanced due diligence after the AML/CTF Act came into force.

Lastly, regarding inadequate monitoring and reporting, DNB's failure to comply and investigate alerts connected with "mass closures" of transactions was identified. Alerts from the transaction monitoring system indicated suspicious transactions which should be investigated. Between 2014 and 2018, the bank carried out 15 rounds of "mass closures" of 1.8 million transaction alerts (over 80 per cent of the alerts), but no manual closure assessment was made and no mass closures were carried out after 2018. Finanstilsynet found that neither Corporate Banking nor Markets complied with the AML/CTF Act's requirement to monitor whether any suspicious activity had occurred, and the bank's overall procedure was not adapted to the business units' product and service offerings and was thus not suitable for providing adequate guidance. DNB's inadequate systems led to suspicious transactions not being reported to ØKOKRIM, the National Authority for Investigation and Prosecution of Economic and Environmental Crime in Norway, in violation of the AML/CTF Act.

In making its penalty decision against DNB, Finanstilsynet took into account that DNB's board and management had been aware of the bank's shortcomings for a long time as the regulator had repeatedly notified DNB of its non-compliance. However, DNB had failed to prioritise and implement adequate improvement measures to rectify the serious issues. Finanstilsynet acknowledged that much of the bank's non-compliance with the regulations was partly due to inadequate measures that existed before the regulatory inspections. However, the regulator emphasised that the 2020 audit revealed clear deficiencies in compliance had remained in areas where recent regulatory changes in the bank's policies and procedures had been implemented.

Finanstilsynet stated that there was no clear link between the offences and the benefits obtained but it assumed that DNB had made savings linked to its insufficient resources on AML/CTF measures, including due diligence, employees not being able to identify and report suspicious conditions internally due to lack of training, and the bank not investing in adequate financial and human resources to operate effective electronic transaction monitoring. As such, Finanstilsynet fined DNB NOK 400,000,000 under the Norwegian AML/CFT Act.[22]

3. What Basel risk category does this event fall under?
4. Discuss the actions of the various regulators; do they all seem reasonable?
5. What was the most important lesson learned? Discuss.

Case 3   Knight Capital Technology Glitch

Read the ORX description of the Knight Capital technology glitch event below and respond to the questions that follow.

Knight Capital Loses USD 440 Million in Automated Trading System Malfunction

Knight Capital Group caused market disruption on 1 August 2012 after a malfunction in newly installed trading software caused the firm to rapidly place millions of erroneous orders into the New York Stock Exchange (NYSE). On 2 August 2012, Knight

(continued)

(continued)

Capital stated that it had exited the erroneous trading positions, realizing a pre-tax loss of USD 440 million (EUR 361 million) after selling stock it had acquired at inflated prices back into the market at lower prices.

The NYSE witnessed high trading volume and large price volatility in around 150 stocks in the first hour after markets opened on 1 August 2012. The NYSE cancelled trades in six of these stocks, reported to be China Cord Blood Corp., American Reprographics, E-House (China) Holdings, Quicksilver Resources, Reaves Utility Income Fund and Wizzard Software.

A Knight Capital press release states that following the installation of new trading software, the firm sent "numerous erroneous orders" in equities listed on the NYSE into the market.

Large trading volume caused prices of certain stocks to experience very large price fluctuations.

Media reports suggest a "rogue" algorithm was to blame for the trades. The Financial Times reports that the trading system at Knight Capital may have executed a large order for a number of stocks over five minutes instead of over a longer period of up to five days. This could have inflated the price of stocks rapidly.

Knight Capital has said it has removed the new software from its systems and that no clients have been affected.

UPDATE 1 (15 August 2012)—Knight Capital Finds Source of Trading Program Glitch
The trading loss at Knight Capital was caused by disused software which was reactivated after a new program was installed on its system, Bloomberg reports. After being reactivated, a glitch in the out-dated trading system began to multiply stock orders by 1,000. Employees at Knight Capital reportedly looked through eight sets of software before finding what had gone wrong.[23]

6. What Level 1 Basel risk category was this event?
7. What was the main cause of this event?
8. What Basel business line did this business event occur in?

Case 4   The UBS Unauthorized Trading Scandal

Read the following excerpts in Figure 18.4 and 18.5 from ORX's and FIRST's records of the UBS event below and respond to the questions that follow.

UBS		BL0201 – Equities	
EL0101 – Unauthorised Activity		USD – 2,347,600,000.00 **LOSS**	USD – US Dollar
GB – UNITED KINGDOM		Western Europe	

Event	Published in Media 15/Sep/2011	Date of Occurrence – From 01/Oct/2008	Date of Occurrence – To 01/Dec/2010	Discovery Date 14/Sep/2011	Date of Recognition / Settlement N/A
Loss Amount USD USD 2,347,600,000.00	Loss Amount EURO EUR 1,714,645,276.00		Provision No		Boundary Risk Other Risk
Industry Event N/A	Scenario ROGUET - Rogue Trader		Product PD0310 - Equity Derivatives		Process PC0603 - Position or Portfolio Mgt (proprietary)
Parent Company N/A	ORX Member No		Role of Firm LS0303 - Employer		AMA Status N/A
Cause 1 CS0206 - Unauthorised Activity		Cause 2 CS0203 - Criminal Activity by Internal or External Staff		Cause 3 N/A	
Counterparty LS0212 - Not Identifiable		Jurisdiction / Choice of Law LS0104 - United Kingdom		Environmental Volatility LS0403 - Market Risk	

© ORX 2012. The contents are provided as part of the ORX News Service and are subject to the General Terms and Conditions for the ORX News Service.

FIGURE 18.4   ORX Case File on UBS Trading Scandal
Source: Operational Riskdata eXchange Association (ORX).

Keywords	
Entity Type	FINANCIAL SERVICES\BANKING\COMMERCIAL\FULL SERVICE BANK
Business Unit Type	TRADING & SALES (BIS)\TRADING
Service/Product Offering Type	TRADING CATEGORIES\PROPRIETARY TRADING
Contributory/Control Factors	CORPORATE GOVERNANCE\GENERAL CORPORATE GOVERNANCE ISSUES,CORPORATE\MARKET CONDITIONS\CORPORATE & MARKET CONDITIONS,CORPORATE\MARKET CONDITIONS\REGULATORY PRESSURE,EMPLOYEE ACTION\INACTION\EMPLOYEE MISDEEDS,LACK OF CONTROL\FAILURE TO QUESTION ABOVE MARKET RETURNS,LACK OF CONTROL\FAILURE TO TEST FOR P/L ACCURACY,LACK OF CONTROL\LACK OF INTERNAL CONTROLS,LACK OF CONTROL\POOR DOCUMENTATION,LACK OF CONTROL\RULES, REGULATIONS & COMPLIANCE ISSUES,MANAGEMENT ACTION\INACTION\LACK MANAGEMENT ESCALATION PROCESS,MANAGEMENT ACTION\INACTION\POOR EXECUTION,MANAGEMENT ACTION\INACTION\POOR JUDGMENT,OMISSIONS\FAILURE TO COMPLY WITH INTERNAL POLICIES AND PROCEDURES,OMISSIONS\FAILURE TO SET OR ENFORCE PROPER LIMITS,OMISSIONS\FAILURE TO SUPERVISE EMPLOYEES,OMISSIONS\FAILURE TO TEST PRODUCTS OR SYSTEMS,OMISSIONS\INADEQUATE DUE DILIGENCE EFFORTS,OMISSIONS\LACK OF PROPER TRAINING PROCEDURES,OMISSIONS\OMISSIONS & LAPSES,OMISSIONS\OUTSOURCING,ORGANIZATIONAL STRUCTURE\UNCLEAR REPORTING STRUCTURE,STAFF SELECTION\COMPENSATION\UNTRAINED/ INEXPERIENCED STAFF
Loss Type:	Known
Loss Impact	DIRECT LOSS\REGULATORY/COMPLIANCE/TAXATION PENALTY (BIS)\FINES/PENALTIES,DIRECT LOSS\REGULATORY/COMPLIANCE/TAXATION PENALTY (BIS)\REGULATORY-ORDERED CHARGE TO CAPITAL RESERVES,DIRECT LOSS\WRITE-DOWN (BIS)\WRITE-DOWNS,INDIRECT LOSS\MANAGEMENT REMEDIATION,INDIRECT LOSS\REPUTATIONAL (NON-MONETARY),INDIRECT LOSS\SHARE PRICE
Loss Detection Sources	PERIODIC INTERNAL REVIEWS\BACK OFFICE REVIEWS
Market Focus	INSTITUTIONAL SERVICES
Event Trigger	PEOPLE RISK CLASS\TRADING MISDEEDS\UNAUTHORIZED TRADING/ACTIVITY ABOVE LIMITS\UNAUTHORIZED TRADING – PROPRIETARY ACCOUNTS
Basel Levels I & II	Internal Fraud\Unauthorised Activity\Trans type unauthorized (w/monetary loss)
Basel Business Line	Trading & Sales\Proprietary Positions
Industry Event	
Rules and Regulations	European Jurisdictions\United Kingdom Jurisdiction\Financial Services Authority\The FSA Handbook\High Level Standards\Principles for Businesses\Principle 2 - Skill, care and diligence,European Jurisdictions\United Kingdom Jurisdiction\Financial Services Authority\The FSA Handbook\High Level Standards\Principles for Businesses\Principle 3 - Management and control

FIGURE 18.5   First Summary of UBS Trading Scandal

(continued)

(continued)

ORX Record and Description[24]

UPDATE 2 (26 November 2012)—UK FSA Fines UBS Million GBP 29.7 Million

UBS has been fined GBP 29.7 million (USD 47.6 million, EUR 36.7 million) by the Financial Services Authority over the 2011 rogue trading incident. The regulator found ineffective systems and controls and inadequate supervision of the synthetic equities desk at UBS allowed Adoboli to cause the unauthorized trading losses.

Though it does not have the power to levy fines, the Swiss Financial Market Supervisory Authority (FINMA) jointly published the findings of its investigation, and has stated it will be appointing an independent investigator to ensure that UBS implements various corrective measures.

On 15 September 2011, UBS reported a loss due to unauthorized trading "in the range of USD 2 billion." This figure was revised to USD 2.3 billion (EUR 1.7 billion) on 18 September 2011 when the bank released a statement providing further details into the rogue trading loss.

The trades were carried out at UBS' Global Synthetic Equity business in the City of London. The losses derived from what the bank called "unauthorized speculative trading" in equity index futures. Whilst the positions taken were within "normal business flow of a large global equity trading house," the trader used fictitious hedges to obscure the fact that risk limits had been violated. The bank stated the positions had been offset with "fictitious, forward-settling, cash ETF positions."

City of London police have arrested and charged trader Kweku Adoboli with fraud by abuse of position and false accounting. UBS stated that the trader had revealed his actions to the bank on 14 September 2011. It has been reported that Adoboli was a market maker in Exchange Traded Funds (ETFs), working on the "Delta 1" trading desk, which replicates stock indices through derivatives such as swaps, futures and options. This is the same desk as Jérôme Kerviel worked on at Société Générale when he famously lost the bank approximately EUR 4.9 billion through falsely hedging large trades.

Appearing in court on 22 September 2011, Adoboli was also charged with fraud between October 2008 and December 2010. Prosecutors referred to "reckless and inappropriate" trades between these dates.

UBS board member David Sidwell has been appointed to begin an internal investigation into the trading loss. The FSA and its Swiss counterpart FINMA have both stated that they will inves-tigate the loss.

UBS said that no client positions had been affected by the loss.

UPDATE 1 (20 November 2012) — Adoboli Convicted of Fraud

Kweku Adoboli has been sentenced to seven years in prison after being found guilty on two counts of fraud by abuse of posi-tion. The jury acquitted Adoboli of four counts of false accounting.

FIRST Record and Excerpts from Description[25]

Control Failings and Contributory Factors

Employee Misdeeds: *A 31-year-old trader in the European Equi-ties Trading Division at UBS' London offices was arrested after the bank discovered he had engaged in unauthorized trades. The employee executed transactions for the bank's account in excess of his defined limits and concealed the risk exposures. Using a variety of methods, he successfully concealed the actual scale of his trading positions and the risk they posed. The methods used included one-sided internal futures positions, the delayed booking of transactions and fictitious deals with deferred settlement dates (T+14).*

Corporate and Market Conditions: *Mr. Adoboli made a series of bets on market indices at times when markets were very volatile, due to concerns about Greek sovereign debt and other economic difficul-ties. "He managed to change his position always at the wrong time,"* an unidentified source told the Wall Street Journal *(September 20, 2011). Shortly before UBS disclosed the loss, equity markets had been very volatile, due in part to concerns about a possible sover-eign default by Greece, a Euro-zone member. To curb what it called "massive overvaluation" of the Swiss Franc, the Swiss National Bank intervened on September 6, 2011 to cap the exchange rate of the CHF against the Euro, a surprise move that led to losses for some hedge funds. Although some have speculated about the possible impact of the SNB's intervention, it is not known whether such externalities contributed to the loss at UBS — or whether it turned a manageable loss into a much larger one.*

Failure to Test for P/L Accuracy; Lack Management Escalation Pro-cess: *Profit and loss suspensions to the value of USD $1.6 billion were requested by Adoboli during August 2011. Prior to 18 August 2011, these were accepted without challenge or escalation.*

(continued)

(continued)

The combined factors of unexplained profitability and loss suspensions should have indicated the need for greater scrutiny.

Lack of Internal Controls: *The front office's monitoring tools established by the line manager responsible for the ETF desk had major deficiencies and were not used properly. The trade capture and processing system had significant flaws, which Adoboli exploited to conceal his unauthorized trading. The system permitted trades to be booked to an internal counterparty without sufficient details; there were no effective methods to detect trades at material off-market prices; and there was a lack of integration between systems. UBS' various control functions did not assemble their information to produce an overall picture. Fulvio Pelli, the party president of the Swiss Liberal Party, commented:"For a bank that has made mistakes in the past, it's absolutely unacceptable. I'm absolutely astonished that internal controls didn't work at UBS."*

Poor Judgment: *Operational risks were assessed mainly through a yearly self-assessment process by traders and internal controllers. Improvements to this process had been in progress since January 2011, but came completed too late, according to Swiss regulator, the Financial Market Supervisory Authority (FINMA), which was working on an independent investigation of this incident with the FSA.*

Inadequate Due Diligence Efforts: *Untrained/Inexperienced Staff: The regulators found that there was a perception amongst personnel supporting the ETF desk that the Operations Division's main role was that of facilitation. Their focus was on efficiency rather than risk control and they did not sufficiently question the front office about its actions. The control functions had insufficient understanding of the trading activities in question and were therefore unable to challenge the ETF desk's actions. Operations saw its role as providing services to Adoboli and raised no serious questions about his activities. Although reconciliation errors remained unresolved over several weeks, explanations provided were far-fetched, and inconsistencies were seldom escalated, Adoboli's managers and controllers were too quick to accept his explanations. Even at a meeting held on August 24, 2011, managers came to the conclusion that no large amounts of money were at risk. In August 2011, Adoboli once again persuaded Product Control that losses of one billion dollars shown in the trading systems were incorrect. His assurance that he would correct these "booking errors"in the near future was accepted without objection. In fact, Adoboli's objective was to eliminate the bank's losses, at least temporarily, from the books.*

Poor Documentation: *An important control report was not produced at all for a period of several months without anyone noticing. This report is described below, under Outsourcing.*

Lack of Proper Training Procedures: *FINMA found that control personnel "had too little understanding of the trading activities in question and were therefore unable to challenge the ETF desk's actions." Moreover, the various control functions at UBS "did not collate their information to produce an overall picture."This was due in part to the outsourcing of control functions, as well as unclear reporting lines.*

Outsourcing: *The Times of India (November 26, 2012) noted that a key internal control for detecting fraud had been moved to India. This function, known as the T+14 report, was maintained by an outsourcing provider, which FINMA did not identify. The T+14 report was designed to identify deferred settlement trades, which posed a greater risk to the firm than trades which settled in three business days (T+3 trades). According to FINMA, the T+14 Report, "was non-operational between May and November 2009, and from November 2010 to September 2011"—shortly before the loss was discovered. If it had been operational it should have flagged the trader's fictitious deals with deferred settlement dates created by Trader X.*

Poor Execution: *FINMA found that unclear reporting lines were a key factor:"Line managers were uncertain of their functions and responsibilities" as to who was monitoring the ETF desk. After an internal reorganization in April 2011, the direct line manager for the ETF desk was located in New York, but"no specific arrangements were made for transferring responsibility for monitoring [the desk]." Therefore, warnings did not reach the new direct line manager in New York.They ended up instead with the previous line manager in London, who received and acknowledged them, even though this was no longer his responsibility."*

Unclear Reporting Structure: *At UBS, responsibility for monitoring and controlling the ETF desk was divided between the line managers in the front office and three separate control functions. The Operations unit was charged with ensuring that the ETF desk's trades were correctly logged and processed. Product Control was tasked with ensuring correct reporting and for checking the plausibility of profits and losses, while Risk Control was responsible for monitoring and evaluating the risks from trading activities. Line managers were uncertain of what their functions and responsibilities were as regards monitoring the ETF desk.*

(continued)

(continued)

Unclear Reporting Structure (more): *Failure to Question Above Market Returns: FINMA and the FSA determined that the three control functions had failed to properly investigate the many red flags triggered by transactions from the ETF desk. FINMA pointed to one example, where unusually large profits generated by the ETF desk starting in the first quarter of 2011 were not critically scrutinized. The regulator said that the bank failed to examine the underlying reasons for the significant growth in profitability of the ETF desk despite the fact that this could not be explained by reference to the end of day risk positions.*

Failure to Supervise Employees: *At UBS' London offices, the manager of the alleged rogue trader resigned shortly after the trader was arrested. Some banks have reportedly urged supervisory staff to be aware of potential risks posed by traders who may have direct knowledge of "back-office" systems and urged them to give those employees heightened supervision. FINMA found that the direct line managers failed to properly monitor the ETF desk in London. Adoboli's relationship with his line manager and the internal control functions relied on trust and not enough on control. The FSA criticized that bank for having inadequate front office supervision. It stated that the supervision arrangements within the Global Synthetic Equities (GSE) trading division, of which the ETF desk was part, were poorly executed and ineffective.*

Failure to Set or Enforce Proper Limits: *Although UBS' London trading room was aware that the ETF desk caused many reconciliation errors, often due to late or incorrectly booked transactions, these concerns were not discussed with either the Product Control unit nor with senior management. Starting in June 2011, the reconciliation errors became substantial, with the unexplained amounts sometimes exceeding USD 1 billion. Between June and July 2011, it became clear on at least four occasions that Adobeli had breached his limits. In one case, he revealed to his manager in New York that he had made a profit of USD $6 million by taking a position of more than USD $200 million, far in excess of his approved risk limit. The line manager first congratulated Adoboli on the profit and only later reminded him that he needed permission to exceed his limit. The inadequacy of the controls was also made clear by an incident in August 2011 in which fictitious ETF trades with deferred settlement dates generated irregularities amounting to half a billion dollars. These warning signals were accepted without further investigation. The ETF Desk breached the risk limits set for their desk without being disciplined for doing so. These limits represented a key control and defined the maximum level of risk* *that the desk could enter into at a given time. This brought about a situation in which unauthorized risk taking was not actively discouraged or penalized by those with supervisory responsibility. According to FINMA, UBS sent out misleading signals by "awarding pay increases and bonuses to a trader who had clearly and repeatedly breached compliance rules, and by accepting him onto a junior management program."*

General Corporate Governance Issues: *Failure to Comply with Internal Policies and Procedures;* Staff Selection/Compensation: *UBS awarded pay increases and bonuses to Adoboli who had clearly and repeatedly breached compliance rules, and by accepting him onto a junior management scheme.*

Omissions & Lapses; Regulatory Pressure: *Reuters reported that the European Union's MiFiD regulations do not currently require the reporting of confirmations from counterparties for over-the-counter (bank-to-bank) ETF transactions until after the settlement date. This would appear to be a major loophole in MiFiD's current reporting requirements.*

Failure to Test Products or Systems: *Although ETFs have been in use for a few years, banks are now using them to hedge their own positions. The risks posed by ETFs remain poorly understood, one analyst told Reuters News (September 20, 2011): "There hasn't been the investment in systems to keep up with the complexity of [ETFs]. When new trading products emerge, often the links to risk and credit controls are an afterthought."*

Rules, Regulations and Compliance Issues: *UBS breached FSA Principles 2 (due skill, care and diligence) and 3 (risk management systems and controls) of the FSA's Principles for Businesses.*

9. What lessons had UBS not learned from the Société Générale case from only a few years earlier? Discuss. (See Chapter 8 for a discussion of the Société Générale event.)

NOTES

1. www.forbes.com/sites/nathanvardi/2012/05/16/london-whale-harpooned-iksil-out-at-jpmorgan/.
2. www.ft.com/cms/s/0/fbab63ae-9b72-11e1-b097-00144feabdc0.html#ax-zz1x77Fp2ct.
3. http://news.yahoo.com/beached-london-whale-loses-2-billion-j-p-213300751–finance.html.

4. For example, www.bloomberg.com/news/2012-06-06/paulson-gold-fund-said-to-extend-slump-with-13-may-loss.html.

5. http://blogs.wsj.com/deals/2012/04/06/deals-of-the-day-meet-j-p-morgans-london-whale/?KEYWORDS=jp+morgan+whale.

6. www.bloomberg.com/news/2012-04-09/london-s-biggest-whale.html.

7. www.reuters.com/article/2012/05/18/us-jpmorgan-crisiscommunications-idUSBRE84H05G20120518.

8. http://blogs.wsj.com/deals/2012/05/10/whale-of-a-call-dimons-best-quotes/.

9. http://i.mktw.net/_newsimages/pdf/jpm-conference-call.pdf.

10. www.nypost.com/p/news/business/jpmorgan_trading_loss_leads_to_us_JYUL-wjSYhaCot9ZrdoakUM.

11. http://online.wsj.com/article/SB10001424052702304192704577406093989791910.html.

12. http://business.time.com/2012/05/17/jpmorgans-london-whale-loss-rises-to-3-billion-as-lawsuits-fly/.

13. www.investorplace.com/2012/05/so-jamie-dimon-what-do-you-think-of-the-volcker-rule-now/.

14. "Report of JPMorgan Chase & Co. Management Task Force Regarding 2012 CIO Losses" (JPMorgan Report), January 16, 2013, http://media.bloomberg.com/bb/avfile/rM8QB5s4.Eoc (no longer available).

15. www.bloomberg.com/news/2013-01-16/jpmorgan-halves-dimon-pay-says-ceo-responsible-for-lapses-1-.html.

16. JPMorgan Report, extracts from pp. 10–13.

17. www.orx.org/orxnews.

18. IBM FIRST Risk Case Studies. Property of IBM. 5725-H59 © Copyright IBM Corp. and others 1992, 2021, IBM, the IBM logo, ibm.com.

19. https://www.credit-suisse.com/about-us-news/en/articles/media-releases/trading-update-202104.html.

20. https://www.credit-suisse.com/about-us/en/reports-research/archegos-info-kit.html.

21. IBM FIRST Report for Loss Event 19072/OpData ID 23123.

22. ORX News Reference 10141.

23. ORX News Reference 0734.

24. ORX News Reference 0012.

25. FIRST Report for Loss Event 11117/OpData ID 15887.

Appendix: Answers to Review Questions

CHAPTER 1

1. c
2. a

CHAPTER 2

1. a
2. d

CHAPTER 3

1. c
2. b

CHAPTER 4

1. b
2. b

CHAPTER 5

1. b

CHAPTER 6

1. c

CHAPTER 7

1. c
2. b
3. e
4. d

CHAPTER 8

1. d

CHAPTER 9

1. b

CHAPTER 10

1. a

CHAPTER 11

1. c
2. a

CHAPTER 12

1. a
2. d

CHAPTER 13

1. c

CHAPTER 14

1. a

CHAPTER 15

   1. d

CHAPTER 16

   1. c

CHAPTER 17

   1. b

CHAPTER 18

Case 1

1. IBM FIRST classified the event as outlined in Table A.1:

TABLE A.1   IBM First Classification of Archegos Credit Suisse Event

Keywords Indexing	
Entity Type	Financial Services/Banking/Commercial/Full Service Bank
Business Unit Type	Trading and Sales (BIS)/Trading
Service/Product Offering Type	Derivatives, Structured Products and Commodities/Derivative Products/Over-the-Counter Derivatives
Contributory/ Control Factors	Corporate/Market Conditions/Corporate and Market Conditions Lack of Control/Failure to Disclose Lack of Control/Lack of Internal Controls Management Action/Inaction/Poor Judgment Management Action/Inaction/Undertook Excessive Risks Omissions/Inadequate Due Diligence Efforts Organizational Structure/Inadequate Organizational Structures
Loss Type	Known
Loss Impact	Direct Loss/Write-Down (BIS)/Write-Downs Indirect Loss/Income Indirect Loss/Management Remediation Indirect Loss/Reputational (Non-Monetary) Indirect Loss/Revenue Indirect Loss/Share Price

(continued)

(continued)

TABLE A.1 (CONTINUED)

Keywords Indexing

Loss Detection Sources	Whistle Blowing/Counterparty Originated
Market Focus	Institutional Services
Event Trigger	Process Risk Class/Transactional and Business Process Risk/Lack of Proper Due Diligence
Basel Levels I and II	Execution Delivery and Process Management/Transaction Capture, Execution, and Maintenance/Collateral management failure
Basel Business Line	Trading and Sales/Proprietary Positions

2. IBM FIRST outlined the following lessons learned:

Lessons Learned

The Wall Street Journal *(April 1, 2021) noted that in July 2020 Credit Suisse had reorganized, "combining risk and compliance and creating a committee to look specifically at big clients. The changes were also described as having 'significant efficiency potential' and cost savings." The merits of such a "cost-saving" combination were under reassessment in early April 2021, as the Credit Suisse announced that former general counsel Thomas Grotzer to be the bank's new global head of compliance.*

The huge losses incurred by some banks' prime broker units suggest that banks need to do a better job of managing collateral when managing credit extended to certain wealthy investors and small firms. In this case, it appears that the banks had very little understanding of the risks they were exposed to when they entered into swap contracts with Mr. Hwang or his firm—and were in the dark as to what other obligations their client faced with other brokers.

Regulators are likely to investigate the whether there were risk management failures at the various prime broker units, the extent to which derivatives contracts (such as total return swaps) were adequately secured by collateral, and whether the institutions faced any potential conflicts of interest. For example, the SEC might be possibly looking into whether Morgan Stanley faced any conflict of interest if it was acting as underwriter of ViacomCBS's share offering if it also was counterparty in some of Archegos' swaps contracts. The scope of disclosures by family firms may also be up for review.[1]

Case 2

3. ORC classified the event as outlined in Table A.2.
4. Regulatory action for anti–money laundering (AML) breaches is generally very severe and can include fines, consent orders, and requirements to restrict business growth until remediations are complete. A Google search of AML regulatory consent orders in the United States will provide further context for discussion.
5. Consider the impact of culture, controls, and risk management in the failings that contributed to this event.

TABLE A.2 ORX Classification of DNB Bank ASA Event

ORX Reference Taxonomy Level 2
RT1004 – KYC and transaction monitoring control failure

Boundary Risk Other Risk	**Industry Event**	**Scenario** SC0006 – AML Failures
Product PD0603 – Commercial Bank Accounts	**Process** PC0401 – (New) Client Account	**Event Closed** No
ORX Member No	**Role of Firm** LS0307 – Position Taking (Principal)	**Jurisdiction/Choice of Law** LS0105 – Western Europe (excluding United Kingdom)
Cause 1 CS0303 – Financial Reporting	**Cause 2** CS0403 – Inadequate Policy/Procedure	**Cause 3**
Counterparty LS0211 – Regulator	**Environmental Volatility** LS0406 – Not Identifiable	**Provision** No

Case 3

ORX classified the event as outlined in Figure A.1.

6. In the ORX standards, EL0601—Technology and infrastructure failure is a risk that relates to losses arising from disruption of business or system failures. This is equivalent to the Basel II risk category of **Business Disruption and System Failure.**
7. ORX states the main cause as CS0503—**Software—Inadequate Maintenance.**
8. ORX classifies the business line as BL0201—Equities, which is a subset of their **Trading and Sales** business line category.

(continued)

(continued)

ORX ASSOCIATION NEWS

www.orx.org/orxnews

ORX News Reference
0734

Knight Capital Group	BL0201 – Equities	
EL0601 – Technology & Infrastructure Failure	USD – 440,000,000.00 LOSS	USD – US Dollar
US – UNITED STATES	North America	

Event	Published in Media	Date of Occurrence – From	Date of Occurrence – To	Discovery Date	Date of Recognition / Settlement
	01/Aug/2012	01/Aug/2012	01/Aug/2012	01/Aug/2012	N/A

Loss Amount USD	Loss Amount EURO	Provision	Boundary Risk
USD 440,000,000.00	EUR 360,844,000.00	No	N/A

Industry Event	Scenario	Product	Process
N/A	Technology & Infrastructure Failure	PD0302 - Equities	PC1001 - IT Development and Maintenance (including IT Project Mgt)

Parent Company	ORX Member	Role of Firm	AMA Status
Knight Capital Group	No	LS0306 - Investor (Principal)	No

Cause 1	Cause 2	Cause 3
CS0503 - Software - Inadequate Maintenance	CS9999 - Not Identifiable	CS9999 - Not Identifiable

Counterparty	Jurisdiction / Choice of Law	Environmental Volatility
LS0212 - Not Identifiable	LS0101 - United States of America	LS0403 - Market Risk

FIGURE A.1 ORX Classification of Knight Capital Event

Case 4

9. IBM FIRST provided the following suggested lessons learned; many are repeats of exactly the same control failings that were identified in the Société Générale event:

Lessons Learned

The Wall Street Journal *on September 16, 2011 said that banks seeking to detect unauthorized trading should supplement their routine electronic surveillance with "an older method of detection: looking out for suspicious behavior." Echoing some findings of the Societe Generale investigation, the WSJ cited several red flags: "traders not taking vacations; traders having a lot of cancelled or amended trades; traders working out of business hours or logging fewer hours on recorded lines; and traders whose trades are questioned by counterparties or exchanges." The size of the loss in this case certainly poses a reputational risk to UBS. In the words of a* Financial Times *(September 15, 2011) report, "Hard questions need to be asked about UBS' internal risk controls. It's hard to believe the Swiss bank's view that it cannot identify the area in which the rogue trades were made, or when more information might become available—everything has an electronic audit trail."*

The loss amount ($2.3 billion) is the largest rogue trading loss ever by a Swiss bank and the third-largest unauthorized trading loss on record, exceeded only by the January 2008 Societe Generale loss of $6.8 billion (Event #7945) and the 1996 Sumitomo Corporation loss of $2.8 billion (Event #1699). These and other cases can be found using the Unauthorized Trading keyword.

Nor is this the first time that the London offices of UBS have suffered from unauthorized trading. In November 2009, the FSA fined UBS GBP 8 million ($13.3 million)—one of the FSA's biggest fines ever—for weak controls that allowed staff to make as many as 50 unauthorized trades a day on at least 39 client accounts and then conceal the losses. (see Event #9481)

The Wall Street Journal *reported on September 22, 2011, that the FSA was looking into several possible rogue trading cases at other institutions in London. "At least three of those cases involve traders who previously had worked in the bank's 'back-offices' where employees enter and confirm trades, handle accounting issues and transmit payments," the paper said. After the Societe Generale fraud, some banks reportedly began asking supervisors of traders who come from a "back-office" background to enhance their supervision. Since the FSA does not have sufficient staff to monitor trades at large banks however, it is incumbent on banks to be aware of risky trades before large losses are found to have occurred. Traders exceeding their risk limits can (at least in theory) return profits, so banks should pay attention to unexpectedly large profits before they are surprised by unexpectedly large losses.*

One of the key questions to be answered by any investigation is how such a large unauthorized trading loss on the "Delta One" desk went undetected, especially after the highly-publicized Societe Generale fraud. Since it appears that Mr. Adoboli's losses were in market index futures (as was the case with trades executed by Jerome Kerviel) it is as yet unclear why his fictitious hedging positions went unchecked. At the very least banks should require confirmations of ETF trades by counterparties.

At least one online analyst, Paul Amery, argues that lax operational settlement procedures for bank-traded ETFs could prove to be a major factor. Firstly, in London the late settlement of ETF transactions is not unusual and is not subject to major sanctions. Secondly, many counterparties do not request trade confirmations, especially for OTC transactions. Mr. Amery concludes: "Taken together, these two loopholes may have enabled the creation of fake transactions in UBS's systems. Even if this was the immediate cause of the fraud, the bank's risk controllers seem to have missed

(continued)

(continued)

> *other warning signs. High gross trading positions, even if the trader reported his position as hedged, plus what were presumably significant cash outflows in margin as the result of losing futures positions, might together have been expected to flag that something was wrong."*
>
> *The* Financial Times *reporter Gillian Tett noted that trading in ETFs requires yet more attention from regulators, since sales of ETFs—which have been very profitable for banks—could pose conflict-of-interest problems if banks were acting as counterparties in the same funds they sold to customers.*
>
> *A few weeks before it disclosed the loss, UBS had announced a plan for 3,500 layoffs—a 5 percent cut in its global work force—half of them in the investment banking arm, in order to meet tougher economic conditions. Press reports said that the loss would also lead to calls from investors and legislators for Swiss banks to reduce their investment banking activities and focus more on private banking and fund management. Regulators could ask for even more stringent capital requirements for investment banking activities, or seek to protect client business from risky proprietary trading.*
>
> *The Swiss parliament was discussing measures to improve the safety of the biggest Swiss banks (UBS and Credit Suisse) even as the event was disclosed. The "too big-to-fail" banks earlier got taxpayer bailouts after losing large amounts investing in mortgage-backed securities from 2006 to 2008. A representative of the Swiss People's Party (SPP) told Bloomberg News: "There can't be another state bailout. It can't be up to the state and taxpayers to rescue large banks that are involved in risky business." Another SPP member found yet another lesson: "It shows that investment banking is a high-risk field and it's important that we clearly separate systemically important functions from the rest of the banking business." Such concerns have also been echoed elsewhere.*
>
> *The proposal to "ring-fence" bank activities on their customers' behalf from risky bets in proprietary trading was a feature both of the Volcker rule (enacted as part of the Dodd Frank Act) in the United States, as well as the recent Vickers Report (available here) into banking in the United Kingdom. Proponents of stricter banking regulation in these and other countries will likely to point to the UBS case to bolster their argument. As Martin Wolf, a columnist for the* Financial Times *wrote: "Thank you UBS . . . I could not have asked for a better illustration of the unregulatable risks to which investment banks are exposed."*

> *In what may be an emerging trend, the Swiss regulator FINMA noted in its summary report that outsourcing of control functions to India was a contributing factor in UBS' failure to detect unauthorized trading. Such outsourcing has also been mentioned in another high-profile case. In August 2012, the New York Department of Financial Services accused Standard Chartered of involvement in laundering financial transactions (11885). The regulator said the bank's compliance function had been moved to Chennai. The New York regulator cited "no evidence of any oversight or communication between the Chennai and the New York offices" with regard to Standard Chartered's compliance with regulations issued by the Office of Foreign Assets Control (OFAC).*[2]

NOTES

1. FIRST Report for Loss Event 19072/OpData ID 23123.
2. FIRST Report for Loss Event 11117/OpData ID 15887.

About the Author

Philippa Girling has more than 25 years' experience in the global financial services industry, working in the fields of risk management, training, project management, and organizational change.

Philippa has held several operational risk leadership roles, including heading the global corporate operational risk functions at Morgan Stanley and Nomura. She was business chief risk officer for Capital One's commercial bank, chief risk officer for Investors Bank, and is currently chief risk officer and a founder of Varo Bank, NA, the first fintech to receive a national bank charter in the United States.

She has delivered operational risk courses at Columbia University, London Business School, Rutgers University, NYU Stern, Baruch University, the University of Connecticut, Claremont University, Wharton, and Carnegie Mellon.

Philippa first authored *Operational Risk Management*, a textbook for the risk and regulation examination of the Global Association of Risk Professionals, in 2009 and authored the first edition of *Operational Risk Management: A Complete Guide to a Successful Operational Risk Framework* in 2013.

She is a regular speaker at global conferences on the topics of systemic risk and regulation, the evolution of the operational risk discipline, and the challenges of risk management in the new digital banking paradigm. She was selected as one of the Top Fifty Faces of Operational Risk by *Operational Risk and Compliance* magazine when the discipline was in its early days and since then has become a recognized leader in the field.

Philippa holds an English law degree from the University of East Anglia, England, is qualified as a New York attorney, is a holder of the GARP Financial Risk Manager accreditation, and received her PhD from Rutgers University. Her area of doctoral study focused on the development of an industry-standard operational risk framework that meets global regulatory expectations and financial services industry business requirements.

Philippa moved from her British homeland to the United States in 1996, and she and her husband share their time between Florida and California.

About the Website

The companion website for this book contains teaching slides and materials and a simple operational risk toolbox. Go to www.wiley.com/go/girling2E (password: wiley13) for access to the following materials:

- PowerPoint slides to support each chapter.
- A fictional case study with instructions for use as a teaching exercise for groups.

The toolbox contains the following items:

- A PowerPoint training presentation that introduces operational risk concepts and fundamentals.
- A simple risk and control self-assessment Excel worksheet with built-in automatic conditional formatting, drop-down risk category lists, and scoring calculations.
- A basic loss event data collection Excel worksheet with standard fields for data capture and one example event.
- A starter kit of key risk indicators in an Excel worksheet with example metrics for each of the seven Basel risk categories of operational risk.
- A sample reporting deck in PowerPoint with examples of operational risk reporting slides and with supporting sample data in Excel.
- An operational risk policy document in Word.
- A loss data standards document in Word.

The site also features links to all of the reference materials in this book.

Index